2

April
1986

ECONOMIC POLICY
A European Forum

Senior Editors
GEORGES DE MENIL
RICHARD PORTES

Managing Editors
DAVID BEGG
CHARLES WYPLOSZ

Assistant Editor
CHARLES BEAN

Board of Governors
GEORGES DE MENIL *Co-Chairman*
RICHARD PORTES *Co-Chairman*
FRANÇOIS BOURGUIGNON
JEREMY HARDIE

Cambridge University Press and
Editions de la Maison des Sciences de l'Homme for
Centre for Economic Policy Research and
École des Hautes Études en Sciences Sociales

Panel

Giorgio Basevi
University of Bologna

Michael Bruno
Hebrew University of Jerusalem

Willem Buiter
Yale University

Rudiger Dornbusch
Massachusetts Institute of Technology

Gerhard Fels
Institut der Deutschen Wirtschaft, Cologne

David Hendry
Nuffield College, Oxford

Ravi Kanbur
University of Essex

Louka Katseli
Yale University and Centre of Planning and Economic Research, Athens

Mervyn King
London School of Economics

Paul Krugman
Massachusetts Institute of Technology

Jacques Mairesse
ENSAE, Paris

Jacques Melitz
INSEE, Paris

Patrick Minford
University of Liverpool

Torsten Persson
Institute for International Economic Studies, Stockholm

Hans-Werner Sinn
University of Munich

John Vickers
Nuffield College, Oxford

Mike Wickens
University of Southampton

Statement of purpose

Economic Policy provides timely and authoritative analyses of the choices which confront policy-makers. The subject matter ranges from the study of how individual markets can and should work to the broadest interactions in the world economy.

Edited in London and Paris, *Economic Policy* offers an independent, non-partisan, European perspective on issues of worldwide concern. It emphasizes problems of international significance, either because they affect the world economy directly or because the experience of one country contains important lessons for policy makers elsewhere.

All the articles are specially commissioned from leading professional economists. Their brief is to demonstrate how live policy issues can be illuminated by the insights of modern economics and by the most recent evidence. The presentation is incisive and written in plain language accessible to the wide audience which participates in the policy debate.

Prior to publication, the contents of each volume are discussed by a Panel of distinguished economists from Europe and elsewhere. The Panel rotates annually. Inclusion in each volume of a summary of the highlights of the Economic Policy Panel discussion provides the reader with alternative interpretations of the evidence and a sense of the liveliness of the current debate.

Financial support from Citibank, the Alfred P. Sloan Foundation, the Esmée Fairbairn Charitable Trust, and the Rock Foundation is gratefully acknowledged.

Subscriptions: *Economic Policy* (ISSN 0266-4658) volume 1 issues appear in November 1985, April and October 1986; thereafter each volume will consist of two issues. Volume 1 subscription price, valid until 31 December 1986, which includes postage, is £16.00 (US $30.00, Ffr 240) for institutions, £9.00 (US $15.00, Ffr 120) for individuals ordering direct from the publisher† and certifying that the journal is for their personal use. US dollar prices apply to USA and Canada. Copies of the journal for subscribers in USA and Canada are sent by air to New York to arrive with minimum delay. Orders, which must be accompanied by payment, may be sent to a bookseller, subscription agent or to the publishers: Cambridge University Press, The Edinburgh Building, Shaftesbury Road, Cambridge CB2 2RU, UK or 32 East 57th Street, New York, NY 10022, USA.

† When exchange control regulations permit, individuals may pay by any of the following methods: Cheque (made payable to 'Cambridge University Press'), UK Postal Order, International Money Order, bank draft, Post Office Giro (a/c no. 571 6055 GB Bootle – *advice of payment should be sent with the order to the Press*), Barclaycard/Visa/BankAmericard or Access/MasterCard/Eurocard (or any other credit card bearing the Interbank symbol).

Advertising: Apply to Cambridge University Press, UK or North American branch.

Contents

Editors' introduction

The five papers in this issue were discussed at the second meeting of the Economic Policy Panel on 11–12 November 1985 in London. Each paper is preceded by a summary of the argument and principal conclusions. In this editors' introduction we place the papers in context, assessing their relevance to the policy issues they discuss.

When this issue appears in print, general elections will have been held in France, and the five years of Socialist rule may have come to an end. Jeffrey Sachs and Charles Wyplosz's assignment was both to evaluate the economic policies of this period and to identify those principles which should guide the next government. Beyond the particular and important case of France, we believe that their analysis is of interest for many other countries. In France, as elsewhere in Europe, the successful battle against inflation has been costly in terms of unemployment. Double digit unemployment rates are now the rule, and the figures for youth unemployment are often above 20%. Most governments feel helpless as a decade of unrelenting budget deficits has resulted in large public debts. Real interest rates remain at unprecedented levels, hampering capital accumulation and thus further darkening the already bleak prospects of long term growth. With 'Europessimism' so widespread, Sachs and Wyplosz's emphasis on the supply side seems to go to the heart of the major issues. Their finding that today's unemployment rate in France is only slightly above the inflationary threshold is a useful reminder that traditional expansionary policies are of limited usefulness. Their analysis of the failed attempt at expansion in the early phase of the Mitterrand period illustrates the importance of policy coordination, especially among EMS countries. Given the official view that massive unemployment is not likely to disappear before the end of the decade, their study would be of little comfort if they did not also provide a detailed account of what could lead to a resumption of sustained growth. No doubt their preoccupation with labour taxes is likely to be controversial and requires confirmation.

Yet their suggestion of restraint in public spending, coupled with negotiated reductions in taxes on labour and production, ought to be taken seriously. The next step, they argue, is to design the proper mix of supply-friendly measures, coupled with compatible demand expansion to ensure that additional supply is fully utilized.

In his comments on Sachs and Wyplosz, Georges de Menil stresses the hidden potential long-term costs of the French nationalizations of 1981–82, which eventually are likely to reduce productivity. A detailed study of the shortcomings of the public sector is provided by George Yarrow. His concern is with privatization, particularly with the current trend in Britain. Here again, the topic is of immediate interest as many countries are now planning, and often have started, to return to the private sector large segments of the state-owned enterprises. Yarrow's central argument is that privatization is likely to improve economic efficiency when markets are competitive. He does not believe that private ownership is necessarily superior to public ownership because of the many existing market failures, ranging from information costs to management control and natural monopolies. Of special interest is Yarrow's insistence that the frontier between government regulation and public ownership is not precisely delineated, and that inadequate regulatory policies can lead to poor performance of large firms whether in the public or private sector.

Even when some form of privatization has been agreed, there are many forms it can take (partial or complete asset sales, franchising, contracting out of services). Here, too, in evaluating the British experience (for example, the offer price for share flotations and the extent of involvement of existing public sector management) Yarrow is highly critical of actual policy. While the privatization debate will continue, this article should at least serve as a warning that privatization is a complex issue and cannot be a universal solution to the problems attributed to public ownership.

The following article by Michael Bruno is an account of the Israeli government's programme to bring inflation down from a rate of about 500% a year to below 10%. As the new policies have been implemented very recently, it is too early to call it a success, yet most of the early observations are reassuring. Shunning simplistic monetary explanations, Bruno brings out clearly the interaction of real and monetary factors, and the role of both the external sector and of institutional aspects such as the timing of wage contracts or price revisions. This diagnosis calls for a direct attack on the real imbalances associated with large budget deficits which spill into external disequilibria, and for anchoring simultaneously several nominal variables such as wages, the exchange rate and monetary aggregates. In this respect, we note that,

Economic Policy   April 1986   Printed in Great Britain

SUMMARY

France under Mitterrand

Jeffrey Sachs and Charles Wyplosz

While French economic performance has not conformed to the enthusiastic promises of early 1981, this paper argues that the widely held view that it has been an unmitigated failure is unwarranted. First, the general deterioration can largely be dated back to the early seventies. Second, the early and unfortunate attempt at a demand-led expansion was both moderate in size and quickly reversed. Finally, the post-1983 anti-inflationary policies have been successful so that, overall, the disappointing French performance has been on a par with, and in some ways better than, the rest of Europe.

But the main theme of the paper is the emphasis on the supply side. The analysis is organized around the NAIRU, the threshold rate of unemployment below which inflation rises. In an attempt to explain the factors which have led to a continuous rise of the NAIRU since 1973, the paper focuses on labour costs, particularly on the 'wedge' between the costs borne by employers and net take-home pay. To achieve and sustain a significantly lower level of unemployment, labour taxes must be cut, thus reducing the wedge and the NAIRU, and there must be a corresponding demand stimulus so that actual unemployment can fall to this level.

The economic consequences of President Mitterrand

Jeffrey Sachs
Harvard University and CEPR

Charles Wyplosz
INSEAD, Fontainebleau and CEPR

1. Introduction

The economic management of France under the Socialists in the 1980s is widely regarded as a major failure. Relative to the enthusiastic promises of President Mitterrand's government following the election victory of May 1981, that harsh assessment is warranted. The government came to office promising rapid growth and a reduction in unemployment. Instead, it has presided over four years of slow growth, and a rise in unemployment from 7% in 1981 to 10% in October 1985. The Socialist attempt to revive the French economy sank on the shoals of rising inflation and a foreign exchange crisis by early 1983, so that the government of the left has in the end introduced a tougher, more market oriented programme than anything considered by the previous centre-right administration of Giscard d'Estaing.

In politics, consistency can be more important than correctness, so that the Socialist U-turn and subsequent policies have garnered less applause than might be expected. The austerity since 1983 has reversed a trend of high and increasing inflation that gripped France in the 1970s and early 1980s. The policies have also stabilized the fiscal accounts and greatly improved France's external balance. Nonetheless, the Socialists remain condemned by the failure of their initial experiment. According to opinion polls within France, they have alienated the left without attracting new electoral support from the centre and the right.

*Useful comments have been received from several participants at the Panel and our discussants, from participants at the Paris Séminaire d'Economie Monétaire Internationale and the Business Economics Workshop at INSEAD. We also thank H. Delestré, P. Dubois, J. Mélitz, G. Laroque and G. Oudiz for assistance with data collection, and Fergal Byrne for useful research help. Financial support from INSEAD is gratefully acknowledged.

Our paper aims to provide a broader perspective on Socialist management of the French economy, by placing recent economic performance in the context of longer-term developments, and by comparing the macroeconomic outcomes in France with the results achieved in the other major industrial economies. We argue that the economic crisis in France did not begin with the Socialists in the 1980s, but in the 1970s, under Presidents Pompidou and Giscard d'Estaing. Macroeconomic policies emphasized aggregate demand management during a period in which aggregate supply conditions seriously deteriorated. Because of this deterioration, both inflation and unemployment rose sharply in the seventies in France as elsewhere in Western Europe.

Certainly, the early Mitterrand period did nothing to reverse this trend; the policies pursued were more naively demand oriented than in any other major industrial country. Starting from a position of double digit inflation, the Mitterrand government blithely stepped on the fiscal accelerator, hoping that the stimulus would raise output, spur investment, and thereby lead to anti-inflationary productivity increases. Labour costs were substantially raised by higher minimum wages, increased paid holidays, and a shorter working week. In the short term, France avoided the deep 1982 recession suffered by its neighbours. However, French inflation remained very high in 1981 and began to rise in 1982, while inflation abroad fell significantly. Also, with domestic demand expansion and a worldwide recession, the trade balance deteriorated sharply. With the Franc under attack, the fiscal expansion was quickly abandoned. Since mid-1983, the fiscal expansion has been nearly reversed, and wage policies have been successful in holding down the growth of real labour costs.

Table 1 shows the time paths of inflation, unemployment, and the external balance, in the past fifteen years. Clearly, President Giscard bequeathed a poorly performing economy to the Socialists in May 1981. The unemployment rate had risen in every year since 1974 to a rate of 6.3% in 1980, and the inflation rate increased to 12.2% in 1980. Both measures were far higher than in Germany, France's major political and economic partner. The current account was in substantial deficit. In 1982, the situation deteriorated, with higher inflation, unemployment, and current account deficits. By 1985, after more than two years of austerity, substantial progress was finally made on two of the three major targets of the government: inflation had fallen substantially, and the current account was back in balance. However, the unemployment rate, once the priority target of the Mitterrand government, had risen sharply to over 10%.

One popular way to compare the relative success of the fight against inflation in different countries is to calculate sacrifice ratios. For a given

Table 1. Macroeconomic indicators

	1974–80	1980	1981	1982	1983	1984	1985
Inflation (% p.a.)							
France	10.5	12.2	11.8	12.6	9.5	7.1	6.0
Germany	4.7	4.5	4.2	4.4	3.3	1.9	2.3
UK	16.1	19.8	11.8	7.4	5.0	4.4	5.0
Unemployment rate (%)							
France	4.8	6.3	7.4	8.1	8.3	9.7	10.1
Germany	3.2	3.0	4.4	6.1	8.0	8.5	8.8
UK	5.3	6.6	10.0	11.4	12.6	13.0	13.2
GDP growth (% p.a.)							
France	3.1	1.0	0.5	1.8	0.7	1.6	1.0
Germany	2.4	1.9	−0.2	−0.1	1.3	2.6	2.3
UK	1.5	−2.2	−1.3	1.8	3.2	1.6	3.3
Current account (% of GDP)							
France	−0.3	−1.4	−0.8	−2.2	−0.9	−0.2	0.1
Germany	0.2	−1.8	−0.8	0.5	0.6	1.0	2.1
UK	0.5	1.8	2.9	1.9	0.8	0.0	0.3
Structural budget deficit (% of GDP)							
France	0.6	−0.7	0.3	0.7	0.8	0.2	—
Germany	3.2	3.2	3.0	1.6	0.4	−0.8	—
UK	1.9	−4.0	−4.4	−4.5	−1.5	−1.8	—
Net public debt (% of GDP)							
France	11.5	9.1	10.6	12.5	15.0	17.6	—
Germany	−8.2	14.3	17.5	19.8	21.5	21.7	—
UK	75.3	48.9	48.2	47.2	49.0	49.8	—

Sources: Price and Muller (1984), DRI data bank. 1985 data are forecasts from OECD *Economic Outlook* (December 1985).
Notes: Current Account data in column 1 refer to 1975–80 for France and Germany, 1977–80 for the UK. Structural Deficit is inflation-adjusted at mid-cycle. Net Public Debt Data in column 1 refer to 1970.

period, the sacrifice ratio is defined as the cumulative increase in unemployment divided by the reduction in the annual inflation rate. It is a crude measure of the additional short-term unemployment burden required to get inflation down 1 percentage point. From Table 1 we see that French inflation fell from 11.8% in 1981 to 16.0% in 1985, a reduction of 5.8%. Over the same period the cumulative increase in unemployment was 12.1%. Hence during 1981–85 the sacrifice ratio was 2.1. For Germany and the UK, over the same period the sacrifice ratios were 10.9 and 4.0 respectively. In this sense, Table 1A shows that France faced a more favourable inflation-unemployment trade-off than other European countries.

Whilst the Socialist experiment has been no great success, French performance in some ways has been better than that in the rest of

Table 1A. Sacrifice ratios, 1981–85

	France	Germany	UK
Cumulative extra unemployment (%)	12.1	20.8	27.2
Reduction in inflation (%)	5.8	1.9	6.8
Sacrifice ratio	2.1	10.9	4.0

Source: as Table 1.

Europe. During the 1970s and 1980s, for most European countries, ever-higher unemployment rates have proved necessary merely to hold inflation in check, much less to reduce it. The so-called 'non-accelerating inflation rate of unemployment' (NAIRU), which measures the lowest unemployment rate that can be sustained without fear of increasing inflation, appears to have risen sharply. Note, for example, that during the Giscard d'Estaing administration, the historically high and rising unemployment rates during 1977–79, between the two oil shocks, did little to reduce French inflation (see Table 1).

In our view, the anti-supply side policies of both Giscard d'Estaing and Mitterrand, like the policies pursued in other countries of Europe, contributed to this distressing development. The post-1983 period under Mitterrand has begun to alleviate the problem, but in spite of the willingness of the government to undertake politically tough policies, it has still not shown a deep appreciation of the need for coordinated supply and demand measures. Some measurements of aggregate supply conditions that we develop later show only slight glimmers of improvement. Our policy recommendations at the end of this paper focus squarely on the need for further improvements in aggregate supply conditions.

We must spell out at the beginning how our approach differs from 'supply-side' economics as preached by the Reagan Administration. The Reaganomics supply-siders focus on the effects of income tax cuts on the incentives to save and work. Individuals, it is argued, will work harder, and undertake more entrepreneurial activities, with lower marginal tax rates. In our view, high sensitivity of household behaviour to marginal tax rates has yet to be demonstrated: we do not depart from the traditional macroeconomic assumption of a fairly inelastic long-term labour supply of primary wage-earners.

In our interpretation, sensitivity of workers to tax rates occurs not at the household level, but at the level of wage bargaining between firms and workers, and in political lobbying for government wage policies (see Bruno and Sachs, 1985, and Knoester and van der Windt, 1985). As we show below, unions will try to pass on labour tax increases by raising wages, even if such wage increases will engender unemployment for other workers, and even if unions faithfully represent the interests of members whose individual labour supply is completely wage inelastic! Because unions have monopoly power, they choose willingly to accept more unemployment in return for higher wages. When labour taxes or oil price increases adversely shift the demand for workers, unions are likely to accept higher unemployment in order to preserve real incomes. The same argument could be applied to political pressures for increases in government salaries, or in government-regulated wage levels (as with the minimum wage). Even those voters who would willingly work at much lower wages will often support government policies that preserve higher wages at the cost of higher aggregate unemployment (of others?).

To quantify the factors that have contributed to a rising NAIRU we construct a variable that measures the 'wedge' between costs to the firm and net-of-tax take home pay of workers. The theory suggests that a rise in the wedge will tend to raise the NAIRU, since unions will resist the real wage reductions that would otherwise be necessary in order to prevent higher labour costs from reducing the demand for labour by firms. We find that the 'wedge' has increased markedly in France, under Giscard d'Estaing as well as Mitterrand, mainly because of the increase in social security taxes. The rise in the wedge seems to be well correlated with the rise in the non-inflationary threshold of unemployment in France. For this reason, we share the Reagonomics emphasis on the efficacy of tax reductions as a way of reducing unemployment, especially since France has had one of the fastest increases in the Social Security tax burden in the OECD in the past fifteen years, as shown by the data in Table 2.

The plan of the paper is to review the Mitterrand experience, emphasising both aggregate supply and aggregate demand factors. Section 2 describes the Socialist outlook at the time of the election victory in May 1981, and its economic program, which combined a Keynesian demand expansion, a Blum-style set of supply-side measures, and nationalization of major industrial groups. Why this initial programme failed is the subject of some dispute. In Section 3, we consider three possible reasons: the world recession, adverse supply conditions, and a crisis of confidence. While all of these explanations have some merit, we make one central point: the NAIRU, or threshold unemployment rate, was simply too high to allow for a *sustained* demand-led recovery, and this was compounded by adverse supply-side measures.

While the debacle of this phase is well known, the brevity and moderation of the demand expansion that actually took place is not widely appreciated. As we show, the expansion was already winding

**Table 2. Social security expenditures
(Structural level as % of potential GDP)**

	France	Germany	UK	US
1970	16.8	13.3	8.5	7.5
1975	19.1	16.2	9.2	9.7
1980	22.6	16.3	10.0	10.0
1981	23.4	16.3	10.0	10.0
1982	24.2	15.8	10.5	9.7
1983	24.1	14.9	10.5	9.8

Source:Muller and Price (1984).
Note: Data measure social security expenditures at full
employment, as % of full-employment GDP. The structural level of social security expenditures is constructed
analogously to the structural budget deficit; it is the level
of spending which the system would produce at a normal
level of economic activity.

down by the second devaluation crisis, in June 1982, a mere 13 months
after the Socialists came to power. However, March 1983 brought the
decisive battle for control of the French economy and the Socialist party.
Since March 1983, demand management has been geared, successfully,
towards a reduction of inflation. Although the supply side has continued
to receive only fragmentary attention, the wage policy has been one of
moderation (at significant political cost). Even so, unemployment has
risen sharply. The outcome to date of 'socialist austerity' is reviewed in
Section 4.

In Section 5, the current macroeconomic environment is surveyed,
and some policy recommendations are offered. According to our estimates, a reduction of the unemployment rate to 5% is achievable in the
next few years, through a combination of demand expansion coupled
with a significant reduction in labour costs. A cut in labour taxes would
be useful in reducing labour costs to firms, thereby spurring employment and investment.

2. The first thousand days

2.1. The political background

The election of François Mitterrand as President in May 1981 was a
major political change. The left had not been in power since 1958, and
Mitterrand's brand of socialism was perceived as more fervent and
dogmatic than the socialism of the countless coalitions in the fifties, the
shift being clearly underlined by the explicit agreement to rule together
with the Communist party.

The changes were to cover the whole spectrum of economic policy: nationalization of several of the largest industrial corporations remaining in the private sector, new taxes (especially a wealth tax), new labour market regulations (the Auroux Laws), and a new orientation for macroeconomic policies. Many of the changes were based on a specifically socialist perspective on the economy, but there was also a general perception in France that the previous economic policies had failed and that a change was needed.

The left wing of the Socialist party, nurturing a strong scepticism toward market forces, was attached to the ideological principles incorporated in the joint programme adopted with the Communist Party in 1972, and enshrined in the 'Programme Commun'. They were prepared to go ahead with a large expansion of the public sector, quickly to redistribute income and strengthen the hand of the government in running the economy. It seems fair to say that this was the dominating view in the Spring of 1981.

At the other end of the spectrum, the approach was more pragmatic and cautious. The examples of the Front Populaire in 1936 and of Chile's Allende government were cited.[1] Several advisers were aware that high unemployment and high inflation, a delicate external situation and very nervous employers and investors required a careful approach.

2.2. The French economy in 1981

A careful study of the economic policies of the Giscard era is beyond the scope of this paper. As later under Mitterrand, there were two periods associated with the two Prime Ministers. Jacques Chirac presided over an expansion in the aftermath of the first oil shock. It led to a quickly rising inflation rate, a stubbornly upward creeping unemployment rate, and severe external imbalances which twice prompted France to leave the European currency arrangement known as the Snake. Raymond Barre replaced Chirac in late 1976 and quickly established his mark as a 'dismal' economist bent on the hard work of deflation. His main themes were balancing the budget, strengthening the Franc and wage moderation. In a later stage he engineered a historical break from the entrenched practice of pervasive price controls. He succeeded in balancing the budget, in leading France into the European Monetary System and in never having to devalue the Franc.

Over the period 1973–81, in France as elsewhere in Europe, the rise in unemployment had been met by a series of measures which con-

---

[1] S. C. Kolm, 'La Transition Socialiste Francaise,' *Le Monde* 17-18 June 1981.

tributed to a further rise of unemployment. Unemployment benefits, mainly financed by taxes on wages, increased faster than actual salaries, along with other social transfers also financed by labour overheads (health and retirement benefits, as well as the elaborate system of family allowances). By 1981, 25% of GDP was being thus redistributed, financed by wage taxes, the single largest tax in France. In this context, stabilizing labour costs would have required either an explicit agreement with the trade unions on wage moderation or relying on the pressure of high unemployment. Giscard and Barre's hostile relationship with the trade unions meant that the former solution was ruled out. Rising unemployment in 1980 allowed for a stabilization of real take-home wages, but increasing overhead charges kept real labour costs rising, although at a slower pace.

The combined rise of inflation and unemployment, along with an emerging current account deficit in 1980, was of course related to the two oil shocks. But, as evidenced by Germany's superior performance, this could not be the only explanation (for some detailed comparisons of France and Germany, see De Menil and Sastre, 1985). Indeed, France had largely followed the general European trend of supply-side mismanagement, with excessive labour costs, a fast growth of the welfare system, and continuously spreading regulation of labour markets. Another liability inherited by Mitterrand was an overvalued exchange rate. Since the creation of the EMS and despite an unfavourable inflation differential vis-à-vis Germany, the parity of the Franc had remained unchanged. In the event, the real appreciation (about 10 to 12%) proved to be the first hurdle on which the Socialists stumbled.

The bright side of Giscard's and Barre's legacy resided in the public finances. With the exception of the early Chirac expansion and the temporary 'locomotive' agreement of the 1978 summit, the budget had remained almost balanced. As a result, France's public debt (relative to GDP) was in 1980 one of the smallest among OECD countries (Table 1). Mitterrand enjoyed from the beginning more budgetary freedom of manoeuvre than was actually available to most other European countries, and it is perhaps not surprising that this is where he chose to move forcefully.

2.3. Policy measures

Fairly quickly, the new government enacted a series of policy measures: a fiscal expansion with monetary accommodation, minimum wage policies, a reduction of the workweek and new laws concerning labour relations.

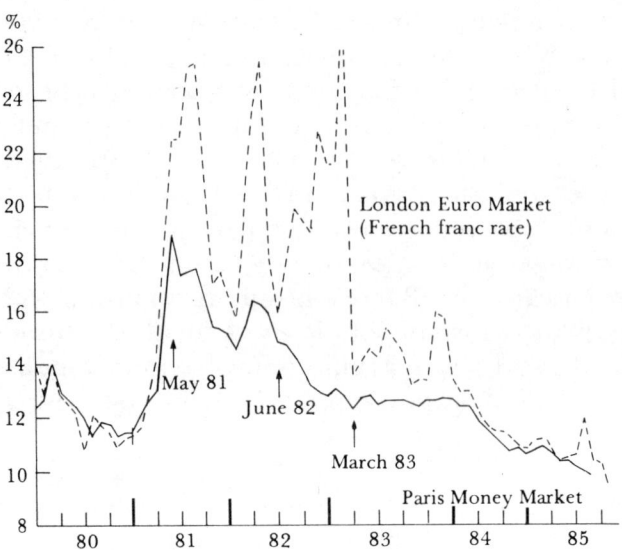

Figure 1. Short-term interest rates

Source: IMF

2.3.1. Fiscal policy. The supplementary 1981 budget increased spending with taxes almost unchanged. In 1981, most of the increased spending was in transfers to households, and subsidies to both state-owned and private corporations, while investment spending by public enterprises was boosted in 1982. Also, the government directly hired 200,000 civil servants in 1981 and 1982.

As a measure of the expansionary impulse, we consider the OECD's inflation-adjusted structural budget balance (for a criticism of *any* single measure of fiscal policy stance see Buiter, 1985), shown in Table 1. The fiscal expansion contributed 1% of GDP in 1981, rising to a cumulative impact of 1.5% of GDP in 1983. As a matter of comparison the Chirac expansion contributed 1.1% in 1975 over 1974, while the post-Bonn summit boost amounted to 1.5% in 1978 (followed by a reduction of 2.8% between 1978 and 1980!).

2.3.2. Monetary policy. Monetary policy was mainly accommodating. The sharp increase in interest rates shown in Figure 1 may be misleading in this respect, because of the French practice of credit ceilings: each year each bank is given a maximum allowed growth rate for its volume of credit outstanding. These ceilings were moderately raised in June 1981 and gradually brought back down in 1982. Interest rates do not clear the market for credit, but rather are directed by the Banque de France with an eye set toward either investment and public borrowing conditions, or the foreign exchange market, depending on the prevailing circumstances. In 1981–83 the main consideration was the perceived need to protect the Franc. Consequently, the 24 hour interbank rate jumped from 10.9% in February 1981 to 18.9% in June, to decline thereafter toward 15% by end 1982. In the event, capital controls prevented an even steeper rise in interest rates in face of an intense speculation. This is shown in Figure 1 as the London Eurofranc rate which is an indication of the level compatible with the expected depreciation (and temporarily falls after each EMS realignment). Yet all this does not signal monetary stringency as the M2 target (10%) was overrun in 1981 (11.4%), leading to an upward adjustment of the reference trend for 1982. This overrun in fact did not correspond to any expansion of credit to the private sector, but rather to direct financing of the government borrowing requirement (one third of the deficit for 1981 was money financed).

2.3.3. Labour market. Mitterrand's election was perceived by the trade unions as a momentous change. The pledge to fight unemployment, together with a host of specific promises to redistribute income and strengthen the hands of trade unions enshrined in the 'Programme Commun', were perceived as the beginning of a new era, akin to the historic transformations achieved during the short tenure of Leon Blum at the head of the Front Populaire in 1936–37. Nationalization and the new tax on wealth were precisely designed to symbolize the shift of power. While it is hard to assess the macroeconomic significance of some of these changes, we shall emphasise the effects of three particular measures concerning the labour market.

The minimum wage: In 1981 a view commonly held in France, and incorporated in some macroeconometric models, was that an autonomous increase in real wages has an expansionary effect. The usual mechanism is a transfer from firms to groups with a high marginal propensity to consume, increasing private consumption which, via the familiar multiplier-accelerator mechanism, generates more investment spending in spite of the profit squeeze. The adverse effect of the profit squeeze on output and investment spending is delayed and is dominated in the interim by a reduction of unused capacity.[2] The sharp increases in the minimum wage (the SMIC) were thus expected to fulfill two major objectives; income redistribution and higher employment. The SMIC was raised by 10% in nominal terms in June 1981, followed by

---

[2] This result was common in 1981 models like METRIC but seems to have been modified recently. Sterdyniak *et al.* (1984) report that in the OFCE model investment spending falls immediately, but total spending increases for two years, followed by a severe recession.

several smaller increments. It rose by a cumulated 38.9% over 1981–82, and in real terms by 11.4% between April 1981 and July 1982. The number of workers receiving the SMIC doubled to about 8% of the labour force (Bourit, Hernu and Perrot, 1982). Overall, the average real hourly wage rate increased by 5.2% during the same period.

The Auroux Laws: Several measures were aimed at changing the relationship between employers and trade unions. The best known of them constituted the 'Lois Auroux', a series of new laws which codified and often enlarged the statutory role of trade unions. These laws, named after the Minister of Labour, Jean Auroux, provide union leaders with increased protection against disciplinary measures and establish the right of workers at the shop floor and factory levels to be involved in production organization choices. They also require wage negotiations with trade unions at least once a year, effectively eliminating the scope for non-union wage settlements. Despite the fact that less than 20% of the labour force formally belong to a union, most of it is de facto unionized, for example because in many low-paid, non-union sectors wages are set close to the minimum wage level, which in turn is set by the government after consultation with the unions.

Other labour measures continued the trend of the seventies in reducing the ability of employers to dismiss redundant workers or to resort to part-time and temporary employment. Since 1975 collective dismissals must be submitted to administrative approval. Such approval, although usually granted, may be, and was, routinely delayed.

Shorter hours and longer holidays: Two decisions were designed to reduce the length of working time. The first extended the length of mandatory paid vacations from 4 to 5 weeks per year. The second reduced the 'legal' workweek from 40 to 39 hours as of January 1982, and was meant to be a first step towards a 35 hour week to be established by 1985.[3] The legal workweek is the number of weekly hours beyond which workers must be offered overtime rates, which increase steeply. The actual system is quite complicated and need not be explained in detail. It is enough to note that average hours per year declined by more than 3% between 1981 and 1983.

After a major debate, Mitterrand expressed publicly his desire to see that monthly pay remain unaffected by the reduction of the workweek. Estimates reported by Marchand, Rault and Turpin, (1983), indicate that such was indeed the outcome for the overwhelming majority of cases. Consequently, real hourly salaries rose quite sharply in 1982: the

---

[3] These decisions were also a powerful symbolic gesture, echoing the introduction of the 40 hour workweek and paid vacations in 1936 by Leon Blum, considered by many people to be his major achievement.

additional vacation week raised them by about 2%, with another 2.5% corresponding to the reduced workweek.

2.4. The nationalization programme

Since the signing of the 'Programme Commun' in 1972, nationalization had been a major commitment for Mitterrand. The arguments behind this programme reached deep into the social history of France, and there was little room in 1981 for questioning the principles involved: the government felt the need to control directly sensitive parts of the economy (banking sector, high-technology, natural monopolies) in order to guarantee more growth and greater equity. Debate concerned only the size of the programme.

The final decision was half-way between the maximalist project of the Communist Party and the shorter list of the Socialists' right wing. It involved 12 industrial firms, 36 banks and 2 financial corporations. As of May 1981, industrial state-owned companies represented about 5% of GDP, with the share rising to about 8% after the new nationalization measures. The newly nationalized industrial groups employed some 550,000 workers, 2.6% of the work force. By 1981, the publicly owned banks already received 60% of all deposits. New nationalization took this share to almost 90%. When it is recognized that the largest insurance companies and a host of financial institutions were already in the public sector, virtually the whole financial sector is now directly controlled by the government.

The question of interest here is the *macroeconomic* impact of nationalization. This would require a difficult analysis, beyond the scope of this article. We limit ourselves to remarks about the conditions under which the macroeconomic effects are likely to be significant.

First, the government may intend to use the nationalized sector to achieve macroeconomic targets. While jobs were created in 1981–82 in the government administration, nothing much was evident in the public industrial sector. At most, lay-offs were postponed. But since 1983 there have been deep cuts in the steel industry, the automobile sector (Renault), and several other newly nationalized corporations.

Second, the government may change the allocation of resources, drawing funds toward state-owned corporations. It is true that between 1981 and 1983 subsidies to the public sector rose markedly, but this trend has now been reversed. By 1984, most of the newly nationalized firms have seen their subsidies fall or disappear *and* have restored their financial equilibrium.

Third, the government may now be tempted to alter its trade policies to protect the public corporations since, while before 1981 the output of the public sector was largely internationally nontradable (electricity, railroad, telephone and postal services), all the newly nationalized firms belong to the internationally tradable sector. Casual evidence suggests that France has always protected its corporations, public or private, when it was deemed necessary. The government has mainly encouraged a wave of mergers (the so-called restructuring), all motivated by the pressure of international competition. As noted by Stoffaes (1985), this is likely to be the major impact of nationalization, and we tentatively conclude that nationalization has probably not had major macroeconomic effects.

2.5. The outcome

The evolution of the French economy during 1981–83 certainly failed to conform to the Government's expectations. The official forecasts for 1982 and 1983 announced a rate of growth of real GDP of 3.1 and 2% respectively, while the actual results were 1.8 and 0.7%. For the inflation rate, the forecasts of 13.4 and 8.2% must be compared with the realized values of 12.6 and 9.5%. Unemployment did not fall, and the Franc was buffeted by several crises. This sequence of setbacks has deeply impressed observers of the French economy, to the point of frequently overshadowing the subsequent economic accomplishments. Yet the episode of expansionary policies was relatively short lived, and a complete explanation of what went wrong does not seem to have been offered. Before turning in the next section to an analysis of this period, we first present the main facts and show how a succession of foreign exchange crises brought about a complete policy reversal.

Unlike other large OECD countries which suffered *two* years of real GDP reduction in the early eighties (Table 1), French GDP never actually fell. On the other hand, inflation, which had remained stubbornly around 10%, started to rise in 1980 after the oil shock and increased again in 1982, while most other industrial countries were achieving significant reductions (see Table 1).

To characterize the employment situation, Table 3 separates the competitive sector from the sheltered sector. The latter includes those industries which are not subjected to market forces because they are dominated by state-owned monopolies. We further separate out the competitive sector into its tradable and non-tradable components (for details see the notes on Table 3).

Total employment, measured by the number of employed workers, had been practically stagnant since the early seventies and declined marginally after 1980, hence the steady increase in the unemployment rate given a trend growth of 0.7% in the labour force. The stability of

Table 3. Indices of employment (E) and manhours (MH) (1980 = 100)

		1973	1979	1981	1982	1983	1984
Competitive sector:	E	100.1	100.2	98.8	98.1	96.7	95.0
	MH	108.5	100.2	96.8	93.7	91.4	88.9
tradable	E	111.0	101.6	98.8	95.0	92.9	90.4
	MH	125.0	103.2	95.7	91.6	87.8	84.7
nontradable	E	90.7	99.0	100.5	100.8	100.0	99.0
	MH	95.6	97.8	97.6	95.5	94.3	92.5
Sheltered sector:	E	92.3	99.1	101.1	103.3	105.1	106.1
Total	E	97.9	99.9	99.4	99.6	99.1	98.1
	MH	101.5	98.5	100.8	98.3	97.7	98.0

Source: INSEE: *Rapport sur les Comptes de La Nation.*
Notes: tradables (those sectors where exports plus imports at least 5% of value added;
agriculture, manufacturing); nontradables: construction, retail and wholesale services;
sheltered: energy, transport, telecommunications, financial.

total employment, in France as in most other European countries, conceals the divergent evolution of a declining traded sector and a growing non-traded sector. Overall employment was maintained close to its 1980 level largely as the result of an increase in the number of workers in the sheltered and government sectors. In conclusion, while the expansionary measures may have insulated France from the world-wide recession in 1982, they certainly failed to deliver the expected increase in employment.

The new government was also confronted with several speculative attacks on the Franc. The first one actually started in the last days before the election and swelled immediately thereafter, prompting the central bank to intervene heavily and to raise interest rates. Minister of Economic Affairs Jacques Delors wanted an immediate devaluation while the President's other advisers did not want to give an impression of weakness in the face of speculative attacks. The latter view prevailed, leaving France with an overvalued exchange rate, that became increasingly so as inflation edged upward while abating abroad. The current account deficit worsened, lending strength to the belief that a devaluation within the EMS could not be avoided. And the Franc was devalued, not once but three times.

The first devaluation occurred in October 1981. After six months of continuing pressure, the Central Bank had exhausted most of its options (high interest rates, strengthening of capital controls, and heavy use of the foreign exchange reserves). The official view was that the exchange rate devaluation represented a technical adjustment prompted by the legacy of a high inflation rate and a wave of unfriendly scepticism on the financial markets.

Paradoxically, the devaluation strengthened the hand of the left wing within the Government. It was, they said, a proof that 'new' policies could not be successful within an economy dominated by the iron law of markets. More control, not less, was required. The Government pressed ahead with the implementation of the Programme Commun. To many observers, France had embarked on a path that would eventually lead it towards more controls, more dirigism and a break-away from the EMS and EEC. Given such expectations, the exchange markets remained sceptical. By March 1982, the pressure built up once again, interest rates were raised and capital outflows swelled to new heights. In June 1982, Mitterrand was hosting the Chiefs of State for the annual summit meeting in the magnificent 'grandeur' of Versailles, while the Banque de France was depleting its reserves. Immediately thereafter, the Franc was devalued by 10% vis-à-vis the DM. This time, the devaluation was accompanied by stabilization measures. First, prices *and* wages were frozen until October 1982. Second, new taxes were raised through higher social security contributions. Third, the budget deficit was targetted at a level not to exceed 3% of GDP. Fourth, some public expenditures were delayed until further notice.

For the first time, the word 'austerity' surfaced, suggesting an end to the expansionary phase of the previous year, and a return to the rules of the game of the EMS. The joint freeze of both prices and wages, for the first time since 1958, signalled a decisive shift towards more controls. In view of this combination of policies, it was unclear whether the Socialists would abandon their macroeconomic policies and return to Barre's medicine, or would go further in restricting the market economy, eventually leaving the EMS. The answer came in March 1983 when, after a further exchange rate crisis, the Franc was devalued by 8% vis-à-vis the DM.

The external constraint had forced Mitterrand to make a political decision he would rather have avoided. For Industry Minister Chevenement and his left-wing backers, the only solution was to leave the EMS, abandon austerity and expand by increasing public spending, especially through the enlarged public sector. The external constraint would be taken care of by protectionist measures, and if need be, a temporary suspension of EEC agreements. For Finance and Economics Minister Delors and the more market-oriented wing, the external constraint required a strengthening of the austerity measures phased in since the previous devaluation, while leaving the EMS would only worsen the situation. The President, after wavering, finally chose to shift towards more restraint at home. This was the end of the short-lived expansionary programme, already shaken after the previous devaluation of June 1982. Hereafter, the Socialists would pursue policies which looked a lot more like those of Barre than those they had advocated during the campaign. Chevenement left the Ministry of Industry and the Cabinet, and was replaced by Fabius, while Delors' responsibilities were enlarged.

3. Anatomy of a policy failure

It took the Mitterrand government no more than two years to reverse its expansionary policy stance, only about a year if one notes that by June 1982 fiscal expansion was already being cut back markedly. It is now official doctrine in the Socialist party that 'we have learned a lesson'. Yet it is not clear what has been learned. One interpretation, articulated by Fonteneau and Muet (1983) is that the main problem was the delay in the world recovery. In this view France was suffering only from insufficient aggregate demand. Accordingly, an expansion was warranted in 1981, and could have been sustained without major external deficits had the world recovery materialized that year, as most forecasts then predicted.

Another possibility, which we strongly endorse below, is that the various early measures affecting the labour markets and the taxes on corporations further worsened supply-side conditions which were already unfavourable by 1981. Several studies (Bruno and Sachs, 1985, Bruno, 1986, Artus, 1984), have previously suggested that an expansionary policy would largely fail to generate more employment and more output, or would do so only at the cost of higher inflation. But we would still have to account for the sharp slowdown in investment spending and the sheer size of capital outflows. Could it be, then, that the mere election of a Socialist government committed to sweeping social changes and income redistribution, prompted a crisis of confidence among investors, forcing the Franc down and provoking a deep slump on the stock market?

This section presents an attempt at disentangling the three explanations. They are not mutually exclusive, and all carry some explanatory power. Each of them, though, has different implications regarding the evaluation of the post-1983 policies and, more importantly, the outlook for France as of 1986.

3.1. Can demand factors explain everything?

One important interpretation of the failure of the 1981–82 expansion is that the world recession of 1982 overwhelmed the domestic demand stimulus in France. Such a view has received widespread expression both in France (Fonteneau and Muet, 1983, Muet, 1985, Beudaert, 1983) and abroad (*World Financial Markets*, 1983). There is certainly much merit to this view. As we show below, the size of the contractionary impulse coming from abroad in 1981 and 1982 was a large proportion of the size of the direct demand stimulus from fiscal policy. If world demand had recovered in 1982, rather than contracting sharply, French growth would probably have been significantly higher, and the external deficit would have been reduced.

But this would not have been the end of the story. Higher growth would almost surely have produced an even faster upturn in inflation than in fact occurred, and the real appreciation of the Franc would have been even more severe. According to our estimates France's 7% unemployment in 1981 represented the inflationary threshold at that time. A lower unemployment rate could certainly have been sustained, but only at the cost of a significant acceleration of inflation.

The Mitterrand expansion did have a temporary effect in boosting growth in the French economy in 1981. A comparison of France and Germany provides a good illustration of this point. Based on the structural budget deficit figures of Table 1, the shift of fiscal policy between 1980 and 1983 amounts to a contraction of 2.8% of GDP in Germany, and an expansion of 1.5% of GDP in France. Over 1981–83, the rise in unemployment in France is a moderate 1.9%, as compared with 5% in Germany, and 4.2% in the EEC as a whole. By bucking the trend of fiscal contraction in the rest of the OECD, the Socialist government clearly bought some moderation in the upward trend in unemployment, at least temporarily, but by less than had been expected in 1981.

To gauge the effects of the world recession on France, we consider the change in the size of the export market in which France was competing. Export volume growth for the industrial countries as a whole slowed down quickly after 1980, actually decreasing by 1.7% in 1982. Given the previous trend, we estimate a shortfall of exports due to the world recession of 4.5% in 1982, and another 0.4% in 1983.[4] The elasticity of demand for French goods with respect to the overall market for industrial country exports is approximately 1.0. Thus, as a rough approximation, we can argue that French exports were reduced by approximately 4.5% in 1982 because of the world recession. Since French exports of goods and non-factor services were about 20% of GDP in the early 1980s, the first-round contractionary effect of the

---

[4] Estimate based on authors' regressions, and is similar to the 5.2% reduction in foreign demand estimated by Fonteneau and Muet (1983).

reduced exports (i.e. before any demand multiplier is considered) was approximately 0.9% of GDP in 1982. This is more than half of the increase in the structural budget deficit in 1981 and 1982.

In this sense, the assertion that the demand stimulus was sharply curtailed by the world recession is probably correct. This conclusion underscores the relatively small amount of fiscal stimulus that was imparted in 1981 and 1982, as well as the severity of the global downturn. However, the world recession was not the only limiting factor in successfully reducing unemployment. For we should ask what would have happened to French inflation, and to the pressure on the Franc, in the event of a larger net expansion domestically. The inflation equations of the next section are emphatic on a key point: France was already at the inflationary threshold level of unemployment in 1981. With more expansion, inflation would have had no place to go but up!

It is important to stress that the rebound in inflation in France in 1982 was home made, rather than imported by the devaluations of 1981 and 1982. Import prices rose at the same rate as domestic prices in 1982 (12.2% for import prices and 12.6% for the GDP deflator). This is not surprising in that the devaluations did little more than keep the Franc depreciating at a rate equal to the inflation differential with France's EMS trading partners. Thus, with no world recession, there is little case for arguing that import price inflation would have been sharply lower.

It is sometimes argued that even with higher, and rising, inflation, the policy would have been sustainable in the absence of a world recession, since the external balance would have been substantially improved. On the first round, exports would have risen by about 0.9% of GDP, with the ultimate current account improved by a somewhat smaller amount (after second-round induced imports are accounted for). Thus, the current account deficit might have deteriorated from about 0.8% of GDP in 1981 to perhaps 1.7% of GDP in 1982, rather than the 2.2% level that was actually reached. Nonetheless, the current account position would still have been adverse (as should be expected after any fiscal expansion).

Furthermore, the current account is not the only channel through which the external constraint is felt. All three realignments which, taken together, led to a 32.2% devaluation of the Franc vis-à-vis the Deutschmark, followed intense speculative runs which all but depleted France's non-gold foreign exchange reserves. As can be seen from Table 4 much of the action in 1981 took place through the capital account: between the first and the second subperiod, the overall balance worsens by 2.1% of GDP, of which only 0.4% is attributable to the current account. As for 1982, the dramatic improvement in the capital account is largely

Table 4. Selected items in the balance of payments: quarterly averages (% of GDP)

	1980Q1–1981Q1	1981Q2–1982Q2	1982Q3–1983Q1	1983Q2–1985Q1
Current Account	−0.8	−1.2	−2.6	−0.3
Long-Term Capital	−0.3	−0.5	1.5	0.5
Short-Term Private Capital	0.6	−0.2	−0.0	−0.1
Errors and Omissions	0.2	−0.4	−0.1	0.2
Overall Balance	−0.3	−2.4	−1.3	0.3
Short-term Public Capital	−1.1	2.9	0.4	−1.0

Source: Banque de France, *Bulletin Trimestriel*.
Note: The Short Term Capital Account excludes the Banking Sector which is included in the Overall Balance. All data are on a quarterly basis and the ratios are averaged over each subperiod.

explained by the increasing use of the time honoured practice of instructing publicly owned corporations to borrow abroad ('emprunts encouragés') as an indirect means of intervening on exchange markets. The current account, therefore, is only a partial measure of the external constraint. Even without the 1982 world recession, the Franc would almost surely have been under stress.

3.2. The supply side

While most European countries went through a period of slow growth and regularly declining inflation in 1982 and 1983, consumer price inflation began to rise in mid-1981 and remained strong until mid-1982 when most prices were frozen. We have already noted that foreign prices and the exchange rate depreciations cannot be held responsible for this development. Rather, 7% unemployment represented a 'tight' labour market in 1981, offering little scope for noninflationary expansion. A NAIRU of 7% was of course extraordinary, given the much lower average employment rates of the 1960s and 1970s, and few analysts showed any awareness of how tight the situation was.

The evidence rejects the key element of simple demand-centred policy analyses: the assumption of a constant NAIRU. When the NAIRU can change over time, movements of actual unemployment rates relative to their historical averages provide little direct evidence as to whether a demand expansion is warranted or is likely to be inflationary. As voluminous recent research has shown, the scope for demand expansion can be determined only after a careful analysis of supply conditions in the economy. This analysis is unfortunately hampered by the absence of an agreed framework.

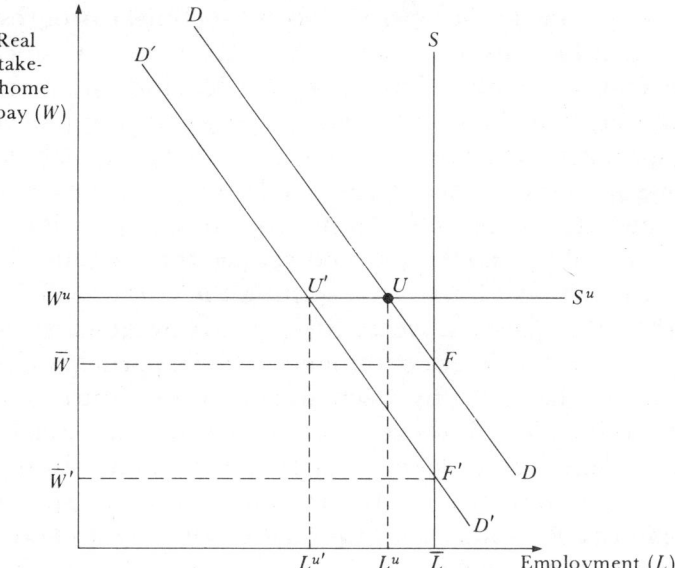

Figure 2. The labour market

Our approach makes the NAIRU the cornerstone of the analysis of supply behaviour. In doing so we seek to answer the question: what is the lowest unemployment rate that can be sustained in the medium and long-term without producing a continuously rising inflation rate? Thus the NAIRU is not a barrier above which a fiscal expansion will not raise output or lower unemployment; it is only a barrier vis-à-vis the long-run sustainability of a demand expansion. In the short-run unemployment may fall below the NAIRU, but ultimately only at the cost of rising inflation. Our model of supply behaviour is compatible with a variety of stories about short-run behaviour. In particular it is quite consistent with an approach that has been especially popular in France which treats wages and prices as fixed in the short run and admits rationing in goods and/or labour markets (see Artus, Laroque and Michel, 1984; Lambert, Lubrano and Sneessens, 1984; Bouissou, Laffont and Vuong, 1984; Malinvaud, 1986). Such models address the different question of whether a demand expansion would be successful at reducing unemployment in the short run irrespective of any effect on inflation.

Figure 2 depicts a simple diagram of the labour market. Firms' demand for labour will, for a given capital stock, be lower the higher is the real cost of labour. However the real cost of labour differs from real take-home pay of workers (W) for three reasons. First, whereas workers deflate nominal wages by *consumer* prices, firms care about the level of wages relative to the *product* price. Second technical progress which increases the productivity of labour for a given capital stock reduces the effective cost of labour and increases the demand for labour even when take-home pay is unchanged. Finally employer and employee taxes drive an additional wedge between take home pay and labour costs. Figure 2 shows a labour demand curve DD for given levels of capital, technical knowledge, taxes, etc. An increase in taxes, or lower level of capital or technical productivity would reduce the demand for labour at any given level of take-home pay, shifting the curve to $D'D'$.

Econometric evidence suggests, at least for primary wage-earners, that real take-home pay has little effect on labour-force participation. Hence we draw a vertical labour supply schedule at $\bar{L}$ in Figure 2. A major theme of our discussion, however, is that if wages are set by unions, rather than by competitive labour markets, the union 'supply' schedule might in fact be quite elastic[5]. In fact, one important special case derived in Appendix B shows that a rational union might choose to fix the level of real take-home pay at a level such as W^u, no matter what the implications are for the employment level. In other words, the union 'supply' schedule would be perfectly elastic at the wage level W^u, as shown in Figure 2.

Now let us consider some alternative scenarios. Beginning with labour demand DD, full employment in a competitive labour market is at point F, with real take-home pay $\bar{W}$ and employment $\bar{L}$.

Now suppose instead that the labour market is fully unionized, with unions demanding real take-home pay level W^u. The union-based equilibrium will be at the point U.

Unemployment is given as $\bar{L} - L^u$, and the (proportional) deviation of the actual union wage W^u from the level warranted by full employment is $(W^u - \bar{W})/\bar{W}$. This deviation of the actual from the warranted wage is called the *wage gap*.

Suppose now that payroll taxes are raised, so that the demand curve shifts to $D'D'$. The full-employment wage falls to $\bar{W}'$. The new equilibrium is given by U' in Figure 2, with employment $L^{u'}$ and real take-home pay fixed at W^u. Note that the vertical shift of the demand curve, and hence the increase in the wage gap equals the amount of the tax increase.

In this union-based theory of the NAIRU, the 'equilibrium' rate of unemployment depends on the size of the wage gap and the slope of the labour demand curve. (Obviously, this formulation abstracts from

---

[5] Although, as a monopolistic supplier of labour, the union does not have a supply schedule that is independent of demand, it is expositionally convenient to maintain this fiction. A rigorous analysis is given in Appendix B.

purely frictional components of the NAIRU, say due to job turnover or search; we assume that such frictional components are constant, for reasons that we outline below.) When the demand curve is DD the NAIRU is then determined as $U^* = \bar{L} - L^u$.

Factors which shift the labour force $\bar{L}$, the demand curve DD, or the target wage W^u shift the NAIRU. Prime candidates for such shift factors include the wedge, the capital stock, and the state of technical knowledge. A fall in the capital stock, a fall in technical productivity, or a rise in the wedge would both raise the NAIRU and raise the wage gap. Our empirical discussion that follows examines these presumptions.

In our interpretation of the Phillips curve, we assume that union wage-setters gradually reach their target employment level L^u and target real wage level W^u. In particular, we assume that unions increase their real wage demands whenever actual employment L exceeds their target level L^u, and lower their demands when L is less than L^u. We therefore specify the nominal wage change π^w as a function of expected or lagged inflation π_{-1}, and the deviation of the unemployment rate from the NAIRU, $U - U^*$:

$$\pi^w = \alpha(U - U^*) + \pi_{-1} \tag{1}$$

Price inflation π is closely related to wage inflation π^w and the preceding discussion of what determines the NAIRU, U^*, coupled with our hypothesis about how unions gradually adjust actual wages and employment to target levels, allows us to derive (in Appendix B) the empirical Phillips curve which forms the basis of our econometric estimates in the next section.

The key novelty in this approach is that the model underscores the factors that shift the NAIRU, and in turn cause shifts in the Phillips curve. Variables that shift the NAIRU should also shift the wage gap. Thus, in examining the evidence for the 1970s and 1980s, we expect to find that both the wage gaps and the NAIRU have risen in France. Indeed we find strong evidence for both of these trends after 1973.

3.2.1. Wage gaps. Wage gaps have been calculated for France's manufacturing sector by Bruno and Sachs (1985), Artus (1984) and Bruno (1986). Such measures are difficult to obtain as they require, in principle, the estimation of production functions, from which to deduce the slopes of labour demand schedules. Our intention here is to update previous estimates and to measure wage gaps for sectors other than manufacturing, as the manufacturing sector represents a small, and secularly declining, portion of France's output (22% in value added terms in 1984, down from 26% in 1963).

Table 5. Wage gaps (% of labour costs, base years 1976–78)

	Manufacturing	Building and Construction	Retail and Wholesale Trade
1976–78	0	0	0
1980	1–7	1–5	1–5
1981	4–9	3–7	0–6
1982	3–9	2–8	0–10
1983	4–12	2–9	2–12
1984	6–17	2–10	4–14

Notes: For details of construction see Appendix A. Range of estimates
assume an elasticity of substitution of between 1/2 and 1 and allow for
either Harrod or Hicks-neutral technical progress. The base years correspond to an average unemployment rate of 5%.

Contrary to the other works mentioned, we do not use econometric
estimates to measure the wage gap. Rather we specify alternative parameters of an assumed production function, and find a resulting range
of estimates for the gap. The procedure is fully presented in Appendix
A and only briefly explained here. First, by observing value added,
factor inputs and factor shares, we directly measure the rate of technological change (which is assumed, alternatively, to be labour augmenting,
or both capital and labour augmenting). The production function is
then fully characterized by *assuming* the elasticity of substitution and
measuring the labour share in the base period. The derived labour
demand is then computed (this is the *DD* curve in Figure 2) which
allows us to find the warranted real labour cost, i.e. the level at which
firms would hire the amount of labour corresponding to full employment. A baseline of sectoral full employment, in turn, is estimated given
an aggregate full employment level and the trend in inter-sectoral
employment shifts.

We present in Table 5 a range of estimates for the wage gaps in three
sectors: the manufacturing sector, the building and construction
industry, and retail and wholesale trade. The range of estimates corresponds to the extreme values obtained allowing the slope of the labour
demand curve to vary within reasonable bounds and for both general
and labour-augmenting technological progress. In all cases, the chosen
base period (defined as 'full employment') is 1976–78 when unemployment averaged 5%.

These numbers are meant to answer the following question: by how
much should labour costs be reduced in a given sector and in a given
year to prompt a demand for labour corresponding to an overall 5%
unemployment rate? The table shows large numbers (around 10%),
with some differences across sectors. These numbers do not differ

markedly from those computed for the manufacturing sector by Artus, Bruno and Sachs.

3.2.2. The NAIRU. In view of the traditional link of the NAIRU with 'frictional' unemployment, it might seem fruitful to try to explain its rise with variables that might shift the frictional rate. Such candidates include: demographic shifts in the labour force, such as a rising proportion of young workers, who have historically had high rates of unemployment even when the aggregate unemployment rate has been low; job mismatch, as evidenced by a shift in the relationship between vacancy and unemployment rates; regional and industrial mismatch, as evidenced by an unusual rate of structural change or compositional change in the labour force. A large number of studies have tried to track down these possible culprits, and the results have been disappointing (see Layard *et al.*, 1984, and the recent country studies presented at an LSE conference on the Rise in Unemployment including a study on France by Malinvaud).

The inability of standard frictional variables to account for much of the increase in the NAIRU in Europe has led us to emphasize explanations drawing directly on the model of the firm-union bargain developed in the previous section, and formally set out in Appendix B. Thus we expect the NAIRU to increase when the unions' target wage increases, when productivity growth slows, and when the wedge increases.

In this section, we verify that such a mechanism has been at work. Recent studies have shown that France, like most European countries, has suffered a rise in the NAIRU in the 1970s and 1980s (See Grubb, Layard and Symons 1984, Grubb, Jackman and Layard, 1982, 1983, Layard *et al.*, 1984, Coe and Gagliardi, 1985). The significant European exceptions appear to be Italy and Austria, and the remaining notable exception in the OECD is the United States.[6]

To estimate these effects we use an equation which generalizes Equation (1). The NAIRU depends on the wedge x, technical productivity ψ, and the target wage W^u. We cannot gather data directly on the target wage, and we adopt the simple device of proxying it with a time trend t. The wedge (the difference between real take-home pay and real labour cost to the firm) depends on labour taxes and on any

---

[6] The following estimates of the NAIRU are taken from Coe and Gagliardi:

	Germany	France	UK	Italy	Austria	Netherlands	US
1967–70	0.7	2.2	2.1	7.5	1.1	3.0	5.4
1981–83	3.6	7.7	9.4	5.4	2.4	8.7	6.1

Table 6. The Phillips curve (Dependent variable: change in inflation rate, $\Delta\pi$, annual data, 1963–84)

Variable	Regression 1 estimated coefficient	*t* statistic	Regression 2 estimated coefficient	*t* statistic
constant	205.64	(3.77)	251.51	(6.69)
unemployment (u)	−4.16	(4.86)	−4.75	(8.41)
lagged change in relative import prices ($\Delta(p^m - p)_{-1}$)	0.07	(2.33)	0.06	(2.81)
productivity minus wedge ($\psi - x$)	−42.57	(3.76)	−52.05	(6.67)
lagged change in inflation rate ($\Delta\pi_{-1}$)	—	—	−0.31	(4.03)
lagged error ($\hat{e}_{-1}$)	−0.58	(3.29)	—	—
time trend (t)	2.76	(4.27)	3.23	(7.47)
dummy variables: DV_1	1.16	(2.48)	—	—
DV_2	—	—	2.01	(8.61)
Standard error (percentage points)	0.98		0.60	

Notes: (a) p and p^m denote GDP deflator at factor prices and import price deflator respectively. Lower case letters denote logarithms and $\pi = 100\,(p - p_{-1})$. ψ is the log of productivity (adjusted for capital deepening) and x the log of the wedge (see Appendix B). (b) Dummy variables are defined thus: DV_1 takes the value minus unity in 1964, 1965, 1974, 1976, and 1983, the years in which severe wage or price controls were in force, and otherwise takes a zero value. DV_2 additionally takes the value plus unity during the years 1963, 1973, 1975, and 1982 to capture the effect of anticipated tightening of price controls.

discrepancy between the prices relevant to firms and to workers. Since income tax rates change little over our sample period, we simplify by omitting income tax rates including only employer and employee pay-roll taxes and the ratio of import to domestic prices.

Rather than assume that unions continuously attain their target real wage, we postulate sluggish adjustment of actual to target real wages. In terms of our estimated equation, this introduces lagged values of some variables to capture this sluggish adjustment of actual to target real wages. Finally, we include two alternative specifications of a dummy variable DV to capture periods in which unusually severe price controls temporarily distorted the wage bargaining process.

Having examined several regression equations for 1963–84 with annual data, we show our preferred equations in Table 6. They differ primarily in the definition of the price control dummy variable (see Footnote (b) to Table 6). Regression (2) uses a dummy variable which allows anticipated as well as contemporaneous effects of severe wage and price controls and produces a better fit, though we also show

Table 7. Actual unemployment and the estimated NAIRU (%)

	1963	1973	1978	1980	1981	1982	1983	1984
Actual	1.2	2.7	5.3	6.4	7.3	8.1	8.3	9.7
NAIRU: Equation (1)	1.1	2.9	5.4	6.9	7.4	7.7	8.3	8.9
NAIRU: Equation (2)	1.2	2.9	5.4	6.8	7.4	7.7	8.3	9.0

estimates for an equation in which the dummy variable only includes contemporaneous effects (Regression (1)). The choice of dummy variable leads us to choose a slightly different dynamic specification in each case, but the two reported equations are very similar in their economic implications.

Both equations show the crucial significance of the level of productivity ψ and the wedge x. In fact, it is an implication of our theory that the two variables should have equal coefficients but opposite signs, an empirical prediction we tested before combining these two variables in Table 6. The time trend and either specification of the price controls dummy have the expected effect, and changes in import prices relative to domestic prices also affect the wage bargain. Other results are reported in Appendix C. Specifically, we could not detect a role, jointly or severally, for the following variables: changes in the unemployment rate, the ratio of unemployment benefits to wages, the level of unemployment benefits or of the minimum real wage, and the ratio of vacancies to unemployment (a crude indicator of mismatch).

As we explain in Appendix B, the equations of Table 6 can be solved to derive an estimate for the NAIRU. Essentially this involves using the equation to determine what value of unemployment would generate no change in inflation, given other variables in the equation. Table 7 shows the values of the NAIRU thus derived. Both regressions give very similar estimates. The NAIRU has increased steadily over the last 15 years, with marked jumps in 1974 and 1980–81. The most striking implication of Table 7 is that actual unemployment has been very close to the NAIRU, at least until 1984. Our procedure cannot distinguish between two competing explanations of this finding: first, that markets adjust very quickly, and, second, that policy makers, being sensitive to accelerating inflation, have chosen or been forced to adjust demand and employment to levels corresponding to the NAIRU.

The role of the different factors in the evolution of the NAIRU can be considered using Regression (1). During 1964–73, productivity growth was strong enough to absorb both a growing labour force and

**Table 8. Changes in unemployment and NAIRU
(percentage points)**

	1973–80	1981–84
Change in actual unemployment	+3.7	+3.3
Change in NAIRU	+4.0	+2.0
contribution of:		
productivity slowdown	+1.6	+0.9
wedge increase	+1.3	+0.5
others	+1.1	+0.6

Note: NAIRU decomposition based on Regression (1) of
Table 6.

expectations of rising living standards. Had productivity growth during
1974–84 remained at the 1963–73 rate (in other words, 5.1% per year,
rather than the actual 2.7%) the NAIRU would have been reduced by
2.5% in 1984 (Table 8). During the same period 1974–84, the wedge
rose from 41 to 69% of net take-home pay, contributing another 1.8%
to the overall 6.0% increasing in the NAIRU. The rest is either unex-
plained or captured by the time trend. The time trend may be interpreted in several ways. First it picks up rising expectations of increased
standards of living, so that the target wage set by unions grows irrespective of actual productivity advances. Second, it may also represent a
gradual increase in labour market regulation. Third, there have been
several demographic factors increasing the labour force, including the
postwar baby boom and the entry of women. Finally, there is a trend
towards reduced working time that we discuss below.

3.2.3. The effects of reduced working time. In January 1982, two changes
were introduced: the legal workweek was reduced from 40 to 39 hours,
with an objective of 35 hours by 1985, and a compulsory fifth week of
paid vacations. As already noted, hourly wage rates were raised to leave
workers' yearly earnings unchanged. While some reductions in labour
taxes were granted on a selective basis (small firms, or large firms which
hired new workers), labour costs nevertheless increased. It was the
official view that reduction of working time should lead to more employment through work sharing.

The argument that employment might rise has been articulated in
the French case by Oudiz, Raoul and Sterdyniak (1979). It explicitly
recognizes that the desired job creation requires that hourly wages do
not increase and argues that the actual measues and the foreseen
reduction of the legal workweek to 35 hours would prompt plant-level
reorganizations which should in fact reduce labour costs and raise the
overall demand for labour. This would be the case, for instance, if a

plant were to use two shifts where it formerly used one. But apart from exceptional cases, the reduction of the workweek is likely to produce rather marginal changes in the plant level organization of labour. It is more plausible to assume that, given the existing equipment and lay-out of most plants, operating less hours with more people will be more costly, if only because if it had been in the firms' best interest to do so, they would not have waited for the mandatory changes to introduce the new system.

A formal analysis of the issue (see Calmfors, 1985; Wyplosz, 1985) in the framework of the union wage model shows that if workers care a lot for leisure, they will accept a reduction in their earned incomes in exchange for a shorter workweek. Their unions would then go along with no, or little, hourly wage increase as it would give firms an incentive to maintain their demand for manhours and increase the chances that work sharing occurs. If, in addition, there are no significant costs of producing with more workers working shorter hours, then employment must rise.

The evidence reported so far is that work sharing did not occur in France in 1982. We know that hourly wage rates were not reduced so that labour costs increased. And there is no evidence of large scale plant re-organization which would have brought about benefits from operating with more workers. Thus the two necessary conditions were not satisfied. Attempts at measuring the effect directly conclude that it was, at best, very limited. For example, Colin, Elbaum and Fonteneau (1984) conclude that some 25,000 jobs were created in 1982, with no further effects thereafter. This represents about 1.25% of the unemployed population and 0.12% of total employment. If we consider that the reduction in working hours and the fifth week of paid vacations reduced the number of hours per worker by about 4.5% (2.5 and 2.0%, respectively), we conclude that these measures reduced the total volume of manhours by about 4%. As actual manhours fell by about 2%, it appears that these 'work sharing' measures in and by themselves more than offset the effects of all the other expansionary measures enacted in 1981–82.

3.2.4. Appraisal. This section has produced evidence that labour costs have increased steadily over the past 10 years, resulting in 'wage gaps' of about 3% in 1973 to 7% in 1981. The 1981–82 expansion, coupled with measures which further increased labour costs, could not have succeeded in creating jobs in the competitive sector in a non-inflationary way. With the actual rate also around 7%, Mitterrand's electoral pledge to reduce unemployment quickly could not, in any case, be fulfilled without an acceleration in prices.

Our estimation of the NAIRU (Table 7) shows that a 10% reduction in labour costs (via increased productivity or a reduction in the wedge) would lower the NAIRU by a little more than 1%. This would require labour costs to fall by about 50% in order to reduce the NAIRU to its 1976–8 level! There is a large discrepancy between the implications of the wage gaps and those of the NAIRU. Clearly, measurement problems may be part of the explanation. Yet there is another one. Given the many labour regulations and the costs of altering the size of the labour force, it may be that in the short run the firms' wage elasticity of demand for labour is quite small[7]. In this case, the Phillips curve estimates capture a short-run elasticity, while the wage gap estimates capture the long-run response of labour demand to wages. Thus, we suspect that the long-run fall in the NAIRU following a rise in productivity or a fall in the wedge is probably greater than is suggested by the estimates of the Phillips curve in Table 6. However, we have not yet investigated the nature of union behaviour under the assumption that the long-run labour demand elasticity exceeds its short-run value.

3.3. The confidence factor

No matter how misplaced, the policy measures of 1981 were of moderate magnitude. This stands in contrast with the very strong reaction of the exchange markets to the change in government in 1981. We therefore offer a third hypothesis to explain why the Socialists failed to sustain their policies, namely that they never inspired much confidence among the investors and private corporations, and that whatever goodwill they may initially have relied on was quickly shattered.

To evaluate the role of these fears in the deterioration on the French situation between May 1981 and March 1983, we focus on two markets where these expectations are likely to have been most powerful; the stock market and the exchange market. Figure 3 shows a monthly index of industrial share prices deflated by an industrial goods price index and the one-month forward exchange rate discount of the Franc vis-à-vis the Deutschmark (the percentage forward discount is stated at an annual rate). In principle, the first variable reflects the market expectation of future discounted profits, while the second is a crude measure

---

[7] The estimates in Tables 6–8 suggest an elasticity of 0.1 of the NAIRU with respect to $(\psi - x)$. Production function estimates (see Appendix B) suggest a value $\sigma/(1 - S_L)$ where σ is the elasticity of substitution and S_L (=0.66 in 1984) the share of labour in value added. Even an elasticity of substitution as low as 1/6 would suggest a long run NAIRU elasticity of 0.5, considerably above the short run estimate given above.

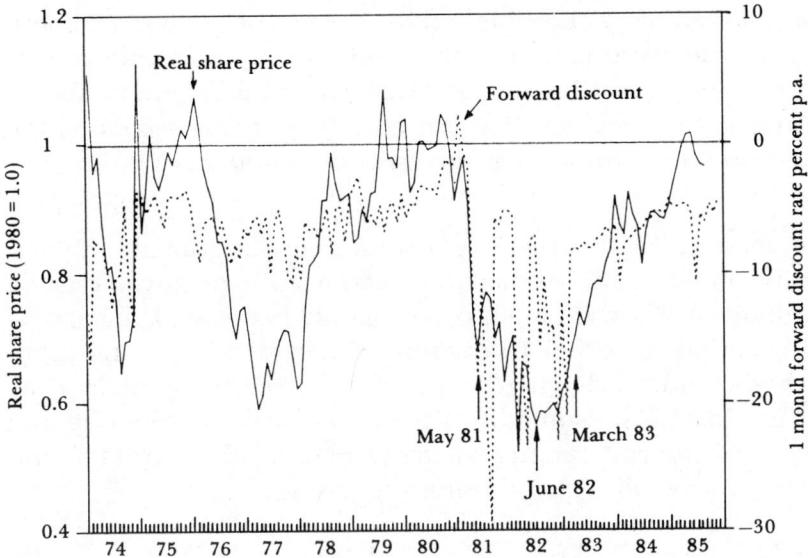

Figure 3. The real share price and the forward discount

Source: DRI Data Bank & IMF

of expected future exchange rate depreciation (a negative value indicates an expected depreciation).

Three subperiods appear. In May 1981, there is a clear and sharp fall in both measures followed by a hectic evolution around a downward trend until June 1982. Thereafter the real share price remains flat up until early 1983 where it enters a third phase with an upward trend. By mid 1985 it is back at its 1980 level, though some 50% below its pre oil-shock level of 1973. The pattern of the forward discount is similar, except for more volatility in the intermediate period. The three subperiods during 1981–85 commence with to the election of Mitterrand in May 1981, the second devaluation accompanied by the first restrictive measures in June 1982, and the definite turn to austerity at the time of the third devaluation of March 1983.

In principle, we would like to be able to say whether the sharp change observed in May 1981 and until March 1983 is a rational anticipation of what was to follow (indeed corporate profits fell, several corporations were nationalized[8] and the Franc was devalued) or whether it reflected exaggerated fears. In the first case, by bringing forward future adverse developments correctly anticipated, the financial markets fulfill the

---

[8] Though compensation was paid (see Langohr and Viallet, 1986).

useful role of reducing possible misallocation of resources, both nationally and internationally. In the latter case, a panic undermines what could have been sensible policies. Unfortunately we are unable to distinguish these two views so that the objective of this section is the more limited one of documenting the crisis of confidence.

3.3.1. The stock market. Share prices are very much expectational variables, incorporating all available information about future movements in profits and interest rates. Changes occur mainly because of the arrival of new information. In order to organize the evidence, we therefore examine whether quarterly changes in this variable are explained by changes in the factors presumed to have an influence: monetary and fiscal policy, real interest rates, real wages (which affect profits), and import prices. We obtain the following regression:

$$\Delta q = 0.03 - 7.21\,\Delta w - 0.04\,\Delta B + 1.70\,\Delta m - 0.08 D_1 + 0.06 D_2 \qquad (2)$$
$$\quad\;\;(1.43)\,(3.23)\qquad(1.74)\qquad(1.24)\qquad(2.07)\quad(1.45)$$

Sample period, quarterly, 1974Q1–1984Q1;

where t statistics in brackets; standard error $= 0.08$; $DW = 1.92$

Δq = quarterly growth in real share price index (nominal index deflated by index of industrial goods' prices), Δw = quarterly growth in real labour costs, ΔB = quarterly change in public deficit as a proportion of GDP, Δm = quarterly growth in the real money stock (M2). Thus higher real labour costs, a larger public deficit, and a lower real money stock tend to reduce real share prices. We also include two dummy variables in Equation (2): D_1 takes the value unity from Mitterrand's election to the major policy reversal of March 1983, zero elsewhere; D_2 is unity thereafter, zero elsewhere. D_1 documents the initial confidence crisis, whilst D_2 provides some evidence for a subsequent restoration of confidence.

Thus, Mitterrand's election had two major effects on share prices. First the direct confidence effect which alone accounts for a fall of 8% during the initial period when share prices actually fell by some 20% in May–June 1981. Second, Equation (2) implies that each 1% increase in real labour costs reduces equity prices by 7%. Since we have argued that Mitterrand's labour market policies added significantly to real labour costs, this reinforced the fall in share prices.

Nor are these effects unimportant. Reductions in real share prices, by hitting investment spending, may have weakened the initial stimulus to aggregate demand. To investigate this possibility, we estimate the following regression on quarterly data from 1976Q1–1984Q4.[9]

$$i = 0.24 + 0.02q - 0.17r + 0.18\Delta_4 y + 0.87 i_{-1} \tag{3}$$
$$(2.72)\ (2.00)\quad (1.67)\quad (2.21)\quad (17.31)$$

t statistics in brackets; standard error $= 0.02$;

where: $q = $ (logarithm of) the real share price, $i = $ (logarithm of) the share of investment in output, $r = $ (ex post) real interest rate, $\Delta_4 y = $ annual growth rate of corporate output.

This regression confirms the usual investment equations of French macro-models which stress the accelerator effect of growth and of the real interest rate. What we add is the role of stock prices, and through them, the impact of market expectations and of profitability. The regression, when simulated to measure the effect of the 40% drop in real share prices during the early Mitterrand period predicts a fall of 0.7% in the ratio of investment to output as compared with an actual fall of 1.7%. These crude computations simply illustrate the plausibility of the story which links adverse expectations in financial circles to a fall of stock prices, and then to a depressing effect on investment spending. Ignoring these links, as do the usual French investment equations, led to unpleasant surprises, as the government was obviously betting on the resumption of growth to boost investment spending. The investment recovery never occurred.

3.3.2. Capital flows and the EMS constraint.

The other gauge of confidence is the international monetary situation. We already noted the high correlation between share prices and the discount on the forward exchange rate. Capital outflows are another channel of interest because they may exacerbate the pressure faced by the monetary authorities as they attempt to maintain a given parity within the EMS. In order to assess the role of capital flight, a certain number of precautions must be taken. First, because exchange controls are widespread in France (see Claassen and Wyplosz, 1985) and have been strengthened in June 1981 and further considerably tightened from March 1983 to January 1984, capital flight is observed both in the short term capital account and in errors and omissions. Second, both directly and through state-owned corporations, the Government has been able to borrow abroad when private outflows swelled. This is why we show in Figure 4 the sum of the short-term private capital account and the errors and omissions, labelled the speculative capital account.

---

[9] Recognising that q is endogenous, we have re-estimated Equation (2) using 2SLS, but obtained practically identical estimates.

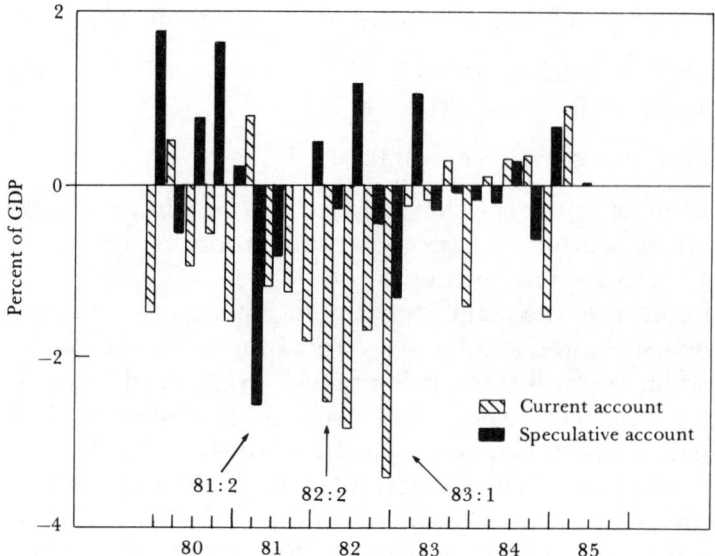

Figure 4. The current account and the speculative capital account
Source: Banque de France

The quarterly figures, the only ones available, probably understate the size of outflows immediately preceding a devaluation, since the outflows become inflows in the aftermath of the devaluation, or when the expectations turn out to be unwarranted. Thus, the quarterly data tend to smooth out larger short-term swings. Yet, we observe massive outflows in 1981 until the first devaluation in October, a reflux delayed until the second devaluation of June 1982, quickly reversed by the crisis in the first quarter of 1983 which led to the third and last devaluation in March.

As in the case of stock prices, capital outflows and the forward discount may well have been rational anticipations of future current account deficits and devaluations, respectively, or else they might have reflected a component of irrational fear. What is important is that they all point toward a significant worsening in confidence.

The role of external pressure was extremely important, since there is good reason to believe that French commitments to the EMS tipped the balance towards austerity. Unlike the much looser commitments under the European Snake in the 1970s, which France abandoned on two occasions, membership of the EMS has been invested with enormous political importance at the very highest levels of the government. That is why the debate over leaving the EMS was treated as synonymous with the debate over abandoning other spheres of cooperation in Europe, including participation in the Common Market. Apparently few participants in the debate opted for an intermediate strategy of continued free trade, but with a floating Franc outside the EMS.

Thus, the episode is an important case study of the possibility of applying international monetary agreements to restrain domestic policies. Economists have long debated whether international exchange rate agreements can really bind national policies, since the sanctions for breaking agreements are so small and diffuse. The example of the Socialist turnaround in March 1983 suggests that an international agreement can help to tip the balance towards domestic restraint.

Perhaps a more interesting aspect of the EMS constraint is that it represented a way for one political party in France to bind the future actions of another. After all, Giscard took France into the arrangement in 1979, but the constraint under the arrangement really only became binding under Mitterrand. Thus, Giscard effectively exercised a strong vote on French policy long after leaving office. This form of future control might be an argument for the Conservative Party under Thatcher to lead the UK into EMS membership: not to bind its own behaviour, which is sufficiently austere by itself, but rather to bind the actions of a successor government, which is likely to be far more expansionary.

Note that the EMS could one day serve the interests of the Socialists by preventing overly contractionary policies of a right-wing government, since excessive appreciation carries responsibilities for intervention and adjustment as does excessive depreciation (of course, the principal burden of adjustment falls on the country with the depreciating currency).

3.4. Summing-up

The Socialist spending expansion added a very modest 1.5% of GDP to total domestic demand, and in the end, employment declined outside the non-competitive and public sectors. We agree that the unexpected world recession in 1982 played an important role in undermining the French attempt at unilateral expansion, yet this is only a partial explanation of the policy failure. Confidence was shaken, and we found that this alone accounts for a fall of private investment spending representing 0.7% of GDP. Coming on top of the 0.9% of GDP lost in exports because of the world recession, we see that there was never much of a net demand stimulus. At best therefore, the monetary and fiscal policy mix of 1981–82 was enough to keep France out of the world recession. The resulting current account deficit, together with confidence-related capital outflows, created the conditions for a balance of payments crisis.

In the end, Mitterrand's choice to remain within the EMS left him with no other choice than to reverse his policy stand and join France's partners in austerity.

The striking element of 1981–83, dating back to the early seventies, was the simultaneous problem of high unemployment and continued strong inflationary pressures. The NAIRU had risen sharply over the 1970s, and continued to rise in 1981 and 1982. The high level of the NAIRU was accompanied by large and growing wage gaps. The proximate cause of the rising NAIRU was the combination of slow productivity growth in France and a continuing increase of real labour costs, due to higher labour taxes, the secular growth of real take-home pay, and cost-raising measures such as the shortened workweek. Hence, even without the problems induced by a world recession and a collapse of confidence, Mitterrand had little scope in 1981 to embark on a sustained demand expansion without quickly generating accelerating inflation.

4. Socialist austerity: a success story

Hesitantly between June 1982 and March 1983, and more boldly thereafter, the Socialist government has completed a turnaround in its economic policies. The fight against unemployment is no longer at the forefront of the government's objectives. The key words are now: external balance, modernization and rationalization of the economy, greater competitiveness and wage moderation. By the time of the March 1986 election, therefore, Mitterrand will have presided over two years of expansionary policies and three years of austerity. In this section we present an overview of these new policies and an early assessment, concluding that the government has successfully fought inflation, restored the current account balance, made some progress on the wage front, but has not yet grasped the full importance of the supply side.

4.1. The external balance target

The decision to stay in the EMS meant that, unless the current account was quickly brought back into balance, a new crisis would erupt. Such an objective was stated explicitly by Mitterrand, and was part of the agreement reached with Germany at the time of the currency realignment. Assigning tasks in 1983 for Mauroy's new government, Mitterrand asked him to 'bring down inflation to a rate compatible with our competitors . . . restore within two years our external trade balance . . . and respect the financial equilibrium of Social Security while maintaining the public budget deficit within its current levels' (*Le Point*, March 28, 1983).

This is exactly what happened. The budget deficit was stabilized around 3% of GDP. This was achieved by freezing budgeted expenses and by raising taxes: a 1% additional income tax to finance Social Security and a compulsory subscription to public borrowing representing 10% of 1982 income taxes.

The OECD measures of structural deficit confirm the restrictive stance of fiscal policy after 1983 (Table 1). Indeed, while the actual deficit rose slightly from 1983 to 1984, the structural deficit was reduced by 0.5% of GDP. Monetary policy also remained contractionary, although the squeeze has come from a different channel. While previous monetary contractions were achieved through binding credit ceilings and (relatively) low interest rates, since 1983, and more so since 1984, interest rates have been kept so high that the credit ceilings have not been binding.

The role of the exchange rate is more difficult to assess. With an inflation differential with Germany running at about 4%, and assuming that the Franc–Deutschmark parity was satisfactory after the March 1983 devaluation, this would imply a gradual overvaluation reaching about 8% by mid-1985. But the Franc–Deutschmark parity is not the only indicator of France's competitiveness. An effective exchange rate index also includes the dollar and reflects its appreciation. From the end of 1980 to the end of 1984, the dollar appreciated in real terms vis-à-vis the ECU by about 50%. Against the dollar the ECU was undervalued, while within the ECU, the Franc was overvalued and the Deutschmark undervalued. Viewed this way, the improvement of the current account in 1983 and 1984 was helped by the dollar appreciation.

Thus, 1983–84 in many respects looks like the mirror image of 1981–82. A standard Keynesian expansion was replaced by a standard contraction, while the rest of the world pulled itself out of recession. In 1982, final domestic demand in France grew by 3.9% while it remained flat in the OECD zone. For 1984, the numbers are 0.5% for France and 5.1% for the OECD. This reversal must have been a major factor behind the balancing of the current account in 1984 and 1985. Unfortunately, the situation is not perfectly symmetric: in the meantime both the public debt (see Table 1) and the external debt have grown, thereby complicating the balancing efforts on the budget and the current account. Also, as noted by Fonteneau and Gubian (1985) the 1981–82 fiscal expansion was based on permanent features (new hirings of civil servants) which are not as easily reversable as increases in spending on goods. Debt service in 1984 represented 4% of public spending, i.e. about 2% of GDP, a figure which can be compared to the budget deficit of 3%. A return to budget balance would now require more contraction of spending or faster growth generating higher revenues. This leaves the French government, present and future, with a limited margin of freedom to use fiscal policy.

The external debt situation is often described with alarmist undertones. Cumulated current account deficits have raised France's *gross* liabilities by some 8% of GDP between 1980 and 1984. But as of June 1985, France's external assets (export credits, foreign exchange reserves, etc.) *exceeded* the external debt liabilities.[10] It is true that many of the French assets are known to be held in LDCs and are therefore at risk. Yet, by all measures, the external debt situation cannot be considered as a major source of concern, as France's ratings on world financial markets amply testify.

4.2. Inflation

The inflation differential with Germany has been more than halved between 1981 and December 1985. Two broad policies have been put to work: a set of direct wage and price controls and the more traditional strategy of demand restraint.

While price controls are part of France's tradition, the imposition of a wage freeze as early as July 1982 was a great surprise to public opinion. This freeze was set for 4 months. The policy adopted after the freeze is interesting as it illustrates one of the many efforts by European countries to achieve effective de-indexation. There has never been formal cost-of-living adjustment in France but in practice, this has been the rule for a very long time. The existence of a de facto full indexation mechanism is confirmed by all the econometric studies (Artus *et al.*, 1981; Oudiz and Sterdyniak, 1985; Feroldi and Meunier, 1984; and the mean lag is found to be between one and two quarters). Similarly there is a strong, fast, and well-documented effect of wage increases on inflation.

The procedure since 1982 is as follows. At the beginning of each year, the government issues inflation rate targets and asks the firms and the trade unions to base their wage increases on these targets. This is simply a wish, backed by a carrot and a stick. The carrot is the fact that the government pledges to follow this target for its own labour force and the prices of public services and utilities. As for the stick, prices are not free but result from contracts at the branch level with the authorities (in the absence of agreement the government *sets* prices).

---

[10] Data computed by the Ministere de l'Economie, des Finances et du Budget (Sept. 1985). Gross liabilities are defined as borrowing for over one year; shorter liabilities are omitted. Gross assets exclude exchange reserves and are mainly export credits or public loans. At June 1985, net external debt was estimated as 5.2% of GDP.

Table 9. Wage guidelines (%p.a.)

	1982	1983	1984	1985*
Official Target	10.0	8.0	5.0	4.5
Actual Increases:				
Gross Hourly Wage	15.4	11.2	7.6	5.6
Gross Average Salary	12.6	10.1	7.6	5.6
SMIC	17.6	12.2	9.4	6.9
CPI	11.7	9.7	7.5	5.6

Source: *Les Notes Bleues* No. 251.
*Note: official forecast.

The interesting feature of this scheme is that it does not state that wages must be de-indexed. On the contrary, it specifically endorses indexation but ties it to *future* inflation, not to past observations. The advantages of a forward-looking indexing mechanism when disinflation is under way are obvious. With targets set at the beginning of each year, the 1 or 2 quarter traditional lag is now replaced (at least in principle) by an average *lead* of six months. While there have been some inevitable slippages above the targets, Table 9 shows that wage growth has been gradually converging toward price inflation since 1983. Because social security contributions borne by employees have risen, especially in 1984, this has meant a reduction in net real wages (−1.8% in 1984).

At the same time, unemployment has been rising quickly, ahead of our estimates of a steadily increasing NAIRU. The interesting question is whether the system of price and wage restraint has added much, if anything, to the normal Phillips curve mechanism. In its 1985 annual survey of France, the OECD reports an INSEE study which has simulated its estimated wage-price equations for 1984 finding a 2% difference between predicted and observed inflation, suggesting that indeed wage and price controls did work. Our own estimates support these calculations. When we re-estimate our Phillips curve (Regression (1) of Table 6) over the period 1963–80 and generate forecasts for 1981–84, we find negative and statistically significant residuals of, respectively, 2.9 and 3.6% inflation for 1983 and 1984.

4.3. Labour costs and employment policies

With real gross wages roughly constant in 1984–85, real hourly labour costs have still increased by about 4% in 1984 because of a further rise in the wedge. As a result, our measures of wage gaps show a further worsening of about 3% in the manufacturing sector. Not surprisingly therefore, while employment measured by the number of registered workers did not fall in 1984, after declining in the years 1981 to 1983, the reduction of effective man-hours worked in the competitive sector has not yet come to a halt.

Thus it appears that the apparently successful effort at curbing wages has not been mainly motivated by the desire to reduce real labour costs and promote employment, but by a concern to break the wage-price spiral in order to fight inflation. Here again we find in 1983–84 a mirror image of the policies followed in 1981–82: reducing real wages is now meant to reduce demand, very much as the earlier wage hikes were supposed to raise it. The demand side is unfortunately still the dominating concern.

A similar interpretation applies to employment policies. In the face of rising unemployment numerous policies have been designed to reduce the number of registered unemployed, without really increasing the number of employed workers; early retirement benefits, training programmes, special contracts with firms for temporary on-the-job training have been continuously expanding in size, scope and cost. By 1983 these measures together with unemployment benefits represented 3.4% of GDP. These numbers underestimate the true cost as they do not include subsidized loans to corporations, but they are large enough to prompt a change of heart. In 1984, for example, the unemployment benefits system has been restructured, reducing the number of beneficiaries and the volume of benefits. Several training programmes are being scaled back. The civil service and state-owned corporations are no longer called upon to hire. There have been spectacular large-scale firings in industries such as steel, coal and shipbuilding which have long been recipients of public subsidies, as well as at state-owned Renault, long a symbol of generous social policies. The government itself is now engaged in a process of trimming its ranks.

4.4. Conclusion

With obvious successes regarding inflation (the official target of 5% for 1985 has been surpassed) and the external balance (with a current account surplus in both the second and third quarters of 1985), the major casualty of the Socialists' policies is paradoxically employment. The combination of demand expansion and supply side errors in 1981–82, followed by demand restriction in 1983–84, has resulted in a continuous rise in the unemployment rate, in line with growing wage gaps and a growing wedge. Only in 1984 did it emerge that the Government had realized the importance of the supply side and profitability.

At the time of writing, there is little factual evidence on which to base a theory that the Socialists have now moved the whole circle towards defending the virtues of competition in a free market economy. Prices are being gradually freed, but controls remain extensive. Foreign exchange regulations have been eased but remain as extensive as before May 1981. The long standing tradition of credit ceilings has been replaced by a market-based monetary policy relying on management of bank reserves, but this change was probably motivated by the very large amount of unused credit below the ceiling (due to the weakness of demand and high real interest rates) which could be absorbed should the economy pick up. Financial markets have been allowed to grow and develop new instruments, with the active support of tax incentives, and stock prices have soared since 1983, but the banks are still almost entirely state-owned and 'selective financing' (i.e. credit allocation by government) does not appear to have fallen.

5. Current situation and policy options

In the third quarter of 1985, with unemployment at 10.2%, the budget for 1986 was being finalized around the general objective of further disinflation and no relapse from austerity. The arguments behind a strategy of continuing austerity are that there is no room for expansion because: the external constraint would again surely undermine any such attempt; the budget is still in deficit, thus ruling out any fiscal policy-led recovery; monetary policy must remain tight in France because it is tight abroad, expecially among EMS countries; the process of rationalization and trimming of French companies is not yet completed, and any expansion would relax the pressure to pursue this fundamental structural effort.

We do not find these arguments convincing, since we believe that if demand stimulus is combined with appropriate supply measures, many of the adverse consequences of a demand expansion could be avoided. We now sketch some policy options which can be enacted fairly quickly and which, according to our analysis, could deliver sizeable gains in employment with only modest costs in inflation or external deficits. The cornerstone of the proposal is a reduction in labour costs designed to reduce the wage gaps and bring the NAIRU down, achieved through a decrease of labour taxes and a social contract. This policy must be accompanied by suitable strategies for the budget and for the external constraint.

5.1. A marginal wedge reduction

A central conclusion of Section 3 is that any attempt at reducing unemployment through a demand expansion alone would quickly hit

Table 10. The wedge. (Ratio of employers' real hourly labour costs to employees' real take-home pay)

1963	1968	1973	1976	1980	1982	1983	1984
1.34	1.41	1.41	1.50	1.60	1.62	1.65	1.69

Source: INSEE, *Comptes Trimestriels.*
Note: The wedge is $(T_1/T_2)(P^c/P^v)$ where T_1 is the ratio of total labour costs to the wage bill, T_2 is the ratio of net to gross take-home pay when employees' social security contributions are deducted, and P^c and P^v respectively are price indices for consumption and value added. As in Table 6, we ignore income tax rates, which changed little over the period.

the inflation threshold, with the attendant external crisis. The immediate implication is that the first priority should be to reduce the NAIRU and the wage gap. One way of doing that would be to reduce hourly wages relative to productivity, either through negotiated concessions, or through 'surprise inflation'. The required reduction, 10 to 15% is such that the inflation solution is untenable, while the reduction in hourly wages via concessions is likely, by itself, to lead only to small progress achieved over a protracted period. A different approach is required.

Our analysis of the Phillips curve directs attention to the wedge, the ratio of total real hourly labour costs to net real hourly take-home salaries. The evolution of the wedge is shown in Table 10. Cutting the wedge at constant real take-home salaries will reduce real labour costs in the same proportion. Thus a 15% reduction in the wedge, which brings it back slightly below its 1976–78 level, would probably eliminate most of the prevailing wage gap. The strategy of achieving wage concessions should be combined with a strategy that reduces the taxation of labour income.

A 15% cut in the wedge would not immediately return the NAIRU to its 1976–78 level of around 5%, since in the meantime several other factors (rising social protection, an increase in the target wage, new labour regulations) have taken their toll. Our estimates show that, in the short run, the NAIRU would only fall by a bit more than 2%, which would leave it in the range of 6 to 7%. However, as we have stressed earlier, we believe that the Phillips curve estimates of the NAIRU probably understate the long-term benefits of a reduced wedge.

Most of the wedge corresponds to labour taxes used to finance social security expenditures, which at present amount to almost 25% of GDP (Table 2). A 15% reduction in the wedge, if achieved by an across-the-board reduction in payroll taxes, would then contribute to a deficit in the social security budget of 3.75% of GDP, a very large amount to recoup through spending cuts. However, if the cuts in payroll taxes can be placed more on the margin, to apply mainly to new workers, and not to existing workers, the budgetary costs of wedge reduction would be very substantially reduced.[11] As a very rough example, if a 15% marginal wedge reduction succeeds in bringing employment up by 5%, the shortfall in social security receipts would amount to about 0.5% of GDP.

It must be stressed that in order to achieve the long-term benefits from payroll tax reduction, and to get those benefits as rapidly as possible, firms must be convinced that the lower taxes will be sustained for several years. One difficulty with a marginal tax reduction is that firms may be able to manipulate the system to their advantage without creating more jobs in total. For example, faced with a subsidy on new workers, firms might be induced to make dismissals for the purpose of subsequent hirings, or to create new businesses to replace, for legal purposes, existing business activities. One possibility would be to relate the reduction in payroll taxes only to new workers that raise the firm's total labour force above the size at the start of the new policy. Thus dismissals by a given firm for the sake of re-hiring the same number of workers will be pointless. It may also be advisable to plan to make a gradual reduction in the level of labour taxes on existing employees, so that average tax rates are ultimately aligned with the lower marginal taxes, thus alleviating the incentive to close down one business and start up another to take advantage of the marginal wedge reduction.

5.2. A Social Contract

A reduction in labour taxes will lead to a distributional fight over sharing the benefits between employers and employees. The union wage model suggests that unions will try to capture a part, though not the entire benefit, of tax reduction. To make certain that the tax reduction translates significantly into reduced labour costs for the firm, it is worthwhile attempting a social compact between the government, trade unions and employers' associations. We envisage an agreement to split the reduction in labour taxes according to a formula of one-third to the employees (in the form of higher take-home pay), and two-thirds to the employers, (as a reduction in labour costs). Note that initially, the employees' average benefits would be very small, to the extent that the tax reduction applies on the margin only. If the average tax rate is

---

[11] Our proposal for a marginal employment incentive differs from that of Steinherr and Van Halperen (1983) in three respects. Our proposal is designed to be permanent rather than temporary; it acts via a reduction in the wedge rather than an explicit employment subsidy; and we do not insist that its budgetary incidence is offset by changes in unemployment benefit.

reduced over time, the average rise in wages would become larger. Also, negotiations should be opened to deal with issues like productivity incentives and labour market regulations (e.g. hiring–firing restrictions, overtime work or part-time job regulations, various unemployment programmes), reductions in subsidies to ailing corporations, and price and wage moderation.

5.3. The need for a demand expansion

Fixing the supply side creates the necessary conditions for a *non-inflationary* increase in employment. But unless demand is present to absorb the increased supply, a fall in the NAIRU will, in the short run only reduce inflation, without denting unemployment. The government could instead aim for a gradual reduction of actual unemployment, trailing behind the reduction of the NAIRU (see e.g. Blanchard *et al.*, 1985). What is the amount of demand expansion that would be required to achieve a gradual reduction in unemployment (assuming a falling NAIRU), say at a rate of 1% a year?

For this purpose, it is useful to turn to Okun's Law, which relates GDP growth to reductions in the unemployment rate. Using simulations of demand expansion performed with METRIC model (Artus *et al.*, 1981) we find that real GDP must grow about 2% faster than its underlying trend (a proxy for supply expansion) if unemployment is to be reduced by 1% a year.[12]

It is difficult to say how much demand stimulus should accompany the supply side measures, in order to achieve the target growth rates. In essence, both monetary and fiscal policies will have to operate on a feedback basis, by setting nominal GDP targets that are sufficiently expansionary to allow for the desired real growth of the economy. The supply measures will of course themselves raise demand, via higher take-home pay, higher investment demand as labour costs fall, and higher international competitiveness. However, the precise details of such an induced demand expansion will require separate study. It should also be pointed out that any precision in the size of the necessary demand expansion is vitiated by the uncertainties in the world economy.

5.4 The external constraint

As has been amply demonstrated by the 1981–82 experiment, no policy measure is likely to succeed unless it pays due attention to the external

[12] As a rough estimate to fix an order of magnitude, if trend annual growth is estimated at 3% the growth rate the government should target is about 5% a year over the five years following the wedge reduction.

constraint. This constraint, in turn has two components: the current account and speculative capital flows. It should be clear that supply-friendly measures of the type envisioned should boost the stock market, build up confidence and therefore, at the very least, leave the capital account neutral.

As for the current account, we already noted that a reduction in labour costs has the important advantage of creating a strong gain in competitiveness. Yet simulations performed with French macromodels (METRIC or OFCE) concerning reductions in employers' social security contributions, find that the current account slightly worsens because such policies generate faster growth and a rise in imports.[13] This result (of which we are a bit sceptical) should at least be taken as a warning that any expansion has a potential for creating current account difficulties. The best way to resolve the external pressures from an expansion would of course be for Europe as a whole to undertake measures similar to the ones that we are outlining. After all, France's difficulties are shared in various degrees by all EEC countries, where one also finds severe labour market rigidities, large wage gaps, and low rates of profit (see Bruno and Sachs, 1985; Bruno, 1986; Dornbusch *et al.*, 1983; Layard *et al.*, 1984). If the other EEC countries refuse such a coordinated expansion, the second best would be a devaluation within the EMS. Our estimates indicate that the Franc is currently overvalued by about 6% vis-à-vis the Deutschmark. Of course with a reduction in labour costs, the extent of the overvaluation is considerably reduced. Yet, with an anticipated growth differential, a devaluation is inevitable.

5.5. Fiscal and monetary policy

The proposed wedge reduction could result in significant budgetary costs, especially if the reduction is generalized to all workers, rather than applying only to marginal workers. A general cut in payroll taxes of 15% would cost the government revenues of about 3.75% of GDP, as we noted earlier. Of course there would be large associated savings in unemployment support programmes, that could be as much as 1.5–2% of GDP if the unemployment rate drops from 10 to 5%.[14]

Assuming that there would remain a significant budgetary cost to the tax reductions, the question is whether that cost should be made up

---

[13] Artus *et al.* (1981) and Sterdyniak *et al.* (1984). In the OFCE model a 10% cut in employers' social security contributions leads after one year to a 0.8% increase in output and a worsening of the current account by 0.1% of GDP.

[14] We assume conservatively that the cost of unemployment programmes (4.5% of GDP in 1985) would be cut by only one third, given the fixed cost of bureaucracy needed to administer these programmes.

through cuts in spending of various sorts, or by increases in other taxes, or by somewhat larger deficits.

We have repeatedly stressed that the supply-side consequences of any other tax increases should be scrupulously examined, and not underestimated. If there is a major conclusion of our analysis, it is that cutting deficits via tax increases and spending cuts have different macroeconomic implications for the French economy. After a decade and a half of tax increases, with the attendant supply-side difficulties, it is probably time to stress spending cuts as a way to resolve the budgetary problem.

Discussion

Willem Buiter
Yale University

The authors' thesis is that France, under President Mitterrand, undertook a modest fiscal expansion in May 1981 which had adverse supply-side effects. There was some increase in the growth of output, but the economy soon ran into both internal and external constraints. First, and more importantly, the non-accelerating inflation rate of unemployment (NAIRU) was too high to permit continued expansion without an increase in inflation. The authors argue that Mitterrand's policies significantly raised the NAIRU and they cite a number of contributory factors; the increase in the minimum wage; employers' payroll taxes were also increased; there was an extension of employee protection legislation; working hours were reduced increasing marginal labour costs; and finally there was nationalization (although its effect on the NAIRU is ambiguous).

Second, the economy also ran into a twofold external constraint. The current account deteriorated owing to the world recession. There was also a lack of confidence in the Socialist administration on the part of the financial markets. This produced increased capital outflows. Together these placed the Franc under pressure and raised doubts about the continued participation of France in the EMS.

The authors argue the original Mitterrand program lasted little more than six months. The first cracks were showing by the time of the first devaluation in October 1981. Further devaluations in June 1982 and March 1983 put the final nails into the coffin. The fiscal stimulus (as measured by the cyclically corrected budget deficit which is not the correct measure) was reversed as early as June 1982.

I will first examine their claims about the increase in the NAIRU. The authors' dismissal of frictional effects, such as increased job or skill mismatch, is perhaps a little hasty since many of these effects are difficult to measure adequately. They are probably nevertheless correct that their impact was small. Instead they focus on what has been dubbed 'household-involuntary, union-voluntary' unemployment. Oil price increases, reduced growth in technical productivity (relative to wage aspirations) and increases in the tax wedge have all raised unemployment. However, I do not find their particular model, with competitive firms facing a real wage set by a monopolistic union, either necessary or useful. A more plausible story is to assume unions set the *money* wage and imperfectly competitive firms set prices and hence also the real wage. The optimizing foundations of the model disappear completely when their purely static model is embedded in an 'error-correction' mechanism to obtain the Phillips curve. The final model looks like a standard expectations-augmented Phillips curve where the difference between the target and warranted wage drives inflation and unemployment.

A crucial missing link in the story is why the extra involuntarily unemployed union members cannot find, or choose not to find, work in the non-union sector of the economy. Is this because wages in this sector are too low relative to unemployment benefits as has been suggested by Patrick Minford for the UK? Or is it because relative wages are rigid across the two sectors? The mechanism at work here needs to be spelt out.

The estimates of the Phillips curve in Table 6 provide the centrepiece of the analysis. However, these are equations with relatively low explanatory power estimated on only twenty-one observations. While there is some attempt in Appendix C to examine the robustness of the results with respect to dynamic specification and the inclusion of other plausible determinants of the NAIRU, they strike me as a very slender basis on which to make the very important policy conclusion that France was supply constrained at the beginning of the Mitterrand experiment. Testing the stability of the equations over 1981–84 would be one useful test the authors could carry out.

Turning now to the wage gap calculations, these are potentially useful although I find it difficult to assess their statistical significance. However, the authors make a crucial non-sequitur in assuming that a positive wage gap implies the absence of a significant margin of unemployment due to deficient demand. The real wage can be too high without this being the binding constraint. The finding of a positive wage gap merely implies that one cannot get back to full employment without an accompanying reduction in real wages.

More generally I do not think the authors examine sufficiently closely the possibility that producers in France were constrained by a lack of demand in the early years of the Mitterrand experiment. Data on capacity utilization and vacancies could give some clues here. Is it the case that if France was in a demand constrained regime any fiscal expansion would nevertheless have failed because of a lack of confidence by the financial markets? In other words did the external constraint bind even if the internal one did not?

Finally the authors suggest that a crucial role was played by the French commitment to the EMS. This is interesting but not altogether convincing. Why did the authorities feel constrained to stay within the EMS? They also argue that Mrs Thatcher could tie the hands of a future UK Labour government by joining the EMS. I find this implausible: a future Labour government would just leave the EMS in order to be free to pursue expansionist policies.

Gerhard Fels
Institut der Deutschen Wirtschaft, Cologne

From the French Socialists' experiment of the early 1980s one can learn an important lesson on economic policy. This episode is highly instructive for other countries as well. At least in Germany it has disillusioned many advocates of a 'soft approach' which unions and Social Democrats still favour as an alternative to the present conduct of economic policy. To be sure, Germany's performance was not much better, and was actually worse on employment. But the external difficulties faced by France demonstrate that Mitterrand-style policies cannot solve internal economic problems. Sachs and Wyplosz provide an interesting evaluation of these policies, though I should have preferred a greater emphasis on comparison with other countries.

I feel much in sympathy with the basic analytical approach of the paper. I do, however, have some reservations with respect to the policy recommendations. In substance, I do not think that the recommended policy option currently exists in France. In particular, the external constraint, which was responsible for France's U-turn in March 1983, must be given more attention. France's experience highlights the fact that in an open economy, it is impossible to conduct an autonomous economic policy independent of conditions in the rest of the world, unless one reverts to trade restrictions and capital controls. I think this also has implications for the therapy proposed by the authors.

I think the authors may overstate the degree of success on the employment front. One reason for France's moderate employment decline in the period 1980–84 may be a substantial amount of hidden unemployment or unemployment on the job. Table 3 lends support to this hypothesis: there was a substantial increase in employment in the sheltered sector. But this was not merely a feature of the Socialist administration; it had already occurred during the seventies.

France's success against inflation also seems overstated. It is true that the inflation differential between France and Germany is substantially smaller today than it was in 1982, but in both countries the inflation rate in 1985 is only about one third of what is was in 1982.

There are differing views about what caused inflation to subside. Sachs and Wyplosz maintain that the main factor was wage and price controls. If that is true, the success may only be temporary. But this explanation does not seem to be very convincing since all major countries experienced a sharp drop in the rate of inflation. This phenomenon has to be explained by monetary restraint abroad. Paul Volker successfully reduced monetary growth in the US, and Germany followed suit. Hence France, too, was forced to adopt a policy of tight money. Otherwise, she would have been forced to leave the EMS. So again it is the external constraint which has to be given credit for the improvement after 1983.

The paper suggests that a macroeconomic strategy for overcoming the problems still exists. I agree with the argument that a reduction in labour costs of about 10% would be warranted and useful. But I doubt whether this can be achieved by a significant cut in labour taxes, i.e., in compulsory social security contributions. Can we really expect a shift of the wedge burden – of whatever magnitude – from employers and employees to the public sector to overcome the rigidities of the French economy? It seems to be more important to reduce the burden than to shift it to the public budget. Although the rationale of the US tax cut policy is different from that of the Sachs–Wyplosz analysis, the structure of the argument is quite similar: more incentives to the private sector at the expense of an increased public debt. If any country at all can afford to have a significant increase in public debt relative to GDP it is the United States, due to favourable conditions with regard to its labour market, profit rates, equity capital and the like. By contrast, the French economy suffers from so many rigidities that the fiscal strategy recommended by the authors would be highly risky given the external constraint and the budget situation. I think the same is, in principle, also true in the case of Germany.

To reduce the wedge burden, the authors propose a social contract and a gradual reduction in public spending, especially in subsidies to corporations and individuals. But has a social contract ever been more than a dream in France? Even the Socialist government has not been able to establish it. And the level of subsidies is as much a subject of the debate over income distribution as wages and salaries. The financial support which is given to declining industries has more the character of social policy than of industrial policy. And what about a *large* devaluation of the Franc as a complementary measure? My guess is that accelerated inflation would be the most likely result. If the unions respond to increased inflation the burden will be shifted back to the business sector.

What is the alternative? Austerity is no solution. But in the environment of a sclerotic European economy, private consumers and investors have lost confidence in macroeconomic policies which lead to a higher budget deficit. Under European conditions, supply policy must be geared towards improving total factor productivity, which will also bridge the wage gap. In the French case I would propose to continue and reinforce the course of economic policy which the government has been pursuing since 1983. This would mean; further efforts to reduce the budget deficit by maintaining only a modest growth of public spending; continuation of monetary discipline to ensure low inflation rates; combating major legislative rigidities which constrain and discourage employers from hiring additional workers; deregulation of the service sector to increase competition, and the privatization of public service activities; easing of the constraints imposed on small and medium-sized firms in the form of worker participation and additional social changes; and finally the introduction of tax shelters for newly established enterprises.

Of course, such a strategy promises only a gradual improvement. However, if supply conditions are improved the freedom for manoeuvre in fiscal policy will become greater. The greater freedom should be used to lower taxes on investment and high-risk activities. My belief is that such a strategy would enable the French economy to grow at a rate of about 3%. The German economy may serve as an example. It is about to recover and will accelerate its growth measures to improve supply conditions which allowed the economy to overcome stagnation without an increase in the budget deficit.

Georges de Menil
Ecole des Hautes Etudes en Sciences Sociales, Paris

After the legislative elections of March 1986, the new French government will try to learn from the errors of the preceding four years. Why did this Socialist experiment fail? My comments will concentrate on the authors' three principal and most provocative conclusions: budget deficits were not the most important problem; reductions in the profitability and competiveness of French enterprise – in short, supply-side disturbances – were the most seriously disruptive aspects of the Socialist programme; and Mitterrand's policies exacerbated these supply-side problems but did not constitute a fundamental departure from the previous trends. They were in essence a ripple on the rising tide of Eurosclerosis. My discussion is organized under three headings: the demand side aspects of the programme, its supply-side consequences, and the implications for present and future policy.

The importance of relative demand stimulus. In their claim for the relative unimportance of the Keynesian stimulus in 1981–82, Sachs and Wyplosz make a myopic error. They point out that the increase of the structural deficit of the French government budget during 1980–82 (1.4% of average GDP) was smaller than in the United States during 1980–83 (1.8% of GDP) and about the same as in Germany (1.2% of GDP during 1977–80) following the Bonn summit (see Muller and Price, 1984). It is not budgetary expansion *per se* which disrupts external balance, but expansion *relative* to the policies being followed by major trading partners. In 1981 these partners were simultaneously moving in the direction of restraint. The substantial divergence between French stimulus and foreign restraint was neither an accident nor a surprise: the French government consciously decided to expand when others were contracting.

Supply-side consequences. The most appealing aspect of the Sachs–Wyplosz study is the crucial emphasis they place on the effect of the Mitterrand programme on supply. The heart of their study is an application to France of the wage-gap analysis which has gained prominence in recent years. A number of economists following Giersch (1981), including most recently Bruno and Sachs (1985), have argued that excessive real costs of labour are the major reason many Western economies, particularly in Europe, have experienced steadily rising unemployment. 'Natural' unemployment is largely determined in this view by the difference between the effective cost of labour and its marginal productivity when all resources are fully employed. This discrepancy is the wage-gap. The authors then estimate a Phillips curve which relates short-run changes in inflation to the difference between actual and 'natural' unemployment. Whilst inflation and actual unemployment are observable the unobservable natural rate of unemployment must be modelled implicitly. Whereas for this I believe that wage-gap analysis is required, Sachs and Wyplosz stress only one aspect of this analysis, the so-called 'wedge' between gross labour costs to the firm and net take-home pay received by workers. In my view this simplification is not warranted.[15]

Moreover, the key role of supply in the authors' analysis is deficient for two reasons. First, inadequate attention is paid to considerations of competitiveness and external balance. It was not inflation or rising unemployment but the deterioration of the current account, and the consequent speculative attack on the Franc, which forced a reversal of budgetary policy in the Spring of 1983. It is regrettable that the authors, in contrast to their careful study of inflation and unemployment, do not bring this same detailed analysis of supply and demand to the external position.

The second deficiency is more fundamental. In their introduction, the authors recognize the long-run structural reforms which, in the eyes of both the Socialists and the opposition, constituted the heart of the programme. In many areas these were major departures. The nationalized sector increased by one quarter, to 18% of total non-agricultural value-added. Marginal tax rates were increased, reaching up to 75% in 1982, and a new annual wealth tax of up to 2.5% was introduced. New labour laws enhanced trade union power, private rented housing was subjected to rent controls, and private medicine was curtailed.

Whilst budgetary policy had been reversed by 1983, and some incentives for enterprise had been restored, by 1985 the full array of the structural reforms were essentially left untouched. What were their effects on productivity and competitiveness? Sachs and Wyplosz are surprisingly silent on the question. Having emphasized the importance of supply-side considerations, the authors have given us Hamlet without the Prince of Denmark. Of these omissions, the most glaring is the neglect of nationalization, especially in the banking sector. Given exchange controls and the underdeveloped nature of French capital markets, bank loans constitute the most important source of external funds for private investment in France. The argument that the 1981

---

[15] The wage-gap, in Sachs–Wyplosz notation is

$$(h + t_1 - p^v) - \psi$$

which may be rewritten as

$$(h - t_2 - p^c) + (t_1 + t_2 + p^c - p^v) - \psi$$

The first term is the log of real take-home pay, the second is the log of the wedge. Having made this decomposition, the authors implicitly assume in their estimation that changes in NAIRU are caused exclusively by changes in the last two terms, and since the data will not support their implicit omission of the first term, take-home pay, they are obliged to introduce an *ad hoc* time trend which only partially captures this omission.

banking nationalization was of secondary importance because two-thirds of the industry had previously been nationalized in 1946, misses the potentially decisive influence on the entire industry of the threat of competition from the private sector. Similar comments apply in the manufacturing sector.

Not only is the reduction in competition likely to reduce productivity and efficiency, each nationalization creates a precedent for future nationalizations and may significantly reduce incentives for innovation and risk-taking in the private sector. If Stephen Jobs or Kenneth Olson, the founders of Apple and Digital Equipment, had been French, they might well have emigrated.

Of course these are long-run effects and difficult to measure. But they should not be neglected on that basis. By concentrating their analysis on short-run phenomena which can be discerned quickly in national statistics, Sachs and Wyplosz give an unbalanced account of the Socialist programme, and may miss more than half the story.

Implications for policy. The message of the Sachs-Wyplosz study for future French policy makers is clear: reverse some of the measures of 1981–82, but do not merely revert to the policies of the previous decade. The relentless increase of structural unemployment over that period is a telling testimony to the cost of social rigidities and misguided policies which push labour costs ever higher. This trend must be reversed. Sachs and Wyplosz propose a 15% cut in labour costs to reduce the NAIRU to 5%. This radical surgery, which would imply that the sum of employee and employer taxes on labour fell from 60% to 35% of wages, could not be implemented overnight. And any attempt to achieve coordinated reductions throughout Europe could only take longer. Given the authors' premise that there is little current slack in French labour markets, neither rapid demand expansion nor a quick solution to the unemployment problem is feasible.

An alternative, and in my view more promising, way to reduce the wage-gap is to erode rigidities and distortions, improve competition, and thus make markets work better. Examples of such measures would include privatization and the abolition of controls on prices, rents, and foreign exchange. By increasing productivity and competitiveness, this offers a more durable solution. It would be a radical departure from trends in France over the last twenty years.

General Discussion

Jacques Melitz believed the comparison with the experience of the Giscard administration was instructive. The Chirac expansion was also short-lived, but the Barre plan stabilized the current account and the Franc relatively quickly. Inflation was allowed to rise over the period 1977–81. By contrast there had been three successive devaluations under the Socialists and even in 1984 the current account was still in deficit. This forced Mitterrand to maintain a contractionary fiscal stance exerting continued downward pressure on inflation. He also felt the model of union behaviour was inappropriate for France. Union membership had been falling rapidly under the Socialists and the preservation of union membership rather than the pursuit of higher wages was probably more important to union leaders.

Patrick Minford supported Buiter's criticism of the lack of an adequate story about behaviour in the non-union sector and why unemployed union members could or would not find jobs there. Even if the whole economy were treated as unionized the story could not be sustained because the shadow wage of displaced workers would fall to zero. He thought that the unemployment benefit system, the 'Aide Sociale', early retirement schemes and the like played a central role in underpinning the model of labour market behaviour.

Torsten Persson suggested the distinction between internationally tradable and non-tradable goods could help in distinguishing between the 'profitability' and 'confidence' explanations for the fall in investment. If firms in the tradable sector found it less easy to pass on cost increases on account of foreign competition than firms in the non-tradable sector one would expect to find the share price of the two sorts of firms reacting differently to increases in labour costs. On the other hand fear of nationalization would affect both sectors equally. He also thought the distinction was relevant to the specification of the Phillips curve which implicitly assumed prices were a mark-up over costs: this would not be valid for the tradable sector.

Mervyn King found the estimated investment equation a peculiar hybrid between 'accelerator' models which stressed the role of output and 'Tobin's q' models which stressed the role of the stock market.

Paul Krugman pointed out a peculiar property of the estimated Phillips curve, which implied that unions were perpetually seeking to return to the trend value of the target wage irrespective of developments in productivity or the wedge in the interim. This did not seem very plausible over time spans of a decade or more.

Giampaolo Galli noted that neither unemployment nor the NAIRU was higher in France than in most other European countries and that the somewhat later deceleration in inflation could be attributed entirely to the later increase in interest rates. Monetary policy seemed capable of explaining most of the differences.

Appendix A. Computation of wage gaps

For each sector we assume a CES production function

$$Y = A[\delta K^{-\rho} + (1-\delta)\bar{L}^{-\rho}]^{-1/\rho} \tag{A1}$$

where Y is real value added, K the stock of capital and $\bar{L}$ is labour in efficiency units

$$\bar{L} = L \prod_{i=1}^{t} (1+\gamma_i) \tag{A2}$$

with γ_i the rate of labour augmenting technological progress in year i and L_t is labour (in man-hours).

If S_L is the share of labour in value added and H represents (hourly) labour costs, $S_L = HL/Y$. Let small letters denote logarithms. Then an approximation to (A1) and (A2) is

$$\Delta y_t = (1 - S_{Lt})\Delta k_t + S_{Lt}(\Delta l_t + \gamma_t) \tag{A3}$$

From (A3) it is easy to obtain estimates of γ_t since all of the other variables are observed. In practice, we smooth S_L by taking a two-year moving average of the original data.

Next we normalize Y, K and L to 1.0 in the base period so that $A = 1$. Maximizing profit given K yields the usual relationship

$$S_{Lt} = (1 - \delta) \left[\prod_{i=1}^{t} (1 + \gamma_i) \right]^{-\rho} (Y_t/L_t)^{\rho} \tag{A4}$$

With the above normalization, we find that in the base period $S_L^0 = 1 - \delta$ so that parameter δ is directly obtained as the share of capital in the base period.

We can now express (A4) as a demand for labour after substitution of (A1) (up to a constant term)

$$h_t = \sum_{i=1}^{t} \gamma_i - \frac{1+\rho}{\rho} \ln [\delta(K_t/\bar{L}_t)^{-\rho} + (1-\delta)] \tag{A5}$$

Thus the real wage rate ensuring full employment L^f given the stock of capital is (up to a constant term)

$$h_t^* = \sum_{i=1}^{t} \gamma_i - \frac{1+\rho}{\rho} \ln [\delta(K_t/\bar{L}_t^f)^{-\rho} + (1-\delta)] \tag{A6}$$

The wage gap is then simply $h_t - h_t^*$ where h_t is the (log of the) observed real labour cost. It is computed for alternative values of $\rho = 0$ and $\rho = 1$. A similar procedure is followed for the case of Hicks-neutral technological progress where Equation (A2) is replaced by an equation in which A grows over time.

Appendix B. The union wage model

1. Firms' demand for labour

We assume that the technology is represented by a CES production function with Hicks-neutral technological progress

$$Y = A[\delta K^{-\rho} + (1-\delta)L^{-\rho}]^{-1/\rho} \tag{B1}$$

where $A = A(t)$ is the productivity factor. The unit cost of labour is the gross nominal wage H, divided by the value added deflator P^V, with a mark-up T_1 for employers' taxes.

$$C = \frac{H}{P^V} T_1 \tag{B2}$$

The firms's optimizing condition is

$$C = \partial Y/\partial L = A^{-\rho}(1-\delta)(Y/L)^{1+\rho} \tag{B3}$$

With lower-case letters denoting logarithms and omitting constant terms, (B2) and (B3) imply

$$c = h - p^v + t_1 = -\rho a + (1+\rho)(y-l) \tag{B4}$$

(B1) can be log-linearized as

$$y = a + (1 - S_L)k + S_L l \tag{B5}$$

where S_L is the share of labour in value added.

Denoting the constant elasticity of substitution $\sigma = 1/(1+\rho)$, (B4) and (B5) yield the demand for labour:

$$l = k - \beta(h - p^v + t_1 - a) \tag{B6}$$

with $\beta = \sigma/(1 - S_L)$.

2. Trade union's wage setting

Following MacDonald and Solow (1981) we assume that a single union maximizes the expected utility of the representative worker (or, equivalently, the weighted average of employed and unemployed workers):

$$E(u) = (L/\bar{L})u(W) + [(\bar{L}-L)/\bar{L}]u(\Omega) \tag{B7}$$

where $\bar{L}$ is the labour force, L the number of employed workers; W the real take-home wage, Ω real unemployment benefits. Real take-home wage is;

$$W = \frac{H}{P^c T_2} \tag{B8}$$

with P^c the consumption deflator and T_2 the employee tax mark-up. The trade union maximizes (B7) with respect to the gross salary level H, given the firm's demand for labour in (B6). If the union is able to impose its optimal salary level, it acts as a monopolist, leaving to the firm the decision to hire labour according to (B6).

The union's optimizing condition is;

$$\frac{L}{\bar{L}}\frac{\partial u}{\partial W}\frac{\partial W}{\partial H} + \frac{u-u^0}{\bar{L}}\frac{\partial L}{\partial C}\frac{\partial C}{\partial H} = 0 \tag{B9}$$

where $u = u(W)$ and $u^0 = u(\Omega)$.

This can be shown to become

$$\frac{W}{u}\frac{\partial u}{\partial W} + \frac{u-u^0}{u}\frac{C}{L}\frac{\partial L}{\partial C} = 0 \tag{B10}$$

If the utility function has constant relative risk aversion, $u = W^{1-\gamma}/(1-\gamma)$, and with (B6) we obtain

$$1 - \gamma = \beta\frac{u-u^0}{u} \tag{B11}$$

or

$$W^u = \Theta\Omega \text{ with } \Theta = \left[\frac{\beta}{\beta-(1-\gamma)}\right]^{\frac{1}{1-\gamma}} \tag{B11'}$$

If the union is able to enforce this real take-home wage, the employment level is given by

$$l^u = k + \beta(a - x - w^u) \tag{B12}$$

where $w^u = \theta + \omega$ from (B11') and x is the logarithm of the wedge separating labour costs and take-home wages:

$$X = \frac{C}{W} = \frac{P^c T_1 T_2}{P^v} \tag{B13}$$

The union sets the salary level as a mark-up over unemployment benefits, with the rate of mark-up depending inversely upon the elasticity of the firm's demand for labour $\sigma/(1-S_L)=\beta$ as in a standard monopoly pricing model. In the Cobb-Douglas case β is exactly constant and the target real wage is constant.

Quite logically, (B12) shows that the equilibrium employment level depends on the difference between factor productivity and labour costs as measured by the sum of the wedge x, the unemployment benefits ω and the mark-up imposed by the trade union θ. Importantly, it also depends on the stock of capital k. While k is taken as exogenous, it should properly be related to labour costs via the factor price frontier, and is another channel through which high labour costs may reduce employment.

3. The Phillips curve

While the previous section presents the labour market equilibrium, the Phillips curve is intended to describe how this equilibrium is approached. It requires some lags in the adjustment mechanism. We adopt two standard assumptions: first, unions are not able to achieve their target real take-home wage but work towards it; second, gross nominal wages are set at the beginning of the current period when the CPI inflation rate π^c is not known and approximated by last period's rate π^c_{-1} (either because of the indexation mechanism or because of myopic expectations). Using (B8), the resulting rate of increase of the gross hourly nominal wage is;

$$\Delta h = \Delta w^u + \pi^c_{-1} + \Delta t_2 + \alpha(l - l^u) \tag{B14}$$

where $\Delta z = z - z_{-1}$ and w^u is the (log of) real wage target of the unions given in (B11') as $w^u = \theta + \omega$. From (B6) we derive the rate of change of the value added deflator;

$$\pi^v = \Delta h + \Delta t_1 - \Delta a - (\Delta k - \Delta l)/\beta \tag{B15}$$

If P^m is the price index for imported goods, $P^c = (P^m)^\lambda (P^v)^{1-\lambda}$ and plugging (B14) into (B15) gives (assuming θ constant):

$$\pi^v = \pi^v_{-1} + \lambda(\pi^m_{-1} - \pi^v_{-1}) - \alpha(U - U^*) + \Delta(\omega + t_1 + t_2 - \psi) - \Delta U/\beta \tag{B16}$$

where: $\psi = a + (k - \bar{l})/\beta$ is the log of the marginal productivity of labour evaluated at full employment (see (B3) and (B5))

$U = \bar{l} - l$ is the rate of unemployment.
$U^* = \bar{l} - l^u$ is the union's target unemployment rate.

This definition of unemployment assumes that hours worked have remained unchanged, which is grossly inaccurate. We return to this issue in the following section.

(B16) is the Phillips curve referred to in the text. The NAIRU corresponds to $\pi^v = \pi^v_{-1}$, $\pi^m = \pi^v$, $\Delta U = 0$ and $\Delta(\omega + t_1 + t_2) = \Delta\psi$, i.e. when inflation and unemployment stabilize and labour productivity gains are exactly absorbed by labour cost increases. Then the NAIRU is the union's target unemployment rate and is given by

$$U^* = \beta(w^u + x - \psi) \tag{B17}$$

4. Hours worked

In the above formulation the number of hours worked is taken as exogenous. A proper treatment of this issue would require introducing three changes in the model: leisure should enter the representative worker's utility function; the production function should recognize that there may be costs in operating given equipment with more workers working less hours; the number of hours worked per worker is in the end a decision taken by the firm given the extra cost of overtime work beyond the normal workweek (39 hours in France since 1982). The resulting problem has been studied in Wyplosz (1985) and in a similar model by Calmfors (1985). Its implications are discussed in the text.

Appendix C. Alternative specifications of the Phillips curve

Table C1 augments the two regressions reported in Table 6. Regression (3) augments Regression (2) by adding further lags in π, U, $(\psi - x)$, contemporaneous $\Delta(p^m - p)$ and separate current and lagged values of x. Individually, their t statistics are very small. An F test on the hypothesis that the additional variables are jointly significant is also comfortably rejected. $(F(6, 8) = 0.33)$.

Having checked that it is not possible straightforwardly to improve on the dynamic specification of the equations shown in Table 6, we then investigate the consequence of omitting certain contemporaneous variables from these equations. (Ideally, of course, one would investigate both extensions simultaneously, but with annual data we exhaust degrees of freedom very quickly.) Regressions (4) and (5) investigate the consequences of augmenting Regressions (1) and (2) of Table 6 with three variables (all in logarithms):

B: real unemployment benefits, the ratio of total unemployment outlay to the product of the number of unemployed and the consumer price index.

Table C1. Augmented Phillips curves (Dependent variable $\Delta\pi$, annual data, 1963–1984)

Variable	Regression (3)	Regression (4)	Regression (5)
Constant	201.38 (0.90)	200.65 (3.64)	242.14 (5.88)
U	−4.34 (1.42)	−3.83 (4.28)	−4.46 (6.82)
$\Delta(p^m - p)_{-1}$	0.07 (1.62)	0.06 (1.79)	0.06 (2.57)
$(\psi - x)$	−40.28 (1.93)	−49.00 (3.54)	−53.90 (6.22)
$\Delta\pi_{-1}$	−0.33 (2.15)		−0.32 (3.97)
$\hat{e}_{-1}$		−0.65 (3.89)	
t	2.69 (0.98)	2.87 (4.32)	3.22 (7.07)
DV_1		1.98 (2.80)	
DV_2	1.92 (3.69)		1.95 (7.69)
π_{-2}	−0.01 (0.02)		
U_{-1}	0.07 (0.04)		
$\Delta(p^m - p)$	0.02 (0.39)		
$(\psi - x)_{-1}$	−2.01 (0.05)		
x	22.82 (0.77)		
x_{-1}	−12.25 (0.29)		
B		−5.39 (0.81)	−3.17 (1.05)
RR		6.90 (1.13)	3.15 (1.24)
UV		−1.51 (1.54)	−0.66 (1.21)
Standard error	0.72	0.96	0.62

(t statistics in parentheses)

RR: the replacement ratio, defined by

$$\left(\frac{1-U}{U}\right)\left(\frac{\text{total unemployment outlays}}{\text{total gross wages}}\right)$$

UV: the unemployment-vacancy ratio.

Again, both individual t statistics and the F tests on the 3 variables jointly, $(F(3, 12) = 1.15$ for Regression (4), and $F(3, 12) = 0.62$ for regression (5)) indicate that their omission from Table 6 is not the source of any serious specification error.

References

Artus, J. (1984). 'The Disequilibrium Real Wage Hypothesis: An Empirical Evaluation', *IMF Staff Papers.*

Artus, P., G. Laroque and G. Michel (1984). 'Estimation of a Quarterly Macroeconomic Model with Quantity Rationing', *Econometrica.*

Artus, P., J. Bournay, P. Morin, A. Pacaud, C. Peyroux, H. Sterdyniak and R. Teyssier, (1981), 'Metric. Une Modelisation de l'Economie Francaise', INSEE, Paris.

Beudaert, M. (1983). 'L'Annee 1982 a travers les Comptes Nationaux', *Economie et Statistique.*

Blanchard, O., R. Dornbusch, J. Dreze, H. Giersch, R. Layard and M. Monti (1985). 'Employment and Growth in Europe: a Two Handed Approach', Centre for European Policy Studies, Paper No. 21.

Bouissou, M. B., J. J. Laffont and Q. H. Vuong (1984). 'Econometrie du Desequilibre sur Donnees Microeconomiques', *Annales de l'INSEE*.
Bourit, F., P. Hernu and M. Perrot (1982). 'Les Salaires en 1981', *Economie et Statistique*.
Bruno, M. (1986). 'Aggregate Supply and Demand Factors in OECD Unemployment', *Economica*.
Bruno, M. and J. Sachs (1985). *Economics of Worldwide Stagflation*, Basil Blackwell.
Buiter, W. H. (1985). 'A Guide to Public Sector Debt and Deficits', *Economic Policy*.
Calmfors, L. (1985). 'Trade Unions, Wage Formation and Macroeconomic Stability', *Scandinavian Journal of Economics*, forthcoming.
Claassen, E. and C. Wyplosz (1985). 'Capital Controls: Some Principles and the French Experience', in J. Melitz and C. Wyplosz (ed.) *The French Economy*, Westview Press.
Coe, D. and F. Gagliardi (1985). 'Nominal Wage Determination in Ten OECD Economies', OECD Working Paper No. 19.
Colin, J. F., M. Elbaum and A. Fonteneau (1984). 'Chomage et Politique de l'Emploi 1981–1983', *Observations et Diagnostics Economiques*, Revue de l'OFCE No. 7.
De Menil, G. and J. Sastre (1985). 'Transfer Policies, Income and Employment in France', in G. De Menil and U. Westphal (eds.) *Stabilization Policy in France and the Federal Republic of Germany*, North-Holland.
Dornbusch, R., G. Basevi, O. Blanchard, W. Buiter, and R. Layard (1983). 'Macroeconomic Prospects and Policies for the European Community', Centre for European Policy Studies Paper, No 1.
Feroldi, M. and F. Meunier (1984). 'La Boucle Prix-Salaires et l'Inflation depuis 1970', *Economie et Statistique*.
Fonteneau, A. and A. Gubian (1985). 'Comparaison des Relances Francaises de 1975 et 1981–1982', *Observations et Diagnostics Economiques*, Revue de l'OFCE No. 12.
Fonteneau, A. and P. A. Muet (1983). 'La Politique Economique depuis Mai 1981: un Premier Bilan', *Observations et Diagnostics Economiques*, Revue de l'OFCE No. 4.
Giersch, H. (1981). 'Aspects of Growth, Structural Change, and Employment – A Schumpeterian Perspective.' in H. Giersch (ed.) *Macroeconomic Policies for Growth and Stability*, Weltwirtschaft an der Universitat Kiel.
Grubb, D., R. Layard and J. Symons (1984). 'Wages, Unemployment and Incomes Policy', Centre for Labour Economics Discussion Paper No. 168.
Grubb, D., R. A. Jackman and R. Layard (1982). 'Causes of the Current Stagflation', *Review of Economic Studies*.
Grubb, D., R. A. Jackman and R. Layard (1983). 'Wage Rigidity and Unemployment in OECD Countries', *European Economic Review*.
Knoester, A. and N. van der Windt (1985). 'Real Wages and Taxation in Ten OECD Countries', Institute for Economic Research, Erasmus University, Rotterdam, Discussion Paper No. 8501.
Kolm, S. C., 'La Transition Socialiste Francaise', *Le Monde* 17–18 June 1981.
Lambert, J. P., M. Lubrano and R. Sneessens (1984). 'Emploi et Chomage en France de 1955 a 1982: un Modele Macroeconomique Annuel avec Rationnement', *Annales de l'INSEE*.
Langohr, H. and C. Viallet (1986). 'Compensation and Wealth Transfers in the French Nationalizations' *Journal of Financial Economics*, forthcoming.
Layard, R., G. Basevi, O. Blanchard, W. Buiter and R. Dornbusch (1984). 'Europe: The Case for Unsustainable Growth', Centre for European Policy Studies, Paper No. 8/9.
MacDonald, I. M. and R. M. Solow (1981). 'Wage Bargaining and Employment', *American Economic Review*.
Malinvaud, E. (1986). 'The Rise of Unemployment in France', *Economica*.
Marchand, O., D. Rault and E. Turpin (1983). 'Des 40 heures aux 39 heures: Processus et Reactions des Entreprises', *Economie et Statistique*.
Muet, P. A. (1985). 'Economic Management and the International Environment, 1981–1983', in H. Machin and V. Wright (eds) *Economic Policy and Policy Making under the Mitterrand Presidency 1981–1984*, Frances Pinter, London.
Muller, P. and R. W. R. Price (1984) 'Structural Budget Deficits and Fiscal Stance', OECD Working Paper No 15.
Oudiz, G., E. Raoul and H. Sterdyniak (1979). 'Reduire la duree du travail, quelles consequences?', *Economie et Statistique*.
Oudiz, G. and H. Sterdyniak (1985). 'Inflation, Employment and External Constraints: An Overview of the French Economy during the Seventies'. in J. Melitz and C Wyplosz (eds.) *The French Economy, Theory and Policy*, Westview Press.
Price, R. W. R. and P. Muller (1984) 'Structural Budget Indicators and the Interpretation of Fiscal Policy Stance in OECD Economies' in OECD *Economic Studies*, No. 3.

Steinherr, A. and B. Van Halperen (1983). 'Approche pragmatique pour une Politique de Plein-Emploi: les Subventions a la Creation d'Emplois', *Economic Paper* No 22, EEC.

Sterdyniak, H., M. A. Boudier, M. Boutillier, F. Charpin and B. Durand, (1984). 'Le Modele Trimestriel de l'O.F.C.E.', *Observations et Diagnostic Economiques.*

Stoffaes, C. (1985), 'the Nationalizations 1981–1984: an Initial Assessment', in H. Machin and V. Wright (eds.) *Economic Policy and Policy making Under the Mitterrand Presidency 1981–1984*, Frances Pinter, London.

World Financial Market, (1983), 'The French Austerity Program'.

Wyplosz, C. (1985). 'A Note on the Reduction of the Workweek'. unpublished, INSEAD.

Economic Policy April 1986 Printed in Great Britain

███████

SUMMARY

Privatization

George Yarrow

This paper examines the theoretical and empirical case for private versus public ownership. Privatization usually leads managers to place greater emphasis on the pursuit of profits. However, whether this is beneficial to society depends on the trade-off between possible market failures due to a lack of competition and deficiencies in government control of public firms. The competitive and regulatory environment is more important than the question of ownership *per se.* In competitive markets there is a presumption in favour of private ownership. Where there is a natural monopoly, vigorous regulatory action is required.

The evidence suggests that privatization has led to improved performance by firms such as the National Freight Corporation and Cable and Wireless which operate in a relatively competitive environment. The benefits are less clear in the case of firms like BP, Britoil and British Aerospace. However, the most worrying case is that of British Telecom and the projected privatization of British Gas where little thought has been given to limiting the abuse of monopoly power. Rather the regulatory environment has been tailored to the needs of the existing management and to ensuring a successful share flotation.

Privatization is also advanced as a weapon for reducing trade union power, encouraging wider share ownership, redistributing wealth and improving the public finances. However, there are other policy instruments better suited to achieving these objectives. The existing privatization programme has not led to a marked widening of share ownership and has resulted in windfall gains to a small group of investors at the expense of taxpayers in general.

Privatization in theory and practice

George Yarrow

Hertford College, Oxford

1. Introduction

The economic case for privatization is not new. Two centuries ago Adam Smith (1776) argued that:

> 'In every great monarchy in Europe the sale of the crown lands would produce a very large sum of money, which, if applied to the payment of the public debts, would deliver from mortgage a much greater revenue than any which those lands have ever afforded to the crown. . . . When the crown lands had become private property, they would, in the course of a few years, become well improved and well cultivated.'

Today, privatization policies are again popular: extensive programmes are under way not only in mature economies such as the UK but also in developing countries from Taiwan to Mexico, and are soon to be initiated in countries as diverse as France and Japan. My purposes in this paper are to set out the basic principles that should guide our thinking about privatization and to offer an assessment of the programme to date in the UK.

Whilst a number of benefits have been claimed for privatization, my themes will be that many of its goals are better achieved by other policies and that it is on its contributions to economic efficiency that privatization must ultimately be judged. Such efficiency has two components: the production of chosen output levels at minimum cost, and the correct overall balance of outputs. To evaluate the effects of privatization against these criteria it is necessary first to compare the incentive structures in

I would like to thank Steven Webb and Mark Oliver for valuable research assistance in the preparation of this paper. I am also grateful to David Begg and John Vickers for numerous helpful comments on the earlier drafts.

public and private industry, and second to assess the implications of those incentives for economic performance.

I shall argue that there is a *prima facie* case, supported by available evidence, that, when each is judged against its own objectives, private monitoring of managers is more effective than public monitoring. That conclusion does not, however, imply a general presumption in favour of privatization. A likely, though not inevitable, consequence of privatization is that managers will place more weight upon profit goals. Whether or not this induces an increase in economic efficiency depends in part of the extent of market failures. Indeed it should be recognized that in many cases it was the diagnosis of such market failures (in industries that can be characterized as natural monopolies, for example) that led economists to advocate nationalization in the first place.

From this it follows that any evaluation of privatization must take account of both the relevant market structures and the competition and regulatory policies that are being simultaneously pursued. For these reasons, my assessment of the UK programme groups particular cases by market structure and emphasizes the provisions for regulation in those industries where competition is likely to be weak. I conclude that competition and regulatory policy are more important determinants of economic performance than ownership *per se*.

I take as my working definition of privatization the transfer from the public to the private sector of entitlements to residual profits from operating an enterprise, coupled with any accompanying changes in regulatory policy. The frequent identification of privatization policy with asset sales is misleading for two distinct reasons. First, asset sales need not be involved, as in the cases of franchises awarded for the running of public facilities (e.g. naval dockyards) or publicly maintained legal monopolies (e.g. TV broadcasting). Second, as I have emphasized above, even where asset sales occur, much of the impact of policy may arise from decisions taken about regulation (e.g. the establishment of OFTEL to regulate telecommunications in the UK).

The paper is organized as follows. To provide a concrete framework for the subsequent discussion, in Section 2 I summarize the main features of the UK privatization programme to date. Section 3 analyses the effect of privatization on managerial incentives and briefly reviews the empirical literature on the relative performance of private and public enterprises. Section 4 examines in detail how privatization may be expected to affect economic efficiency in industries where inter-firm competition is moderate to high, and assesses the out-turn in such cases in the UK. Section 5 repeats this exercise for industries where competition is weak. The next four sections discuss a series of other explicit or implicit objectives of privatization: reducing trade union power (Section 6), widening share ownership (Section 7), redistributing wealth (Section 8), and improving the public finances (Section 9). Section 10 assesses the transactions costs of asset sales and, finally, Section 11 summarizes my main conclusions.

2. The UK privatization programme

In Britain the emergence of privatization as a major aspect of economic policy dates from the return of a Conservative government in 1979. Although that party's 1979 election manifesto made little mention of privatization, both the priority attached to transfer of production to the private sector and the scale of operations in that direction increased rapidly in the following few years so that, by the time of the 1983 election, these policies had become a major political issue.

The most visible components of the privatization programme have been sales of existing public sector housing, contracting out of services to private businesses, and complete or partial sales of public enterprises. In the early years it was the first component, implemented at the local government level, that was dominant. Between 1979 and 1983 nearly 600,000 housing units were sold, more than in the whole of the 1945–79 period, and receipts climbed from around £300 million per annum in 1979 to nearly £2,000 million in 1982.

Contracting out – the substitution of private for public production in the provision of *publicly financed* goods and services – has taken longer to implement. Typically it implies the establishment of more complex contractual arrangements than those surrounding housing sales and it requires the continuing involvement of public authorities in contract enforcement and renewal. Nevertheless, by early 1984 over fifty local authorities had each privatized at least one service using this method. The services most commonly 'contracted-out' have been various types of cleaning (streets, offices, schools, hospitals, etc.) and refuse collection, but others have included pest control, catering, architectural services, grass cutting, provision of parking facilities, laundries and housing repairs.

Until 1984, the sale of public enterprises was in many ways the least important of the major strands of the privatization programme. The position changed, however, with the sale of slightly over 50% of British Telecom (BT) in November 1984, and current projections indicate asset sales averaging close to £4,000 million per annum over the next three years. The fact that enterprise sales are largely the responsibility of central government has also tended to place them at the centre of political controversies over privatization.

2.1. Objectives of privatization

The UK programme has never defined a comprehensive list of goals ranked by priority or weight. Indeed, objectives can be expected to differ between ministers and to change over time. The following list, however, summarizes what appear to have been the principal aims:

   (i) improving efficiency by increasing competition and allowing firms to borrow from the capital market,

  (ii) reducing the public sector borrowing requirement (PSBR),

 (iii) easing problems of public sector pay determination,

 (iv) reducing government involvement in enterprise decision making,

  (v) widening the ownership of economic assets,

 (vi) encouraging employee ownership of shares in their companies, and

(vii) redistributing income and wealth.

The last of these objectives has been only implicit but has been a crucial influence on a number of key policy decisions.

In assessing privatization against these objectives the later sections of the paper will be chiefly concerned with the enterprise-sales strand of the UK programme, although parts of the theoretical discussions are directly relevant to the other two components (and to contracting out in particular). This choice of emphasis arises from the combination of space constraints and the easier availability of data in this area. It should not be interpreted as implying a belief that other aspects of the UK programme are relatively unimportant.

2.2. Main features of the UK central-government asset sales programme

Table 1 sets out the principal asset sales to date. It can be seen that, until 1984, the proceeds from asset sales were a relatively minor element in government finances: the figures in the final column should be seen in the context of government expenditure totalling over £700 billion between 1979 and 1984 inclusive, and a public sector financial deficit averaging close to £10 billion per annum over the same period. The proceeds jump sharply in the second half of 1984 – although actual accruals grow more steadily due to the staggering of the payment dates for BT shares – and are projected to remain at a higher level, at least until the next general election.

Disposals of the remaining holdings in Britoil, British Aerospace, and Cable and Wireless generated revenue of over £1,300 million during 1985, and the total would have been considerably higher if the planned sale of British Airways had not been delayed by litigation connected with the Laker Airways case. Plans for the sale of the British

Table 1. The UK privatization programme (Principal asset sales 1979–84)

Company	Industry	Sale date	Net proceeds £ million
British Petroleum	Oil	Oct. 79	276
		June 81	8
		Sep. 83	543
British Aerospace	Aerospace	Feb. 81	43
		May 85	346
British Sugar Corp.	Sugar refining	July 81	44
Cable & Wireless	Telecommunications	Oct. 81	182
		Dec. 83	263
		Dec. 85	600
Amersham	Radio-chemicals	Feb. 82	64
National Freight Co.	Road haulage	Feb. 82	5
Britoil	Oil	Nov. 82	627
		Aug. 85	425
Assoc. British Ports	Sea ports	Feb. 83	46
		Apr. 84	51
International Aeradio	Aviation communications	Mar. 83	60
British Rail Hotels	Hotels	Mar. 83	51
Wytch Farm	Oil	May 84	82
Enterprise Oil	Oil	June 84	380
Sealink	Harbour/Ferries	July 84	66
Jaguar	Cars	July 84	297
British Telecom	Telecommunications	Nov. 84	3,600
Others			716

Notes: (i) Others include sales of 25% of ICL (1979), Fairey (1980), 50% of Ferranti (1980), 75% of Inmos (1984), subsidiaries of British Steel, British Shipbuilders, and the National Coal Board, and other parts of the British Technology Group. (ii) The government still retains a 31.7% stake in British Petroleum, and a 49.8% stake in British Telecom (BT). (ii) Only the BT privatization was accompanied by specific regulatory action, the establishment of OFTEL.

Airports Authority and the much larger British Gas Corporation (BGC) are well advanced and, together with British Airways and possible further disposals of shares in BP, will imply new issues in the next year or two on a scale exceeding that of 1984. Other planned sales include the interesting case of the Trustee Savings Bank – which is not technically owned by the state and where the proceeds will go to the newly formed private company – the Royal Ordnance Factories, Unipart (a part of BL) and Rolls Royce.

In the longer term, Table 2 indicates considerable scope for further, substantial asset sales. In particular, the Electricity Supply Industry (the largest of the nationalized industries) would be an obvious candidate for privatization.

Table 2. Turnover (1984, £ million) of enterprises in the public sector at Autumn 1985

Electricity Boards	10,621	Rolls Royce	1,409
British Gas Corp*	6,392	British Shipbuilders	965
National Coal Board	4,669	National Bus Co.*	754
BL (vehicles)	3,402	London Regional Transport	578
British Steel	3,358	British Nuclear Fuels	460
Post Office	2,884	British Airports Authority*	316
British Rail†	2,832	Civil Aviation Authority	228
British Airways*	2,514	Scottish Transport Group	154

Notes: * Privatization plans at an advanced stage; † 1983 turnover.

A second feature of the programme revealed by Table 1 is that, until 1984, ownership transfer was limited to enterprises that already faced significant competition from private sector firms in most of their activities. Again the BT case marked a significant departure, raising for the first time questions of how to regulate a privately owned firm with dominant positions in major parts of its business (telecommunications networks, switching facilities and equipment sales). Thus, while market failures are not completely absent in some of the earlier cases, the scale of the problem is of a different order in the Telecom case. Recognition of this fact led to the establishment of OFTEL, a regulatory body with powers to constrain monopolistic behaviour by the dominant firm. Gas (and, if it occurs, electricity) privatization gives rise to similar, but generally more severe, natural monopoly problems. It will therefore also involve the formation of a new regulatory agency.

3. Privatization and incentives

In this section I will first outline the differences between the monitoring arrangements for otherwise similar privately owned and publicly owned firms, and then examine some of the implications of those arrangements. While it can be expected that privatization will lead managers to place greater weight on profit goals, the changes involved are far more complex than a simple shift from 'public interest' objectives to profit maximization. The immediate effect of privatization is to substitute shareholder for governmental monitoring and control of the firm's management. Under private ownership, management is directly responsible to shareholders although it might be constrained in its actions by a regulatory body. Under public ownership, management is monitored by government, which in turn can be viewed as an agent of the voting population.

3.1. Private ownership

Consider first the factors affecting managerial incentives in privately owned firms. Although, in general, shareholders will not be unanimous in their rankings of alternative managerial policies (Ekern and Wilson, 1974) I shall proceed on the assumption that shareholders wish the firm to maximize profit. Managerial incentives will then depend upon: the separation of ownership and control, the availability of performance information to shareholders, the effectiveness of the takeover mechanism, and legal constraints such as limited liability.

The simplest case occurs when there is a single manager/shareholder (what Alchian and Demsetz, 1972, call the classical firm). Here the owner-manager has strong incentives to increase the internal efficiency of the firm and thereby raise its profits. Moreover, the marketability of the property rights means that the manager/shareholder, by selling shares, will be able to capture immediately any future returns that flow from current activities.

More usually, however, there is separation of ownership and control. The principals (the shareholders) then need to provide incentives to the agents (the managers) to ensure that the agents do in fact act in the principals' interests. There are two main problems at this point. First, monitoring activities by one owner confer external benefits on others, and there is therefore a tendency towards sub-optimal levels of monitoring. Second, the arrangement gives rise to asymmetric information – managers typically know more about the firm's opportunities than owners. Thus, even if shareholders could formulate and impose optimal profit-related incentive schemes, these are unlikely to reward a manager with the full incremental benefits of extra effort: the dependence of profit on risky factors beyond management's control gives rise to a risk sharing pressure for remuneration to be less highly geared to profit (Shavell, 1979).

The first of the above problems can be overcome if there is a reasonably efficient *market for corporate control.* By purchasing shares on the market an individual or firm can quickly concentrate ownership and thereby wrest control of the target company from its incumbent management. This possibility gives rise to a potentially powerful incentive effect. If the performance of a particular management is poor the share price of the firm will drop and the returns from a takeover raid designed to introduce a new management team will increase. Hence, the threat of replacement serves as a disciplining factor on incumbent managements.

Unfortunately, there are strong grounds for believing that the market for corporate control exhibits a number of significant imperfections. For example, Grossman and Hart (1980) have shown that the marketability of property rights does not, *per se*, correct the market failure arising from dispersed shareholdings. Put simply, a small shareholder can neglect the consequences of his or her sell/hold decision on the outcome of a takeover and, if the bid is expected to succeed, will prefer to hold so as to participate in the profit gains accruing from the change in control. But, if enough shareholders behave in this way, the raid will in fact fail. There are various ways of mitigating this effect, including compulsory acquisition rights in company law (Yarrow, 1985), but they tend to require costly regulation. Most importantly, empirical work on takeovers indicates a far from perfect market in corporate control (Singh, 1975). Very large firms appear to be less vulnerable than smaller companies to uninvited raids, a result of considerable significance when assessing the effects of privatizing public utilities. There is also evidence that the threat of involuntary takeover is not strongly related to a given management's relative profit performance.

3.2. Public ownership

For publicly owned firms the task of monitoring managerial performance is entrusted to government. There are no marketable shares, and hence no *market* for corporate control. However, this need not imply that managerial incentives will be weaker than for private enterprise. Williamson (1975) has shown how hierarchical arrangements can, in appropriate circumstances, lead to more efficient monitoring than capital markets. Thus, government can provide profit-related bonuses and/or fire personnel where performance is poor.

Government monitoring has two potential advantages over the market alternative: it does not encounter the public goods problem associated with dispersed shareholdings, and it can take immediate account of deviations between social and private returns in goods and factor markets. In other words, public ownership provides an instrument for correcting failures (inefficiencies) in the markets for goods, factors *and* corporate control.

These arguments frequently serve as the basis of the case *for* public ownership. For example, vigorous pursuit of profit by natural monopolists can lead to a variety of anti-competitive practices that operate against the public interest. The difficulties of devising and enforcing simple tests of anti-competitive behaviour may render nationalization superior to regulation of privately owned firms. Alternatively, imperfections in the market for corporate control of private firms could lead to cost inefficiencies as a result of the emergence of non-profit goals, the sleepy monopoly case. Finally, the public enterprise option may facilitate information gathering and reduce the informational asymmetries between management and those responsible for monitoring their performance.

The key to dissatisfaction with the performance of public enterprises must, therefore, lie elsewhere. If governments are the guardians of the public interest, the question is *quis custodiet ipsos custodes?* The answer, of course, is the voting public, but the 'market' for political control is highly imperfect and the incentives for efficient *monitoring* of public enterprises can, as a result, be rather weak. Thus, lack of detailed knowledge on the part of voters about actual and potential performance of nationalized industries, coupled with an inability to vote *separately* on this issue, means that monitoring performance will often have a rather minor effect on a government's electoral prospects. Where decisions do have an impact on political prospects it is likely to be because the actions have highly visible impacts on the wealth of identifiable interest groups, generating pressures to use public enterprises to transfer income to favoured groups, often at the expense of efficiency.

3.3. Assessment

The arguments thus far imply that the relative merits of private and public monitoring depend upon the trade-off between market inefficiencies and incentive failure (arising from the nature of political systems) in government departments or agencies. That being so, it cannot be expected that one form of ownership will be superior to the other in all industries and in all countries. Nevertheless, it might be argued that the evidence on comparative performance indicates that the weaknesses of public sector monitoring are so serious, and so pervasive, that a general *presumption* in favour of private ownership is justified.

In a recent review of the empirical literature on this question, Millward (1982) concluded that there appeared to be no general ground for believing that managerial efficiency was lower in public firms. My own view of the evidence, set out more fully in the Appendix, is slightly different. It is that private sector monitoring is more efficient in cases where the relevant firm faces strong competition and other forms of product and factor market failure are relatively unimportant. It is based on the frequency of the empirical finding that, in such cases, private firms tend to operate with lower costs.

While this view implies that the weaknesses in public monitoring are empirically significant, it is *not* sufficient to establish a presumption in favour of private production in *all* circumstances. The evidence on comparative performance in cases where product and factor market inefficiencies are substantive is much less clear cut. Indeed, in examples such as electricity supply it tends to point in the other direction, towards better performance by public firms. I conclude that general evaluations of privatization policies must necessarily take account of factors such as the degree of competition in relevant markets and the effectiveness of regulatory policies in dealing with market failures, including those arising from monopoly power.

4. Privatization and competition

The incentive structures of firms' managers are affected by a number of factors, of which the ownership structure of the enterprise is only one. In this Section I analyse the impact of product-market competition on incentives and evaluate those asset sales in the UK where the relevant markets can be classified as competitive or 'workably' competitive.

The sale of a public enterprise has, in itself, little immediate impact on market structure. Privatization via franchising or contracting out, however, is different in this respect because, where it involves competitive tendering for the contract, it has the effect of eliminating a crucial entry barrier. I will therefore analyse the role of franchising in a separate subsection.

4.1. Markets and information

In setting incentive structures for managements, shareholders and governments alike face difficulties arising from lack of information. They cannot directly observe managerial inputs or the firm's true opportunities. Observations of the performance of competing firms in the same market, or of firms in similar markets do, however, provide relevant information for the development of more efficient incentive schemes (Holmstrom, 1982).

To illustrate, consider the problem of interpreting a performance statistic such as profitability. In any year it will depend on the levels and quality of managerial inputs and a series of other factors outside of management's control. Inability to distinguish between the contributions of management and external factors limits the ability to correctly reward the former. Suppose, however, that the same performance statistic could be observed for other firms that were similar in the sense that, holding managerial inputs constant, the performance measures are correlated. For example, the profitabilities of firms operating in the same market all tend to change in the same direction when there is an exogenous demand shock. Then the performance of 'similar' firms yields information about the external factors affecting performance and hence, indirectly, about the contribution of the given management. It follows that, by linking rewards to the observable measures of *relative* performance, monitors will be able to implement more effective managerial incentives.

Note, however, that competition among firms is not a necessary condition for the availability of additional, informative signals. Economy-wide disturbances lead to correlations between performance in different industries. Similarly, the results of independent regional monopolists producing the same goods can provide valuable information about the performances of the various managements (Shleifer, 1985). It can, however, be expected that the quality of the signals will tend to be better where several firms are in direct competition.

4.2. Competition and incentives

As well as providing information for monitors, competition among firms also serves to reduce the difficulties faced by the latter in setting incentive schemes. This follows from the fact that competition itself can be regarded as a form of incentive system (Hayek, 1945; Hart, 1983). Given the likely deficiencies of both private and public sector control mechanisms, it is a property of markets that is of the utmost significance for economic performance.

The performance of any one firm depends on the actions of its rivals' managements as well as those of its own. Thus, profit related incentive schemes will automatically link rewards to the behaviour of managers *relative* to competitors in the marketplace. Competition may also lead to reasonably effective incentives even where rewards are not primarily profit-based. Managerial objective functions will typically include a number of variables that reflect a particular management's performance relative to other economic agents. Such variables include market share, power, and prestige. Hence, if a management team performs poorly in competition to reduce costs, its market share, power and prestige (and hence managerial utility) are all likely to suffer as a consequence. Of course, in the case of privately owned firms, shareholders still face the problem of attenuating profit appropriation by management, but that is a less complicated task than detailed monitoring of all decisions and, from a wider perspective, is more a matter of income distribution than of economic efficiency.

4.3. Franchising and contracting out

I have attempted to show why the extent of product market competition can be expected to have quite powerful effects on managerial incentive structures and, hence, on economic performance. The efficiency consequences of enterprise sales are therefore likely to be *dependent* upon the degree of competition, although the sales themselves may not have much impact on the latter. In contrast, where privatization is achieved by allowing firms to compete *for* the right to serve a market or supply a good that was previously served/supplied by a *protected* public sector organization, competition is immediately increased.

Franchising and contracting out are attractive policy options precisely because they possess this property. Moreover, they are capable of reconciling single firm production with competition: firms can be asked to place bids for the *sole* right of supply of the given commodity and, to prevent monopolistic pricing, the right can be awarded to the firm that offers to supply at the lowest price (Demsetz, 1968). Franchising therefore offers a possible solution to the natural monopoly problem.

It should, however, be noted that the replacement of a public firm by a private firm is not the most important aspect of the policy. For example, after receiving a set of competitive tenders, a local authority might decide that it can supply a service more efficiently than outside, private contractors. Nevertheless, the existence of a competitive bidding process will have provided the authority with information about feasible costs of provision and created incentives for cost-efficient operation by public sector workers.

Franchising and contracting out are likely to be most effective when problems of contract specification and renewal are relatively simple. Unfortunately, for several reasons, these conditions will not always be satisfied (Williamson, 1976). First, the goods or services to be supplied may be packages of distinct characteristics. In adjudicating between rival bids, officials may then substitute their own preferences for those of the final customers (as has happened for some cable TV franchises in the US.) More importantly, monitoring and enforcement of the contract may be difficult. Second, the existence of sunk costs may give one firm a decisive advantage in the competition for the contract, causing other firms not to enter and leaving the incumbent with an uncontested monopoly. Alternatively, the inability of an incumbent firm to recover costs in the event of failure to win the franchise in later periods could lead to underinvestment. Third, market and technological uncertainties may imply that incomplete contracts – which allow for adjustments as new circumstances are revealed – are more efficient than complete contracts. Incomplete contracts, however, often require extensive monitoring and their administration is then simply a particular form of regulation (see Section 5).

Except in simple cases, therefore, franchising cannot be regarded as a substitute for regulation, and its potential role in industries such as telecommunications, gas, and electricity supply is relatively limited. On the other hand, many goods and services currently produced by the public sector do satisfy conditions such as simplicity, low sunk costs, and relatively low levels of market uncertainty. In such circumstances franchising and contracting out are promising policy options.

4.4. Assessment

Although the above arguments point to the potentially powerful and beneficial effects of competition, the resulting outcomes may, nevertheless, be inefficient because of the existence of one or more sources of market failure. In the following discussion of UK policy I have therefore divided the cases on the basis of a subjective assessment of the likely importance of such market failures.

4.4.1. No significant market failure.
Where privatization involves an enterprise that is already operating in competitive markets and other, significant market failures are absent, evaluation of performance is, in principle, relatively straightforward. Changes in the internal efficiency of a firm are the main factor of interest, and they can be assessed by examining indicators of financial performance such as measures of profitability.

UK cases in this category include Cable and Wireless, Amersham, National Freight, Associated British Ports, International Aeradio, British Rail Hotels, Wytch Farm, Sealink, and Jaguar. Of these only Amersham provides an example of a single, complete sale of all the state's interest in a previously independent enterprise achieved via the creation of a quoted company. Jaguar (also a 100% sale) had been part of BL; National Freight was sold to a consortium of managers and employees; British Rail Hotels and Sealink were part of British Rail; the Wytch Farm case involved the sale of the British Gas Corporation's 50% stake in the oilfield (the other 50% being held by BP); and both Associated British Ports and Cable and Wireless were sold off in stages – a method that has typically been favoured for the larger enterprises, presumably in the belief that a large share issue might depress the market price.

Apart from the question of constructing appropriate counterfactuals (i.e. forming hypotheses about the performance of the firm in the event that privatization had not taken place), three immediate difficulties are encountered in attempting to evaluate the effects of privatization on the financial performance of these enterprises. First, little time has elapsed since the asset sales. Second, some of the enterprises were either parts of larger publicly owned firms and/or were absorbed at the time of sale into larger private companies, so that evidence for the pre- and/or post-privatization periods is difficult or impossible to construct.

Table 3. Real turnover (£ million, 1980 prices) and profit margins (%) 1981–85

		1981	1982	1983	1984	1985
Amersham	T	43.3	51.5	61.4	65.7	76.5
	PM	9.5	14.1	15.0	15.6	15.8
Assoc. British Ports	T	114.7	125.3	121.5	103.4	94.0
	PM	−8.0	3.6	9.4	−4.6	4.2
Cable and Wireless	T	262.8	289.5	317.3	487.6	609.6
	PM	21.8	25.4	38.9	29.2	28.4
Jaguar	T	174.4	251.5	371.8	475.3	567.0
	PM	−16.2	3.1	10.6	14.4	15.7
National Freight	T	391.4	379.7	388.1	421.4	474.6
	PM	2.3	2.1	2.3	4.1	4.2

Notes: (i) Vertical lines drawn closest to initial sale of shares. (ii) Profit data is pre-tax (except for National Freight where trading profits are used). (iii) All data for accounting periods ending in designated calendar years. (iv) 1985 data for ABP, Jaguar and NF based on doubling their figures for the first half of the financial year.

Third, the pre-privatization period sometimes involved laundering of figures, capital reconstructions, and the like, which reduce the comparability of performance statistics in the pre- and post-sale periods.

These difficulties should be borne in mind when interpreting the figures in Table 3, which shows turnover and profitability for the five companies for which data is most readily available. Note, for example, that, with an accounting year ending in March, the 1982 figures for Amersham relate mostly to a period when the company was in the public sector. Thus, the biggest jump in its profit-to-sales ratio occurs in the run up to privatization. The same is true for Associated British Ports and Jaguar, although the major factor in the latter case was the depreciation of sterling against the US dollar, North America being the company's principal market.

For purposes of comparison, Table 4 shows similar statistics for some of the 'workably competitive' enterprises that have remained in the public sector, and also the pre-tax profit of all commercial and industrial companies (excluding North Sea Oil companies) as a fraction of GDP. The former show that some quite substantial improvements in financial performance have been achieved without change of ownership, while the latter indicates that, irrespective of privatization, some improvement in performance could have been expected as a result of the gradual expansion in economic activity since 1981.

Looking at UK nationalized industries more generally, there has, on average, been a tendency towards better financial performance over the past three or four years. This can be explained in large part by partial economic recovery, higher prices in monopolistic industries (e.g.

Table 4. Real turnover (T) (£ million, 1980 prices) and profit margins (PM) (%), 1981–84

		1981	1982	1983	1984
BL	T	2,564	2,528	2,692	2,550
	PM	0.1	−4.1	−7.1	−8.6
British Steel	T	2,640	2,834	2,542	2,502
	PM	−23.1	−9.2	−12.6	−5.1
British Airways	T	1,842	1,884	1,965	1,885
	PM	−3.3	0.4	8.2	11.7
Rolls Royce	T	1,290	1,229	1,047	1,056
	PM	1.2	−6.1	−8.6	4.5
National Bus	T	543	547	559	565
	PM	4.2	5.9	6.8	6.1
All commercial and industrial companies*	PM	7.4	8.0	8.8	10.4

Note: * pre-tax profit as a % of GDP, excluding North Seal Oil.

gas and electricity), and the aforementioned accounting adjustments, made in anticipation of later sale (e.g. British Airways). Performance gains not explained by these factors have been interpreted in one of two ways: either that they can rightfully be attributed to privatization since, without the spur of the impending sale, they would not have occurred, or, conversely, that they indicated what can be achieved when government simply tightens the financial constraints on its enterprises, and hence show that privatization is not necessary for better performance.

My own reading of the situation is that both views are somewhat overstated. Substantial performance improvements by non-monopolistic, publicly owned firms could have been, and were, achieved simply as a result of a shift in government priorities. I am, however, sceptical that the pressure could be maintained over long time periods, and believe that the goal of privatization has provided greater short-term incentives to government for more efficient monitoring.

Further evidence on the effects of privatization can be obtained from share price movements since the date of sale (see Table 5), although here again there are problems of interpretation. Thus, if market participants fully anticipate all of the ensuing changes, any benefits of privatization will be reflected in the opening price. There is also an argument that, because institutional investors were allocated a smaller fraction of the shares than would be required to hold the market index, their later purchases (motivated by a desire to hold the market index and implemented slowly to prevent a large price hike in a thin market) led to gradual upward drift in prices. Despite these points, I would argue that relative share price movements do still convey information

Table 5. Share prices from issue date to 28 June 1985

	Relative price increase (%)	Relative to:
Amersham	−16.5	FT chemicals
Assoc. British Ports	+37.6	FT industrials
Cable and Wireless	+112.4	FT electricals
Jaguar	+13.0	FT motors

Note: The initial price is the equilibrium price on the opening day of trading. The comparison is with *Financial Times* indices.

about privatization. The learning effect is of some interest: that markets are now more optimistic about future returns constitutes circumstantial evidence in favour of this part of the privatization programme. The market index argument is also not entirely convincing. Given a run of supernormal returns; any individual institutional investor would have done better by purchasing more shares at an earlier date.

The National Freight Corporation is missing from Table 5 because it is not traded on the stock exchange. Shareholders can buy and sell equity from and to the company at a price that is fixed at periodic intervals by accountants – a procedure designed to safeguard the controlling interest of managers and other employees of the company. By the beginning of 1985 a £1 share had increased in value to £8.60, and there was a further upward revision to £12.40 in the Spring of that year. Thus, the most spectacular improvement in performance has occurred in that company with the greatest restrictions on the transferability of its shares, which may indicate the potentially powerful effects of profit-sharing schemes.

It is also noteworthy that National Freight yielded very little in the way of direct financial return to the exchequer (see Table 1). Here was a case where government was prepared to forgo sales proceeds to restructure the company in a way permitting a manager/worker buyout (a pension scheme deficit was paid off and limited interest free loans were offered to assist share purchases), and the decision appears to have produced substantial returns in the form of increased efficiency.

In terms of financial performance then, the success stories of this part of the privatization programme appear to have been the National Freight Corporation and Cable and Wireless, both of which have registered substantial improvements relative to the obvious benchmark indicators. For Jaguar, the early signs are good but judgement should be suspended until there is more information about how well the firm has coped in a period when the US dollar has been weaker. In the other two cases, Amersham and Associated British Ports, it is harder to find evidence that privatization has had significant effects on internal efficiency and a neutral judgment is warranted at this stage.

Taken together, these initial results of the UK programme do nothing to undermine the presumption that, given workable competition and an absence of serious market failures, private ownership is generally to be preferred to public ownership.

4.4.2. More extensively controlled industries. Whether public or private, industries such as oil, aerospace and air transport are typically subject to a high level of government intervention. Hence, ownership transfer cannot be discussed in isolation from other aspects of industrial policy, and the latter will be an important determinant of performance.

Enterprise sales in this category include Britoil, Enterprise Oil, and British Aerospace. The planned privatizations of British Airways and the British Airports Authority are also best considered here (although the latter shares some of the features of the natural monopoly cases to be discussed in the next section).

The argument for public ownership in these industries is that it improves the effectiveness of industrial policy. To illustrate, government may seek to extract the maximum tax yield from the offshore oil industry consistent with retaining production and exploration incentives. Public ownership may assist in this task by hindering collusion amongst oil producers. Similarly, in aerospace, it might be judged the most effective means of maintaining a domestic industry to meet security objectives, acquiring information to prevent overcharging on defence contracts, and controlling overseas arms sales.

The principal question then is whether, despite information that is readily available, the monitoring performance of public bodies has been, and will continue to be, so poor that a switch to capital market monitoring produces benefits that dominate possible losses arising from a reduced number of industrial policy instruments.

The post-privatization performance of firms in this category is difficult to assess for a number of reasons. First, given significant market failures, financial performance alone should not be the only criterion of evaluation. Greater emphasis on profit objectives *may* lead to more vigorous exploitation of market power (oil and aerospace) or deterioration in safety standards (airways). The size and significance of such effects therefore need to be considered (alongside any improvements in cost efficiency) before a final judgement is reached. Second, the flotations that have occurred are small in number and have been concentrated in the oil industry. Third, Enterprise Oil was formed out of the BGC's offshore oil interests, and therefore didn't exist as an independent

Table 6. Real turnover (T) (£ million, 1980 prices) and profit margins (PM) (%), 1981–84

		1981	1982	1983	1984
BP	T	23,000	24,127	25,477	28,436
	PM	9.4	7.9	8.0	9.1
Britoil	T	744	895	985	1,191
	PM	52.5	47.2	46.8	44.4
British Aerospace	T	1,485	1,690	1,810	1,850
	PM	4.2	4.1	3.6	4.9

Note: Figures constructed as in Table 4.

Table 7. Share prices from issue date to 28 June 1985

	Relative price increase (%)	Relative to:
BP	−8.6	FT oil
Britoil	−30.9	FT oil
Enterprise Oil	−16.2	FT oil
British Aerospace	−10.7	FT industrials

entity before privatization, while almost 50% of BP's equity was privately owned *before* the 1979 share issue.

Thus, even restricting the focus to financial performance, the evidence is extremely limited. The statistics shown in Tables 6 and 7 do not immediately suggest a major success story, but it must be remembered that the oil company figures are dominated by (from their perspective) adverse movements in the oil price. Moreover, the FT oil index, which is used as a benchmark for share price comparisons, probably does not adequately correct for this external factor in the Britoil and Enterprise cases, because it also covers petrochemical operations whose results are less sensitive to oil prices.

The most informative figures are those for British Aerospace. No dramatic improvement in financial performance is visible against the benchmarks of the profitability of industrial and commercial companies as a whole (c.f. Table 4) or the share price performance of companies included in the FT industrials index. Given that any improvements in internal efficiency would be expected to show up in financial performance, the results offer little in the way of support for the view that privatization has made a major contribution to microeconomic policy goals. Indeed it is hard to resist the conclusion that the enterprise sales in discussion were motivated largely by their implications for public sector borrowing targets (see Section 10).

Looking forward to future privatizations, the prospects for improvements in policy formulation do not appear to be good. Regulation of airways in Britain will continue in the crucial areas of route allocation, international pricing agreements and safety controls, and there is the danger that the lure of higher sale proceeds from a company with a more monopolistic market position may slow down the process of de-regulation of European routes that has only recently begun. Whilst it may be argued that the operations of British Airways offer more scope for improvements in internal efficiency than, say, British Aerospace, it is far from clear that they are unachievable within a framework of public ownership, as the recent improvements in financial performance demonstrate (see Table 4).

Likewise, there are doubts about the benefits of privatization of the British Airports Authority. Current proposals envisage price regulation to prevent exploitation of market power, and the operation of the company will be heavily influenced by decisions on airport expansion and location. Privatization offers no escape from extensive government involvement, and regulatory effectiveness is therefore likely to be a much more significant factor than ownership in determining performance. Again it appears that policy will be dominated by the desire to capitalize future rents associated with locational advantages (Heathrow) and tax concessions (duty free shops), rather than by considerations of economic efficiency.

4.4.3. Franchising and contracting out. Systematic evidence on changes in economic efficiency following privatization via franchising or contracting out schemes is as yet unavailable for the UK. As noted in Section 2, this approach has been popular at the local government level, and the various indicators of performance have not yet been centrally collated.

Support for the proposition that franchising arrangements tend to improve efficiency where problems of contract specification, monitoring and renewal are relatively simple can, however, be found in the more general economics literature on the comparative performance of public and private enterprises (see Appendix). Refuse collection is a good example of this type of service and the consensus of empirical work on this activity is that the unit costs of private collectors tends to be significantly lower (by margins up to the 30–40% range) than their public sector counterparts (who tend not to have to face competitive tendering). Given the right conditions, then, this method of privatization does appear to offer considerable scope for improving efficiency.

5. Market power and regulation

The UK asset sales programme has increasingly focussed on industries such as telecommunications and gas supply where the market shares of the newly privatized companies will be extremely high. In this section I first examine arguments that regulation of such industries is not appropriate. Having rejected the validity of those arguments in the cases of interest, I then go on to consider some of the lessons of the US regulatory experience. Finally, I present an assessment of UK regulatory policies in the telecommunications and gas industries.

5.1. Privatization without regulation

There are two arguments, deriving respectively from the theory of contestable markets and the Austrian tradition of economic activity as a discovery process, that, even where an industry has few firms, economic inefficiencies may be of minor significance. Both are central to the privatization issue, and I will consider them in turn.

5.1.1. Contestable markets. That only a small number of firms operate in a particular market does not in itself imply market power if barriers to entry and exit are absent. These barriers emerge from asymmetries between the cost and demand conditions of incumbent firms and potential entrants, which in turn depend heavily upon the existence of *sunk costs*. The role of sunk costs has therefore been the principal theme of recent literature on conditions of entry (Vickers, 1985).

Contestability theory is concerned with a world in which, on exit from the industry, firms can fully recover undepreciated, prior investments in capacity, reputation and marketing, (see Baumol, Panzar and Willig, 1982). In these circumstances, even a monopolist will be unable to earn supernormal profit, since, if price were above average cost, there would be opportunities for the adoption of profitable 'hit and run' strategies by potential entrants. The result has obvious appeal to proponents of privatization of monopolistic nationalized industries and a bowdlerized version of it – to the effect that, if markets can be made 'more' contestable, there is little need to worry about inefficiencies due to market power – has been highly influential.

There are, however, at least three problems associated with contestability theory. First, the restrictions on cost functions that are necessary for the existence of a contestable equilibrium are very stringent. In many, if not most, industries there will be no equilibrium. To illustrate, consider an industry where firms have U-shaped average cost curves. If firms are either not producing at outputs that minimize unit costs, or are making positive profits, they will be displaced by new entrants. But if firms *are* minimizing unit costs and are making zero profits, all consumers will be served only if market demand divided by the output level that minimizes unit costs happens, by accident, to take an integer value. Second, the efficiency results of the theory are dependent upon the *complete* absence of sunk costs, and it is extremely difficult to conceive of, let alone find, economic activities where this condition is satisfied. Third, small deviations from contestability can radically alter the properties of the equilibrium. Thus if post entry competition drives prices down to unit variable cost or lower, any level of sunk cost incurred on entry, no matter how small, will serve to deter potential competitors, implying that the incumbent can act as an unconstrained monopolist. Put simply, the equilibrium is not robust (Vickers and Yarrow, 1985). It follows that the idea of ranking markets by their degree of contestability is inherently unsound.

That said, I believe that developments in economic theory (contestability theory included) have rightly emphasized the influence of entry conditions on market behaviour and I share the presumption that beneficial incentive effects can be obtained by judicious choice of policies in this area. However, feasible policies are constrained to operate in a second best world, where policy impact is likely to be contingent on a range of market-specific factors. In particular, the idea that policies directed to the elimination of certain forms of entry barrier will, in all cases, be sufficient to eradicate monopolistic abuse is one that should most definitely be resisted.

5.1.2. Austrian arguments.

Economists in the Austrian tradition recognize that markets will frequently be characterized by monopolistic behaviour. Supernormal profit is seen as being an integral feature of a well functioning market process, providing incentives for the discovery and use (through innovations) of commercially relevant information. Emphasis, therefore, is placed upon the competition *for* monopoly positions achieved via superior performance in non-price aspects of competition.

On this view, barriers to entry resulting from sunk costs may actually be beneficial. If firms had free access to the information of rivals and could quickly enter the market without disadvantage, there would be no incentive for the discovery of new information. *Some* form of entry restriction at the production stage of the competitive process is therefore necessary if badly inefficient outcomes are to be avoided. Sunk costs may partially serve this purpose, although other possibilities, such as the establishment of patent and copyright protection, are clearly available.

As with contestability theory, this reasoning seems to suggest that state monopolies can be privatized without much concern for the harmful consequences of market power. Again, however, cautionary notes need to be sounded, as the following two points seek to demonstrate. First, the Austrian arguments depend heavily upon reasonable freedom of entry at the pre-production stages of the competitive process. Potential entrants must have access to opportunities for innovative developments similar to those of incumbents. But consider the situation when this is not so. Suppose that an incumbent firm, by virtue of its previous R&D record, has cost advantages in the acquisition of new knowledge. Entry into the pre-production stage of competition will be deterred and the incentives for technological progress will be diminished. Instead of Schumpeterian 'gales of creative destruction', we may simply find sleepy monopolists. Second, if barriers to entry into production are high, entry is also deterred at the earlier stage. A new firm may believe that it could develop a more cost efficient technology more cheaply than an incumbent, but if the obstacles to later, profitable production are expected to be severe it may not find it worthwhile even to try.

Formal analysis of these types of issue is developing rapidly and, although much work remains to be done, I believe that the results thus far offer little support for the view that market dominance is either unimportant (because it is sustained by superior competitive performance) or relatively short-lived (because inefficient monopolists will steadily lose market share to rivals). Thus, for example, there are some extremely interesting models of competition for patents that show strong advantages to incumbency or initial technological leadership (Gilbert and Newbery, 1982; Harris and Vickers, 1985). Similarly, work on predatory pricing in conditions of incomplete information illustrates the difficulties entrants face in competing against established firms with multi-market dominance. These follow from the incentives for such incumbents to develop or maintain reputations for aggression in the face of new entry (Kreps and Wilson, 1982). In some cases, therefore, erosion of monopoly may only occur where the efficiency of new firms *greatly* exceeds that of the established firm.

I conclude that potential inefficiencies connected with market power power should not be lightly dismissed when evaluating privatization policies. A *laissez faire* approach to monopolies is therefore unlikely to provide a generally satisfactory basis for public policy. Public ownership constitutes one response to the problem. The alternative is regulation of private monopolies, to which I will now turn.

5.2. Regulation

The term regulation can be applied to any activity of government or its agencies that seeks to influence behaviour via the establishment of rules to guide or constrain economic decisions. In the context of market power, regulation aims to reduce the economic inefficiencies associated with monopolistic positions.

Ironically, public sector monopolies have often been protected from competition by government-imposed restrictions that prevent entry by private sector rivals. Similarly, entry restriction has been a common feature of US regulatory activities. Theoretical rationales for the deliberate creation of entry barriers by government can be provided in terms of the potential cost advantages of single firm production or the possibility of 'destructive competition' when entry is free. However, the performance records of both publicly and privately owned firms in these regulatory environments indicates that policy mixes have, in the past, leaned too heavily in the direction of protection. Hence the current popularity of policies of de-regulation (removal of market restrictions) and liberalisation (measures to increase competition).

Unfortunately, simple de-regulation is unlikely to produce the desired results in cases of very extensive market power. Removal of statutory entry barriers may simply lead to their replacement by strategic entry barriers that are created (at some cost) by the firm itself, or to an increasing recourse to predatory practices by the incumbent(s). Thus, more vigorous regulation of anti-competitive practices will often be required. Liberalization involves more than just the removal of constraints on behaviour.

The task of policing anti-competitive behaviour is generally entrusted to anti-trust agencies, but the practical difficulties faced by such bodies are formidable. Controversies over the issue of predatory pricing bear witness to the problems, which are even greater where non-price competition is concerned. How, for example, should the anti-trust authorities decide whether or not a particular investment programme or advertising campaign is anti-competitive? Given the complexity of the issues, I believe that, for very large, dominant firms, there is a strong case for the establishment of industry-specific regulatory commissions (to facilitate the build-up of the specialized information and expertise that is required for effective monitoring) with price fixing powers in markets where workable competition is not feasible.

Neither liberalizing measures nor the formation of more specialized monitoring units are necessarily connected with privatization, and arguments in their favour apply equally well for public sector monopolies. If, however, privatization of a monopolist leads management to place a greater weight on profit objectives the impact on economic efficiency *will* be significantly influenced by the regulatory framework: the relative incremental returns from, say, cost reducing and entry deterring expenditures will be a function of the operating regulatory constraints.

If liberalization, supplemented by price regulation where opportunities for competition are very limited, is desirable, public policy should focus on the design of regulatory institutions and incentives that best contribute to its efficiency goals. At this point some of the major lesson of US regulatory experience, summarized below, are of direct relevance.

5.2.1. Information. The most significant problem faced by regulators is lack of information. They depend upon information flows that are subject to strategic manipulation. For example, in setting maximum allowable prices lack of detailed knowledge of the market and technological opportunities of the firm tends to lead to a relatively high weight being placed upon the *observed* costs of the monopolist. US style 'cost of service' regulation is a good illustration of the point: allowable prices are set equal to the estimated cost of supply, including provision for a 'fair' rate of return on capital. The result is rather poor incentives for cost efficiency (see 5.2.2).

When informational asymmetries between regulators and regulated firms are taken into account it may be optimal to have more than one firm in the market even though single-firm production *by a cost-efficient enterprise* would be preferable. This is just the informational argument for competition again.

Alternatively, state monopolies might be split up into independent regional companies at the time of privatization to increase the number of information sources. Finally, regulators might insist on accounting separation for different parts of the firm's business. This is likely to be the least effective of the options because the information sources all remain within a single organization.

5.2.2. Cost inefficiency. If prices are set so as to allow a firm a fair rate of return on capital, an incentive will be created for the adoption of excessively capital-intensive production techniques (Averch and Johnson, 1962). With allowable prices fixed according to a rate of return criterion at less than (unconstrained) monopoly levels, a small increase in capital by increasing the base rate, will induce a small increase in prices and thereby raise profit. The source of the problem is again the limited information available to regulators.

Even if the economic cost curve *were* observable, and prices were set so as to allow a fair rate of return to a *cost efficient* firm, the incentives for cost-reducing innovations would be weak. Such innovations would lead regulators to reduce allowable prices, leaving the company with the same rate of return as before. There would be some profit increase, arising from the increased scale of operations associated with falling prices, but the carrot would tend to be rather small. In this case the underlying problem is regulators' lack of information about the economic *opportunities for innovation* of the firm.

5.2.3. Regulatory lag. A partial restoration of incentives for cost-efficiency can be achieved via regulatory lag (i.e. the time interval between reviews of allowable prices), and use of this mechanism is one of the interesting features of the British Telecom privatization in the UK. During a given regulatory period, cost reductions add to profits because the path of prices is independent of the firm's actions. The longer the lag, the greater will be the incentives for improving internal efficiency. However, longer lags will be associated with greater losses of allocative efficiency because of larger and more persistent price-cost deviations. Thus, in choosing the length of the regulatory period, the gains from increased cost-efficiency have to be traded off against the allocative losses, as in the optimum patent life problem (Nordhaus, 1969).

5.2.4. Incentives of regulators. Although regulation can be viewed as an attempt to bring 'public interest' objectives to bear upon the behaviour of monopolistic firms, it cannot automatically be assumed that actual regulatory policy and institutions will always operate along these lines. I have argued that the difficulties of monitoring government performance in its stewardship of nationalized industries is the central weakness of public ownership, and the regulatory approach offers no automatic escape from these problems. As earlier, we need to ask: *quis custodiet ipsos custodes?*

That regulation should not be viewed simply in terms of policy interventions guided by public interest criteria has been a recurrent theme of writers in the Chicago tradition (Stigler, 1971; Posner, 1971 and Peltzman, 1976). Instead they stress the point that politicians 'supply' regulation in response to well defined 'demands' from various interest groups (including, rather frequently, the firms themselves). Supply incentives – first to politicians establishing the institutions and policies, later to their agents who implement those rules – are provided by a variety of side payments such as votes, future employment, or political funding.

An extreme version of the Chicago theory of regulation emphasizes the vulnerability of regulatory bodies to *capture* by one of the interest groups concerned. Most usually, the threat is assumed to arise from producers who, being often small in number, are more easily able to overcome the free-rider problems associated with collective action. Much depends, however, upon the particular institutional arrangements. If regulators are elected, myopic consumer interests may predominate. Thus, in industries with long lead times in durable, non-recoverable investments, suppliers may be subject to ex-post expropriation by regulators keen to keep prices low to satisfy their constituents, a problem that appears to have occurred in some parts of the electricity supply industry in the US over the past decade.

Regulatory activities, by virtue of their distributional effects, are constantly subject to interest group pressures. While I believe that monitoring of regulatory performance, and consequently the performance itself, can frequently be improved by explicitly separating out these activities from, say, government departments (an exercise which, it may be noted, does not necessarily require privatization) it would be wrong to think of this as a panacea for market power maladies. Moreover, while it is possible to conceive of institutional arrangements that impede capture by interest groups, the point at which the regulatory process is most susceptible to these pressures is when institutions and policies are first being established. At that moment, politicians are necessarily the decision makers and the stakes are high for all concerned. Hence, public policy should be particularly vigilant in guarding against the danger that regulatory frameworks set up for newly privatized monopolies will be badly flawed at the outset.

5.3. Assessment

The telecommunications, gas and electricity industries – which, in terms of both proceeds and microeconomic importance, are collectively likely to account for the bulk of the UK enterprise sales programme – are all natural monopolies in major parts of their transmission/distribution networks. As a consequence, potential inefficiencies arising from market power are of great significance. Whilst other, major market failures exist (e.g. environmental side effects in electricity, safety in gas and electricity), and may form part of the case for public ownership, the focus here will be on UK policies aimed at curbing monopoly power in these industries.

In 1984 British Telecom (BT) was turned into a private company without any major restructuring. The flotation was characterized by a number of concessions designed to make the shares attractive to employees and small investors, including free and matching offers, vouchers for reductions in telephone bills, and bonus shares. A regulatory body – the Office of Telecommunications (OFTEL) – was established, charged with policing the industry and preventing anti-competitive behaviour. The maximum allowable price of a basket of BT's outputs (composed of services where little or no competition existed and accounting for approximately half of the company's revenue) is constrained to fall by 3% per annum relative to the retail price index, a pricing formula that will be reviewed after a five year interval. In addition, BT is required to provide a number of 'public service' facilities, including public telephone boxes and emergency services. Licences to run public networks were granted to BT, Mercury (a new private company owned by Cable and Wireless), and Kingston-upon-Hull Council (an idiosyncracy arising from the previous arrangements). No further licences are to be granted for public networks within an initial six-year period. Competition in the provision of value added network services (VANS) is permitted, but unrestricted resale of BT's capacity is disallowed, and cable companies can offer phone services only in conjunction with BT or Mercury.

These were the key features of the BT privatization, and a broadly similar approach is being taken to gas privatization. Thus, the British Gas Corporation (BGC) is to be offered for sale without restructuring, a regulatory body similar to OFTEL will be formed, and maximum average prices for tariff customers (mostly domestic) will be determined by a modified 'RPI $-x$' formula that will allow the company to pass on to its customers any increases in gas purchase prices (which, to a first approximation, are regarded as being outside its control).

At first inspection, the BT privatization might be judged a great success. Hundreds of thousands of small investors bought shares, the net proceeds from the sale will amount to approximately £3.6 billion, customers for network services are guaranteed falling real prices on average, and the share price has risen 20% from its market clearing level on the opening day. Since profit expectations have thus been significantly increased since the flotation date, and since BT's output price in monopolized markets is effectively regulated, this suggests a significant reassessment, even since the flotation date, of BT's ability to increase its efficiency and reduce its costs.

Even so, this fails to address the central question of how else regulation of BT might have been conducted. Thus, even if the privatization has actually increased efficiency, there remains the possibility that alternative policies might have produced (or, in the BGC case, might yet produce) superior results. To tackle this issue, therefore, I will next consider the policy decisions in some detail, drawing on the arguments of Sections 2 and 3 at the relevant points.

5.3.1. Regulatory structures. There is little to criticise in the decision to establish OFTEL (and, now, a similar regulatory body for British Gas), and, in particular, in the decision to regulate the prices of British Telecom. Other options did, of course, exist, of which complete deregulation and franchising solutions were the most notable. Economic conditions in the telecommunications industry, however, like those in gas and electricity (natural monopolies in transmission/distribution coupled with substantial sunk costs) justify scepticism about the efficacy of competition (alone) in preventing monopolistic pricing and imply that the complexity of the contractual process in franchising solutions would pose severe monitoring problems. Put simply, the markets are not contestable and franchising would, in effect, reduce to regulation under another name (Vickers and Yarrow, 1985).

5.3.2. Organization. The UK government rejected the option of restructuring BT prior to flotation, and has repeated the decision for BGC. In contrast, the US authorities adopted a much more radical line in dealing with AT&T. The regional operating companies of AT&T were split off, leaving the parent with only its long distance and manufacturing activities intact.

In this aspect of privatization policy the UK government has been heavily influenced by the managements of both BT and BGC, which have strongly opposed re-organization. What has happened can be viewed as a limited form of regulatory capture. Management opposition would cast a serious cloud over the asset sales and, in order to eliminate the threat of such opposition, government has given undue weight to managerial preferences in the two cases. As a result the advantages of re-structuring have been systematically downplayed and decisions about the organization of the industries have been taken without a thorough and open public debate.

Establishment of independent, regional, transmission/distribution companies in the utility industries has a number of potential advantages. First there would be greater (albeit still limited) competition in output markets. For example, regional companies could compete in long distance services (telecommunications), or boundary and localized industrial markets (gas). Second, there would be greater competition in input markets. Gas distribution companies could compete for supplies and equipment: telecommunications operators could compete for supplies in the apparatus markets. At the moment, for example, BT can use its monopoly position in networks to favour its own equipment businesses thereby transferring profit from regulated to unregulated activities, and the share price improvement mentioned earlier might simply reflect this more sophisticated use of market power, rather than an efficiency effect. Third, regulation would be more effective. Re-organization would increase the number of independent sources of information available to regulators and generally improve their strategic position vis à vis the regulated firm(s). The information could be used to construct more effective incentive structures by linking allowable prices to measures of relative performance, as suggested in Section 4. Fourth, capital market monitoring would be improved. More information would be available to shareholders and the smaller market capitalizations of regional companies (as compared with a single national firm) would tend to strengthen the threat of takeover when internal efficiency performance is poor.

5.3.3. Regulatory policy. With only one firm to regulate, pricing formulae of the RPI $-x$ variety are probably the best that can be managed. The rule was explicitly designed to incorporate dynamic efficiency incentives by allowing the monopolist to reap profit gains from improvements in internal efficiency over a reasonably long period (five years in the BT and BGC examples). The approach does not, however, eliminate the problem that the regulated firm's own costs may have an important bearing on allowable prices when the rule is reviewed, and strategic behaviour by the firm, aimed at influencing regulatory decisions, can be expected as the review date approaches.

The problem arises because, with single-firm production, there is only one source of information for regulators. Between reviews the performance yardstick is the retail price index, not some measure based on other, comparable firms. At the review date, regulators are forced to search for alternatives (small firms, such as Mercury, operating in the market; foreign enterprises; internal cost information) but these are likely to be weak signals, expensive to obtain, or both. In gas the problem is compounded because supplies to contract (larger industrial) customers will be unregulated and there will be no requirement on the BGC to provide separate accounts for the *regulated* part of its gas supply business. To repeat the earlier point, failure to restructure has hindered the regulatory task.

More generally, UK policy has shown little appreciation of the difficulties faced by regulators in attempting to prevent abuse of monopoly power by dominant firms. The extent and subtleties of strategic behaviour have been a recurrent theme of recent work in industrial economics, yet the resources necessary to detect and prevent anti-competitive practices have been seriously underestimated. Further, UK policy provides for virtually nothing in the way of punitive sanctions that would provide deterrents to abuse of dominance. There is a policy trade-off here, between the structure of the industry and the resources required for policing the behaviour of its firms. By opting for a combination of single firm production at the national level and regulation 'on the cheap', the UK policy mix appears to be seriously sub-optimal.

5.3.4. Competition. Apart from the inadequate resources allocated to OFTEL for the policing of anti-competitive practices, two other decisions in the BT case suggest that the UK government attaches a relatively low priority to the objective of increasing competition. The first is the decision to license only one rival to BT in the public network market before 1990. The justification – that an initial period of protection is necessary to allow Mercury to become a credible competitor – is unconvincing. The main threat to a firm such as Mercury arises from predatory actions by the dominant firm, not from other firms moving into the market, and this is better countered by restrictions on British Telecom than by preventing further entry. The outcome will be a highly asymmetric duopoly, Mercury being much smaller than its rival, which does not augur well for the emergence of intense competition. Furthermore, both firms will, in 1990, share a common interest in preventing liberalization of the market. Thus the framework of competition and regulation chosen by the government could hardly be more favourable to the ultimate emergence of some form of tacit collusion between BT and Mercury.

Second, the UK government has declared its intention not to license unrestricted resale of British Telecom's capacity before 1989. Unlike the US, entrants are therefore prevented from moving into the market and offering new services by leasing some of the dominant firm's existing capacity. Increasing competition this way raises some regulatory problems, since BT could not be left free to block entrants by charging exhorbitant prices. Nevertheless, the beneficial effects of increased competition would more than compensate for the increased regulatory costs.

The privatization of the BGC raises an important issue analogous to resale in telecommunications. New entry will be possible only if there is close regulation of the terms on which other companies can use pipeline facilities. If a North Sea operator wanted to sell gas to an industrial customer, the BGC could attempt to block the entrant by overcharging for pipeline transport facilities or by predatory pricing. Both forms of anti-competitive behaviour must therefore be prevented if entry threats are to be made real.

On paper, some progress towards liberalization has already been made in the Oil and Gas (Enterprise) Act (1982), which is aimed at reducing obstacles to the use of pipeline facilities by entrants. New competitors have, however, been notable by their absence, suggesting possible deficiencies in the legislation. One problem is that there is virtually nothing to prevent BGC immediately engaging in predatory pricing. Indeed, BGC's prices are generally below marginal costs at the moment (Hammond, Helm and Thompson, 1985). Stricter regulation of pricing behaviour is therefore required if effective competition is to be promoted. In practice, however, UK competition policy provides little in the way of protection against predatory pricing, and it is currently proposed that the new Director General of Gas Supply will *not* be able to regulate the prices charged for the conveyancing of gas for others.

The low priority given to competition objectives by the government is also visible in its attitudes towards imports and exports of gas. Both are stringently controlled, and it is quite possible that they will continue to be restricted after privatization. A principal aim of this policy has been to keep prices down by strengthening the BGC's position *vis-à-vis* its own suppliers. Since gas prices are held below marginal opportunity costs and electricity prices are above marginal costs, the market share of gas is unjustifiably high.

Ironically, moves to increase competition in the gas industry would, initially at least, lead to higher prices and thereby allow the government to increase its proceeds from the sale. Thus, restructuring of the industry, the ending of trade restrictions, and moves to prevent predatory behaviour (facilitated by BGC's access to low-price supplies on long-term contracts settled many years ago), would reduce BGC's monopsony power and push prices up towards marginal opportunity costs. The government has not, however, followed this course (the restructuring option having been already rejected), apparently in deference to interest group pressures: both gas consumers and BGC's management (as a result of market share objectives) would prefer regulated prices to be kept low. I will take up this point again in Section 8.

6. Labour market effects

Privatization may have both efficiency and distributional effects in the labour market. Thus it might be argued that nationalization increases the monopoly power of labour: unions can extract higher wages since, unlike their private sector counterparts, public sector managers and supervising ministries have relatively weak incentives to reduce unit labour costs (see Section 3).

This claim, however, is not self evidently true. The fundamental question concerns the credibility of a tough negotiating stance by employers. Privatization may, in some circumstances, enhance credibility by creating a commitment (in the form of obstacles to involvement) that a weak government will not step in to accommodate union demands. Then, because it knows that government faces greater costs of intervention, the union will be less inclined to pursue strategies aimed at extracting greater concessions via political involvement. If, on the other hand, government has greater incentives to acquire a reputation for toughness than a private sector employer the argument is reversed: privatization will now increase union bargaining strength.

There are at least two reasons why this latter condition may frequently be operative. First, the state has greater resources at its disposal to withstand union pressure and this ability to tolerate losses may enhance the negotiating strength of management. Second, government will take account of the demonstration effect of a generous settlement in one enterprise on negotiations in other parts of its extensive domain. That is, a concession in one area is likely to be read as a signal of weakness by public sector negotiators elsewhere, leading to settlements that are more generous to labour in these other areas. The government is effectively playing a repeated game characterized by imperfect information in which its indirect participation in each of a set of negotiations provides it with incentives to develop a reputation for toughness (c.f. Kreps and Wilson, 1982).

These arguments demonstrate that there can be no presumption that privatization will always reduce trade union power. If such is the aim, a policy of increasing competition is likely to be more effective than ownership transfer *per se*, provided that collective bargaining in the industry is not fully centralised. The downward pressure on unit labour costs induced by deregulation of airlines and trucking in the US is a vivid illustration of this point. Thus, only where privatization is accompanied by increased competition – as it usually is when franchising or contracting out policies are adopted – is it likely that trade union power will be reduced.

Three recent examples from the UK experience serve to reinforce the above conclusion. The first is the 1984/5 coal miners' strike, where the government was content to sustain large financial losses in both the coal and electricity industries in order to defeat the National Union of Mineworkers (NUM). Further, the government had instructed the electricity supply industry to build up coal stocks in the period preceding the strike to increase bargaining strength in the coal industry. It is unlikely that privately owned enterprises would have had either the financial capacity or the inclination to adopt such a tough stance in the negotiations. Thus, one of the benefits of victory for the government was the demonstration (signalling) effect on other wage bargains in the economy – a factor that would have been largely discounted by private sector negotiators.

Although it could be argued that the initial power of the NUM would not have been so great had the coal industry been privately owned, this view rests largely upon a confusion between ownership structure and competition. Trade union power derives chiefly from the monopoly power of the National Coal Board, which in turn is sustained by policy

imposed entry restrictions, including controls on the level of imports.
Nor is it possible to argue that such restrictions are themselves simply
a consequence of public ownership: the most extensively protected
industry in the UK (agriculture) is characterized by a large number of
private producers.

The second example concerns the privatization of the Jaguar car
company in 1984, which was quickly followed by a sharp increase
in wage rates. Before its sale Jaguar had been a relatively profitable
part of the much larger, unprofitable BL group. Management would
therefore have had strong incentives to resist high wage claims
(based, say, on Jaguar's financial record) because of the possible effects
of a generous settlement on union attitutes elsewhere in the group.
Once privatized as an independent company, however, this strategic
element of management's position disappeared and their bargaining
power was weakened.

Finally, although the desire to reduce union strength appears to have
been a factor in the decision to privatize British Telecom, it is the
licensing of a second public network operator, Mercury, that is likely
to have the more decisive effect. Recognition of the threat posed by
greater product market competition accounts for the hostility of BT's
unions to the development of Mercury. Given BT's existing market
power, however, the diminution in union strength is likely, in this case,
to be relatively limited.

7. The pattern of share ownership

By giving preferential treatment to small investors, sales of public
enterprises can be structured so as to encourage wider share ownership.
However, whatever the underlying motivation for this policy objective,
privatization will generally be a poor instrument in comparison with
alternatives such as changing fiscal incentives for individual share
ownership. The pattern of shareholdings resulting from privatization
will tend to be arbitrary and investors who acquire shares only by this
route will wind up with relatively unbalanced portfolios.

The case for encouraging employee share ownership at the time of
privatization is somewhat stronger, although again, if this is a general
policy aim, instruments with more wide-ranging effects (e.g. tax concessions) are more appropriate. The case rests upon the incentive effects
of employee participation in the profits of the firm. Although property
rights theorists have claimed that these incentive effects are negligible
in all but the smallest organizations – each worker receives only a small
fraction of any profit increase generated by his/her increase in effort –
the point is not altogether convincing since it ignores non-pecuniary

rewards and collective choice at the workplace. Thus, contributions to performance that benefit other workers will be partially reciprocated in non-pecuniary transactions (prestige, status, etc.) between employees, and for those decisions that are made collectively (in bargains between management and labour representatives, for example) the underlying externality does not arise.

Judged by its share ownership objectives, the UK privatization programme has been relatively unsuccessful. A number of enterprises – including International Aeradio, British Rail Hotels, Wytch Farm, and Sealink – were sold to other companies and therefore made no direct contribution to spreading ownership. In other cases, while the flotations were designed to favour small investors, most of those subscribing to the share issues quickly sold their holdings. That is, individual investors have typically regarded the flotations as an opportunity to make a quick killing, rather than as a chance to acquire a longer term asset. Within one month of flotation, the number of shareholders in Amersham had fallen from 62,000 to 10,000; within one year year of flotation, the number had fallen from 150,000 to 26,000 in Cable and Wireless (first tranche) and from 158,000 to 27,000 in British Aerospace. Britoil (first tranche) and Enterprise Oil showed less dramatic drops in the number of shareholders since the initial offers were pitched at levels that did not produce anticipations of large, short-term capital gains. Hence, fewer small investors applied for shares in the first place.

The BT offer was structured to encourage the retention of personal holdings by means of vouchers (that shareholders can use in part-payment of their telephone bills) and the promise of bonus share issues in the longer term. Even so, it is estimated that nearly one third of the shares changed hands on the first day of trading, and it is to be expected that there will be a steady reduction in the number of small investors as the various concessions become less valuable and are eventually exhausted.

The outcome has been much the same with respect to employee share ownership. Despite a variety of concessionary offers, the proportion of the ordinary shares taken up by employees has generally been small. For example, some of the initial percentages were: Amersham 3.7%, Associated British Ports 4.3%, Cable and Wireless 1.4%, Jaguar 1.3%, Britoil 0.1%, Enterprise Oil 0.03%, British Aerospace 3.6%, and British Telecom (including former employees) 4.6%. The major exception to this pattern was the National Freight Corporation, which was sold to a consortium of managers and employees (with a syndicate of banks taking a 17.5% interest). Over a quarter of the workforce initially applied for shares, and by early 1985 the number of worker-shareholders had *increased* to 16,000, almost 60% of the workforce. Thus, as in the evaluation of financial performance (see 4.4.1), the National Freight privatization can be classified as an unambiguous success.

8. Privatization and income distribution

In practice, the transfer of ownership is likely to give rise to non-trivial shifts in income distribution. Indeed, as argued in Section 5.2, government policies can be heavily influenced by demands for income redistribution from various interest groups. Since privatization presents opportunities to politicians for income and wealth transfers to favoured groups, it would be naive simply to ignore this aspect of the policy process.

Three factors give rise to redistributional effects. The first is the change in both the level and structure of output prices that may occur following privatization. The second is the price at which shares in an enterprise that is being sold are offered to the market. Discounts on the market clearing price represent a transfer of wealth to the new owners from the wider public, and, more particularly, from taxpayers. Third, privatization may also redistribute income towards those associated with the provision of services that can be regarded as inputs into the process of selling assets: for example, financial institutions responsible for underwriting and placing or advertising agencies running the campaign (see Section 10).

The influence of implicit and explicit distributional objectives is readily visible in recent UK policy decisions. Privatization of telecommunications is leading to significant adjustments in the relative prices of business/domestic, long/short distance calls as cross subsidization is reduced. The aim of regulatory policy, however, has been to achieve a *gradual* shift away from cross subsidization. This delay in implementing a cost-based pricing structure arises chiefly from a desire not to impose two large an initial price hike on domestic telephone subscribers, the main beneficiaries of the earlier tariff structure. Hence, short-run efficiency gains have been foregone to accommodate an interest group pressure. Similarly, in privatizing the gas industry the UK government is seeking to avoid increases in competition that would in this case lead to significant increases in prices towards marginal costs. The fear of offending politically powerful interest groups is therefore pushing the government towards the establishment of a less competitive environment for the new gas company.

The most obvious distributional impact of asset sales, however, has occurred in the capital market. Table 8 shows the premium of the opening (first day) price over the offer price and the accompanying increase in the market value of the issued equity. Thus the £1.34 billion

Table 8. Offer and opening prices on sale date

Company	Offer price (p)	Opening price (p)	Undervaluation (£ million)
British Telecom	50	95	1,337.2
Amersham	142	190	21.3
Cable & Wireless	168	203	46.6
Assoc. British Ports	112	130	3.5
British Aerospace	150	171	20.9
Jaguar	165	179	25.0
Enterprise Oil	100	100	0
Britoil	100	81	−48.4

increase in the market value of BT's shares represents a transfer of this magnitude from taxpayers as a group to the successful applicants. Of the latter, institutional investors accounted for 47.4% of the shares, British nationals for 34.3% and overseas investors for most of the rest. The overseas holders' first-day capital gain, amounting to over £180 million, should, of course, be viewed as a *real* economic loss to the UK.

As the privatization programme has progressed there has been increasing emphasis on the desirability of channeling more of the shares to the small investor. While political rhetoric has concentrated on the goal of wider share ownership, it has already been shown that the typical pattern is for small successful applicants to sell quickly. The result is that millions of punters have learned how to stag a rigged market, not that a major advance towards wider share ownership has been made.

How then should the flotations be viewed? I would suggest that the appropriate framework to adopt is a variant of Richard Posner's 'taxation by regulation' thesis (1971). Posner argued that much of the regulation we observe can be explained as a form of indirect taxation that allows fairly precise targeting of income transfers to favoured groups behind a veil of public interest arguments. Because the transfers are less visible than explicit taxes or subsidies the opportunities for deceiving the losers are greater. Hence the attraction of the approach to vote-seeking politicians.

The UK privatization programme can, in part, be seen as the other side of the same coin. Instead of 'taxation by regulation' we have 'taxation by privatization'. As the programme has developed, and the scale of new share issues has increased, this redistributional aspect of ownership transfer appears to have become an ever more prominent influence on policy decisions. Thus, in the BT case, large numbers of middle class voters (those successful in purchasing shares at the offer price) received highly visible, short-term benefits, while the 'RPI − 3%'

pricing formula was supplemented with a further restriction to prevent rapid movement to a cost-based tariff structure that would have implied sharp increases in domestic charges. In addition, the Conservative Party has plans to write to BT shareholders to inform them of the danger that their gains will be expropriated in the event of a Labour victory in the next general election. Finally, all the signs are that the government's approach to gas privatization is based upon the same principles.

9. Privatization and the public finances

An important motive for privatization is the government's need to raise revenue or reduce expenditure. Here it is essential to distinguish the consequences of ownership transfer *per se* and the attendant effects, if any, on the actual operation of the enterprise. Consider, for example, the sale of a profitable, publicly owned firm. The government receives an initial payment in exchange for claims on a future income stream. If the operating characteristics of the enterprise are the same in both cases, the sales proceeds are equal to the present value of future income and the net worth of the public sector will be unchanged by the act of ownership transfer. Equivalently, the government could use the sale proceeds to repurchase an equivalent value of its outstanding fixed-interest debt. The stream of future interest payments on the national debt would be reduced by the same amount as the incomes stream which would have been available from the public enterprise to finance these interest payments. Again we see that the net worth of the public sector is unaltered.

Thus, as a first approximation, selling public sector assets is equivalent to selling fixed-interest debt. Both imply the mortgage of future income to improve current cash flow. For this reason, it would be surprising if asset sales represent a free lunch through which current government deficits can be financed without upward pressure on interest rates and consequent crowding-out of private sector expenditure.

This argument should be qualified in two respects. First, by historical accident, in the UK asset sales are treated as reducing the government deficit as measured by Public Sector Borrowing Requirement, whereas sales of fixed-interest debt are treated as financing a given level of the PSBR. For the reasons given above, this distinction is largely spurious (see Buiter, 1985). The second qualification is more convincing. A government may wish to establish the credibility of its claims that future monetary and fiscal policy will be tight. With a high level of fixed-interest nominal debt, there will always be a future temptation to reduce the real burden of interest rate payments by an unanticipated inflation. Since real equity in actual businesses is much better inflation-linked than nominal fixed-interest debt, raising current finance by asset sales may increase the credibility of the fight against inflation by reducing the temptation for future monetary explosions. Notice, however, that the same credibility could be obtained by the alternative policy of selling index-linked bonds.

Thus it is not the transfer of ownership but rather the associated change in the operation of these enterprises which has the potential to make substantial contributions to the public finances, the point so lucidly made in the quote from Adam Smith in Section 1. Here two cases have to be distinguished.

First, consider the case in which privatization induces an improvement in the internal efficiency of the enterprise and where there are no offsetting market failures. Since the assets are more productive under private than public operation, privatization will raise more revenue than the income stream which would have been earned had the assets remained under public ownership. Privatization improves both economic efficiency and the public finances.

On the other hand, a critical policy trade-off emerges if the superior financial performance of the private firm is the result only of greater exploitation of market power. Efficiency and financial objectives are now in conflict. Sale proceeds will be higher if the enterprise is privatized against a background of light regulation and a sheltered market environment, but economic efficiency is then likely to be damaged. Alternatively, stricter regulation, coupled with other measures to open up the firm to greater competitive pressures, promotes efficiency but reduces the revenue which is likely to be raised from the initial asset sale. Faced with this conflict, I argued in Section 5 that the UK government had leaned too heavily in the former direction.

10. Transactions costs

Privatization through sales of shares in an enterprise will typically involve transactions costs. In the economics of business finance, such share issues are often viewed as the most costly way to raise new capital, and in the UK a relatively small fraction of company funds is raised from this source.

Some care must be exercised when evaluating these transactions costs. Fees to advisers, and parts of marketing expenses and sales commissions, will approximately reflect social opportunity costs. They are payments for factor inputs to the process of transferring claims on assets. On the other hand, especially when the success of privatization policy is portrayed in terms of whether or not the shares are fully subscribed, and hence when there is a temptation to set share prices below the market

Table 9. Gross proceeds and expenses of selected asset sales (£ million)

	Sale proceeds	Expenses
Cable & Wireless (C&W)	224	7
British Aerospace (BAe)	149	6
Amersham	63	3
Britoil	548	17
Assoc. British Ports (ABP)	22	2
Enterprise Oil	393	11
British Telecom	3,868	268

Notes: (i) C&W expenses exclude £35 million subscribed by the government
for new shares. (ii) BAe expenses exclude £100 million capital injection and
£55 million Public Dividend Capital dividends foregone by the government.
(iii) Amersham proceeds exclude those paid to the company, and interest on
money held temporarily in respect of unsuccessful applicants; expenses
exclude £88 million debenture repayment. (iv) Britoil proceeds exclude £0.86
million stamp duty; expenses include top estimate of cost of incentive schemes
for small shareholders. (v) ABP proceeds exclude £25 million paid by company
to the government, and interest on money held temporarily in respect of
unsuccessful applicants.

clearing level, part of underwriting fees simply represents a transfer
of wealth from taxpayers to underwriters. They are a transfer payment
but not a real social cost corresponding to physical resources used up
in the process of selling off the assets.

In addition to the transactions costs associated with the actual share
issue, account should also be taken of any costs borne internally by the
enterprise itself. Preparation for privatization will absorb managerial
time and effort, and there will be costs associated with any organizational
changes that occur as part of the privatization exercise. For example,
quite extensive reorganization may be required if the ownership of only
one part of an enterprise is to be transferred to private investors.
Unfortunately, information about such internal costs is likely to be
difficult to obtain.

Table 9 shows that government expenses associated with the UK
flotations were far from negligible. The figures quoted exclude expenses
borne by the companies themselves: BT, for example, is estimated to
have paid around £8.4 million to its own advisers and spent approximately £25 million on its own pre-flotation advertising campaign.

Since the BT figures are so large, Table 10 presents a more detailed
breakdown of the expenditures involved. Items such as employee share
concessions, bonus shares, bill vouchers, and a part of the underwriting,
placing and commitment commissions represent income transfers,
rather than resource costs, and once these are netted out the efficiency

Table 10. Estimated receipts and costs of BT share flotation (£ million)

Receipts		Costs	
Sale of shares at offer price less employee discounts	3,916	Direct UK sale costs: underwriting, placing,	
or free shares	−56	commissions	87
a premium from sale of		bank & legal fees	20
retained shares	3	marketing	14
contribution from		advisers' fees	6
British Telecom	1		
Interest on application		Total direct UK sale costs	127
money	4		
	———	Total overseas sale costs	30
	3,868	Small shareholders	
	———	incentives:	
		bill vouchers (a cash cost)	23
Net proceeds	3,600	bonus shares	88
			———
			268
			———

Note: Costs of small shareholder incentives and employee bonuses assume complete take up by those eligible.

consequences of the flotations appear relatively minor. However, the transfer payments to overseas investors should be counted as a real economic cost to the UK.

11. Conclusions

Privatization affects economic performance indirectly, via the behavioural changes induced by shifts in incentives. In policy evaluation, therefore, the fundamental question concerns the efficiency, judged in terms of given objectives, of alternative incentive structures.

The principal objective of privatization *should* be to increase economic efficiency. In the absence of efficiency gains, the public finance goals of the policy are generally misguided and their pursuit may actually damage efficiency. Similarly, privatization is usually a poor policy instrument for the attainment of such goals as reducing trade union power, widening share ownership, and redistributing income: in each case it is dominated by superior policy instruments.

Privatization is likely (but not inevitably) to lead managers to place greater emphasis on profit goals. Whether or not this in turn leads to an increase in economic efficiency depends upon a trade-off between

market failures and deficiencies in governmental monitoring and control of public firms. In particular, it depends heavily upon both the
degree of competition in product markets and the firm's regulatory
environment.

In general, competition and regulation are likely to be more important determinants of economic performance than ownership. Hence,
where there are deficiencies in these areas, the policy priority should
normally be to increase competition and improve regulation, not to
transfer productive activities to the private sector. Indeed, preoccupation with the ownership question is likely to be damaging if it distracts
attention from the more fundamental issues.

Where markets are reasonably competitive, and there are no other
significant market failures, available evidence justifies the presumption
that private ownership is to be preferred. However, where market
failures are more substantial, and particularly where the firm has extensive market power, the evidence is much less clear cut. In these cases
there should be no presumption in favour of either type of ownership:
each case should be evaluated on its merits.

In the case of state monopolies there are good arguments to support:
the establishment of specialized regulatory agencies, separated from
the main government bureaucracies, and the splitting up of dominant
firms – to increase the number of independent sources of information
and facilitate monitoring of performance – where this can be done
without too large a loss of scale economies. Such structural reforms
should be evaluated and decided *before* any final decisions are taken
on the ownership question: it is easier to change the framework of
competition and regulation before privatization.

For natural monopolies, it would be unwise to rely solely on the
disciplines of product market competition and capital market monitoring to produce reasonably efficient outcomes when firms are privately
owned. Strong measures to deter anti-competitive behaviour, coupled
with price regulation in the monopolized activities, offer the best
approach.

Regulatory agencies are open to the same types of interest group
pressures that confront politicians. As far as is possible, they should be
designed to minimize the threat of interest group capture. Thus, they
should be given resources adequate to their tasks, their personnel
properly rewarded, and their activities made as visible as possible.
However, the moment at which there is the greatest danger that interest
group pressures will lead to sub-optimal decisions is during the period
when regulatory agencies are being first established. The threat is
heightened when governments become preoccupied with rapid ownership transfer, as has been the case in the UK.

Discussion

Mervyn King
London School of Economics

Privatization is a phenomenon that has attracted much attention both in the UK and elsewhere as governments have become increasingly concerned with the inadequate supply performance of their economies. The word 'Privatization' does not, however, appear in my Oxford English Dictionary, which indicates the rate at which attitudes have changed. Political support for privatization in the UK derives in part from the disappointing performance of the nationalized industries since the war. Equally important, however, has been the comparative failure of those policies that were introduced in order to try to control these industries – such as the White Papers on investment and pricing policy in the 1960s. These advocated conventional marginal cost pricing rules and appropriate target rates of return on new investment but were never effectively implemented, partly because these criteria were derived from a model of a world of perfect certainty and partly because the problems of enforcement and monitoring were not taken seriously at the time. Disillusion with that sort of policy has thus led to interest in what could be achieved by privatizing the assets in the public sector. What comes across in this paper very clearly is the extent of the changes that have already taken place and those that are planned for the future. There is nothing cosmetic about Mrs Thatcher's policies.

Nevertheless, there are many parts of the economy which privatization has not reached. Yarrow's paper deals with the issue of those productive assets that have been or will be transferred from the public to the private sector. But to put this in perspective one could point to the many fields in which privatization has *not* taken place. Health and education are clearly areas in which privatization has not been secured to any significant extent, and although there has been some transfer of ownership of public housing, this has been small, only a few percent of the substantial assets that the public sector holds in this form.

What have been the objectives of privatization in the UK? Yarrow discusses a number of these aims and correctly observes that until rather recently asset sales have not made a significant contribution to the PSBR. Indeed government ministers have actually denied that this is a major objective of privatization. Reducing trade union power is an objective which surely must have played a role. Whether there has actually been any change in trade union power is an open question that merits further research. A further objective is, of course, the traditional one of greater efficiency. Mrs Thatcher likes entrepreneurs and believes that efficiency is increased by giving the private sector a free rein. But as every student knows, and as Yarrow documents clearly in the paper, there is no necessary presumption for the superiority of the private over the public sector. Indeed one can make quite a good case for saying that in many contexts public management would do better than selfish private management wishing to exploit a natural monopoly.

The most elegant expression of this viewpoint is contained in the following lines of W.H. Auden:

> Private faces in public places
> Are wiser and nicer
> Than public faces in private places
>
> Collected Poems IV

Unfortunately, as economists we are thrown back on a more agnostic conclusion, and one which we are unable to express so vividly.

Ownership may not, however, be the most important question. The main theme on which the paper concentrates, quite rightly in my view, is that the real issue is competition and not ownership as such. Whereas it may be true that privatization is necessary it certainly is not sufficient. The difficulty which the privatization policy has run up against has been that when dealing with natural monopolies some sort of regulatory agency inevitably has to be set up, and this raises the question of what sort of rules it will follow? This is particularly relevant in the case of British Telecom, and the future privatization of British Airways, British Gas and perhaps the electricity supply industry will pose similar problems. What has been disappointing about privatization in the UK to date is that so little attention has been given to the rules of the game under which OFTEL, the regulatory agency that deals with British Telecom, is meant to operate.

The one theme which I think deserves more attention, although it is mentioned briefly in the paper, is the role of the existing managers in the firms that were privatized. It seems to me that the way in which these assets were privatized and the policies that have been pursued have been very much geared to the objectives of the managers of the firms themselves. It is well known that some of the problems of running nationalized industries result from interference by politicians, but it is also clear that managers can frustrate a privatization policy if politicians want to carry it out quickly. For rapid privatization to be feasible depends to a large extent on the cooperation of the managers of the firms that are privatized. As a result the methods used to float these companies, and the regulations that they will face once they are in the private sector, have been dictated to a large extent by the managers of the existing enterprises. That cannot be an attractive policy if the aim is to improve efficiency and stimulate competition.

Another issue on which there is more to be said is the method by which public sector assets are sold. It is clear the sale price of assets has generally been much below the value subsequently determined by the market. The government has not appropriated for the tax-payer as much money as it might, and there is scope for more experimentation in the way in which assets are sold. One possibility would be a much greater use of tap stock. A good example of the problems that can arise if things are not thought through very carefully is the case of the Trustee Savings Bank. The government announced to Parliament that it wanted to privatize the Trustee Savings Bank. They then discovered that, having decided to sell it off, the government didn't actually own it! Now it is somewhat difficult for a government committed to a policy of law and order to sell off things that it doesn't own. This government is, however, an honest government, and it said: there is no way we can keep the money if we don't own the bank, so why don't we give the sale proceeds back to the Trustee Savings Bank? Such a decision prompts the following question. How much would you be willing to pay for the Trustee Savings Bank when you know that you get not only the assets of the Trustee Savings Bank but also your money back? It really is the kind of offer you cannot refuse. Indeed, in the absence of any transactions costs, the equilibrium price for which the Bank would be sold if it were auctioned is unbounded. Of course what the government does is to sell it off by fixing a price in advance. The result is a massive over-subscription for the issue – at any price.

Let me conclude with three points. First, I agree very much with Yarrow that the major issue is competition and not ownership as such. Privatization is clearly not a sufficient policy though in the light of the experience of the post-War period a certain amount of privatization does appear to be a necessary policy. But the main implication is that we need much more analysis and thought about the appropriate form of regulation. We should learn from the experience of other countries and try to think things through much more carefully than appears to have been done in the case of British Telecom. Second, the methods of sale will have to be improved. Third, the managers of the firms that have been sold off have had things very much their own way. It is not clear that this is the right way to usher in a new era of competition.

Jacques Mairesse
ENSAE, Paris

A remarkable feature and quality of the paper is its effort towards both comprehensiveness and objectivity. Yarrow's views and conclusions are specific rather than general, and I think this is correct. Among the many issues raised, I shall briefly discuss three.

First, who guards the guardians? Whereas Yarrow emphasizes how, in monitoring public sector firms, the government is more likely to be influenced by powerful special interest groups than by the voting public, he draws too sharp a contrast with monitoring in the private sector. Here too, particular interest groups may be powerful within the company or its shareholders, e.g. customers on whom it is especially dependent, or within the bodies responsible for regulation or the provision of information.[1] Hence Yarrow overstates the monitoring gains, if any, to privatization.

Second, since it is the existence of large sunk costs which constitutes a crucial barrier to entry for potential competitors, it may be that investment of this kind should be nationalized or regulated, with the fruits of this investment being made available to different competitors. Public intervention, and even public ownership, need not be bad for competition and efficiency. The paper only alludes to such opportunities in investment in infrastructure, for example telecommunications, radio and television, energy and transportation.

Third, technological or product innovation arising from R&D can lead to another form of economies over scale and over time. Uncertainty about R&D outcomes, spillover effects on other firms, and difficulties of appropriating the full returns to one's efforts, all suggest that market competition will lead to inadequate and inefficient R&D. Again, public intervention is warranted.

In France, if the Right win the legislative elections in March 1986, a sweeping privatization programme may well be high on the agenda. Even so, unlike the Anglo-Saxon world, French policy is still likely to attach an important, and respected, role to public intervention. In part, this derives from French views on industrial policy and national independence. Quite apart from the weight on distributional or social issues, French policy may continue to reflect the belief that it is important for the government to have a strategic interest in industry and in the financial sector.

In these brief remarks I have tried to argue that, whilst the historical performance of public enterprises may leave much to be desired, there are countervailing and powerful arguments why we should not leave everything to the market. Jacques Rueff once wrote 'Be socialists or liberals, but don't be liars.' Yarrow's careful study serves to expose our ignorance as well as our understanding. It should make us all,

---

[1] Editors' comment: Speaking in November 1985, Mairesse anticipated several issues which were to be illustrated during the struggle to put together a rescue package for the UK helicopter firm Westland in early 1986.

economists and policy makers alike, more cautious in advocating sweeping solutions when, in reality, we are only beginning to scratch the surface.

Jacques Melitz
INSEE, Paris

Yarrow's discussion of privatization in the UK calls for a few comments about the prospect of a far-reaching privatization programme in France, following the coming March legislative elections. If fully implemented, this programme would make Mrs Thatcher's pale by comparison. A major segment of the French Right has advocated denationalizing every private firm that the Mitterrand government brought into the public sector in 1981, plus every firm that was nationalized in 1945, and further has proposed privatizing a number of firms that were never private but have belonged to the public sphere since their inception. This would mean bringing virtually all of manufacturing and insurance into the private sector and most of finance too. The only ordinary financial institutions that would remain public are the savings banks, the postal checking system, and maybe the *banques populaires*. On conservative estimates, the sale of equities involved would be of the order of F120 billion, or three times the value of the British government receipts from the sale of British Telecom. However, this figure is based on book values which are unrealistically low in some cases and figures of the order of F200 billion are entirely reasonable.

New issues of equities on the French capital market have recently been of the order of F10 billion a year. In part, this reflects the relatively modest size of the private corporate sector in postwar France. Still, even if we add the entire current annual bond issue of F80 billion, the Right is talking about equity issues of the order of twice what the Bourse currently accommodates in a year. Privatization on this scale raises several important issues.

Let me first consider the macroeconomic implications. Assume for the moment that the government revenues from privatization are simply turned back to the private sector through a reduction in taxes. In the aggregate a rise in the present value of marketable assets matches a rise in future tax liabilities. So far as the equities are sold to foreigners, at the macroeconomic level there is instead a reduction in current taxes matching the rise in future tax liabilities. At any rate, French national wealth does not necessarily change, but its composition and liquidity do. The government asset sales will depress equity prices and raise interest rates and the exchange rate, but also increase the fraction of total French assets that are marketable. Consequently, the aggregate demand for goods may either rise or fall. Increased liquidity will tend

to push demand up; higher interest rates and an exchange rate appreciation will tend to depress it. The traded goods sector will suffer with a
worsening in the current account offsetting the improvement in the
capital account.

These macroeconomic effects can be attenuated by using the proceeds
of the equity sale to acquire bonds, either by retiring government debt
or acquiring bond claims against the newly privatized corporations
(though the scope for the latter may be limited). This way of easing the
adjustment process deserves serious consideration. Gradual privatization is another way of easing the pain, but has obvious political limitations. Still it is questionable that the macroeconomic effects can be
completely erased.

Now let me consider the redistribution effects. Clearly the issues will
vary depending on whether the proceeds from asset sales are used to
purchase claims against newly privatized corporations, or to reduce
current or future taxes. Two factors, however, ensure that distributional
issues generally arise. First, potential equity holders constitute a small
part of the population. The purchase prices must be such as to guarantee
that they will buy up the entire flotation by a given calendar date. This
puts the group in a favourable position relative to everybody else. A
sort of bargaining game may arise, allowing equity purchasers and
their representatives (a few brokerage houses) to exploit the government. Other taxpayers are likely to be losers since they are underrep-
resented. The experience of large overnight profits to the buyers of
British Telecom in England and those of Comsat in an earlier decade
in the States provide a vivid illustration.

Second, privatization and full compensation of the taxpayer are not
entirely compatible in so far as the taxpayer receives current benefits
in kind from the public firms. In this case the two can only be reconciled
through regulation. The benefits in question may be in the form of
subsidized services, such as below-cost transportation, or free goods,
such as checking account services. But regulation alone cannot resolve
the problem in France, since any effort to undertake all of the required
regulation would bring the entire philosophy of the privatization programme – and therefore the programme itself – into question.

Finally let me consider the effects on industry, and management in
particular. The effect of the privatization programme on management
turnover is more complicated than meets the eye, since there are some
beneficial side effects. Every French government tends to name leaders
of public firms of its own political colour. This means an existing
problem of management turnover at the time of elections, which the
nationalization programme of 1981 has only aggravated. Privatization
would alleviate this problem in the long run. However, the French

Right, if electorally successful, will face an immediate dilemma in 1986: to privatize quickly, which will be difficult without continuity and cooperation of existing management, or to delay the privatization until management transfers can be easily achieved, which will damage the credibility of the programme.

In sum, there are some really important asymmetries between nationalization and denationalization, to which a democratic state like France must pay particular attention. Most importantly, in the case of nationalization the equity problem centres on compensation of the expropriated. But in the case of denationalization, a similar equity problem arises concerning compensation of the taxpayer. The whole French denationalization programme could turn sour politically if the privatized firms were sold for vitually nothing, leading to fabulous profits for a minority.

I will end on a general note. The ideological issues that Yarrow deliberately avoids in his discussion may need to be brought to the forefront in France. Precisely because of the scale of state involvement in industrial management in postwar France, the senior French public servant may be a person of considerable entrepreneurial experience. Further he and his peers in industry are likely to come from the same cultural background, to hold the same diplomas, and may even be potential occupants of the same industrial posts. The world of government and the world of big business have always merged in France. This is all the more reason why the issue of the choice of society cannot and should not be suppressed in the French privatization debate. Privatization means more decentralization of decision-making. It means the prospect for the individual to climb the social ladder independently of performance in school and/or diplomas. It means an avenue of erosion of the *cloisonnement* of French society that has been the subject of various sociological treatises. These aspects cannot be disregarded in France.

General Discussion

Georgio Basevi suggested that the issue of who guards the guardians and the rules for selling were interconnected and related to the political structure of the country in question. Italy was currently undergoing a wave of privatization but paradoxically under a Socialist led government. However, this government is a coalition of parties and one reason for privatization may be a mechanism for changing the balance of political power within a company. A recent example of this was provided by the privatization of one particular bank. The privatization of this bank was seen as an opportunity for changing the balance of political power.

Hans-Werner Sinn emphasized the distinction between private and public goods. The market mechanism was inadequate to ensure a sufficient supply of the latter. A related issue was the question of industries subject to decreasing costs. With marginal cost pricing, these industries would necessarily make losses, but this was not necessarily a sign of inefficiency. Under private ownership a competitive industry was unsustainable and would tend to degenerate into a monopoly which would be profitable and would set prices too high.

Patrick Minford felt that it was possible to generalize about the benefits of privatization. He believed that the UK privatization programme had been a great success. Yarrow's emphasis on the privatization of productive industries was misplaced. The great success of the UK privatization programme was in the areas such as refuse disposal, and ancillary services in hospitals and education. The evidence suggested that the contracting out of such services could reduce costs by as much as 30%. A second reason for privatization was to de-politicize the agency process. The public sector had been captured by various interest groups and privatization had been successful at reducing the influence of such groups. In many cases privatization alone might be a necessary step *prior* to encouraging competition if there were powerful vested interests involved. Third, he thought the natural monopoly argument for public ownership was overstated. The break-up of AT&T in the United States had proved extremely successful. In the United Kingdom the performance of natural monopolies under public ownership had been uniformly terrible (with the exception perhaps of the Central Electricity Generating Board) and this hardly provided an argument against privatization. Where natural monopolies did exist, competition for services and tendering should be encouraged.

In response to this John Vickers pointed out that competition was actively discouraged in the case of British Telecom. The government's argument was that a degree of protection was necessary to protect Mercury, an infant industry. However, the restrictions not only aided Mercury, they helped British Telecom even more and were naturally conducive to collusive behaviour.

Louka Katseli argued that the distinction between private and public ownership was separate from the question of whether control was concentrated or diffuse. In Greece the running of the electricity, telephone and transportation industries had been transferred from government bureaucracies to local representative assemblies, comprising consumers, workers and representatives of local authorities. This process of 'socialization' represented a different approach to the problems posed by the bureaucratic control of industries.

Richard Portes suggested there could be strategic reasons for preferring the public rather than private ownership of companies. Defence considerations, or a desire to foster national champions, could provide a reason for keeping companies such as British Aerospace in the public sector.

Georges de Menil pointed out that there were significant differences between British experience and French proposals in respect of the structure and character of the markets affected by privatization. In Britain much of the privatization programme involved public utilities. In France the oppositon parties did not envision the early sale of public utilities but advocated the sale of major nationalized companies in the competitive manufacturing sector, and of the nationalized banks and other financial institutions. The *prima facie* case for privatization was stronger in such industries. He also suggested that in evaluating a change from a public to private ownership or vice versa it was not sufficient to consider the relative efficiency of the two regimes in isolation. Thus a major episode of nationalization could discourage entrepreneurs from creating new firms now while an irreversible programme of privatization could lift that disincentive.

Gerhard Fels agreed that competition and deregulation were more important than ownership. However, he did not think ownership was totally unimportant. Even if the benefits were not obvious in the short-term, privatization changed the environment within which managers and workers interacted, and could lead to a change in attitudes in the long-run.

Appendix: Evidence on the comparative performance of public and private enterprises

Table A1 below lists some of the empirical studies that have attempted to assess the relative performance of private and public enterprises, indicating the principal criteria adopted in each study and the general stance towards public ownership implied by the findings. The evaluations tend to be based upon a few, easily observable performance indicators and generally avoid systematic cost-benefit analyses of alternative ownership structures. Nevertheless, some tentative conclusions can be drawn from this evidence.

First, cost comparisons in the US utility industries (electricity and water) tend to slightly favour public ownership. For electricity, the listed studies (De Alessi, Peltzman) that found private firms to be the more efficient based their comparisons on the extent to which US firms had adopted time-of-day pricing. However, had De Alessi and Peltzman

Table A1. Empirical studies of comparative performance

Industry	Authors	Conclusion on public ownership	Means of comparison of public and private
Airlines	Davies (1971)	Anti	passengers, revenue, freight per employee
	Pryke (1982)	Anti	daily flying hours, capacity tonne km, profitability
Appliance showrooms	Pryke (1982)	Anti	expenditures/staff, mark-up, market share, profitability
Electric utilities	De Alessi (1977)	Anti	pricing policy
	Meyer (1975)	Pro	costs and prices
	Neuberg (1977)	Neutral	cost-efficiency
	Peltzman (1971)	Anti	pricing policy
	Spann (1974)	Neutral	operating costs, investment costs
	Yunker (1975)	Pro/neutral	unit costs, customer costs
	Pescatrice et al. (1980)	Pro	costs
Fire Services	Ahlbrandt (1973)	Anti	costs
Ferries	Pryke (1982)	Anti	turnover per employee, profitability, growth in traffic
Insurance	Finsinger (1984)	Pro	premia, dividends, complaints
	Frech (1976)	Anti	costs, service, number of errors
Medicine	Wilson et al. (1982)	Anti	productivity
Railways	Caves et al. (1980)	Neutral	total factor productivity
Refuse	Hirsch (1965)	Anti	costs
	Kitchen (1976)	Anti	costs
	Pier et al. (1974)	Pro	costs
	Pommerehne (1977)	Anti	costs
	Savas (1974)	Anti	truck utilisation
	Savas (1977)	Anti	overall costs
Steel	Rowley et al. (1981)	Anti	total factor productivity, technological diffusion
Urban transit	Pashigian (1976)	Anti	profitability, revenue/mile, demand
Water	Mann et al. (1976)	Pro	costs
	Crain et al. (1978)	Anti	costs
	Bruggink (1982)	Pro	costs
	Feigenbaum et al. (1983)	Neutral	costs

compared the pricing practices of representative, US private electric utilities with those of, say, the CEGB in Britain or EDF in France, their conclusions would have been reversed. Both of the latter, publicly owned enterprises have sophosticated multi-part tariffs, and the French industry in particular has been in the forefront of theoretical and practical developments in peak load pricing.

Where product markets are less monopolized, the comparative performance studies suggest a more favourable verdict on private enterprise, implying that incentive failures associated with government monitoring are empirically significant. Even here, however, the evidence is far from overwhelming. Caves and Christensen, comparing Canadian National and Canadian Pacific Railroads, conclude that 'public ownership is not inherently less efficient than private ownership' and that the 'oft noted inefficiency of government enterprises stems from isolation from effective *competition* rather than public ownership *per se.*' Rowley and Yarrow found a slight deterioration in the productivity performance of the British Steel Industry following nationalization, but the sample period ended before the dramatic productivity improvements that have occurred (under public ownership) in the last five years as the British government has increased the priority given to financial performance as compared with output and employment targets. Nevertheless, taken as a whole, the results do point to a *presumption* in favour of private ownership, provided that other market failures are insignificant or can be adequately corrected by means of alternative policy instruments.

Finally, Table Al indicates the near consensus of those evaluations of comparative performance that have been concerned with activities that can be franchized on the basis of relatively simple contracts. Refuse collection is a good example of this type of service and, among the studies quoted, the only dissenting note is sounded by Pier *et al.* who investigated the performance of public and private firms in Montana. The remainder of the authors all found that private collection had substantial cost advantages.

References

Alchian, A. and H. Demsetz (1972). 'Production, Information Costs and Economic Organization', *American Economic Review.*

Ahlbrandt, R. (1973). 'Efficiency in the Provision of Fire Services', *Public Choice.*

Averch, H. and L. Johnson (1962). 'Behavior of the Firm under Regulatory Constraint', *American Economic Review.*

Baumol, W., Panzar, J. and R. Willig (1982). *Contestable Markets and the Theory of Industry Structure,* Harcourt Brace Jovanovich, New York.

Buiter, W. H. (1985). 'A Guide to Public Sector Debt and Deficits', *Economic Policy.*

Bruggink, T. M. (1982). 'Public versus Regulated Private Enterprise in the Municipal Water Industry: a Comparison of Water Costs', *Quarterly Review of Economics and Business.*

Caves, D. W. and L. R. Christensen (1980). 'The Relative Efficiency of Public and Private Firms in a Competitive Environment: the Case of Canadian Railroads', *Journal of Political Economy.*

Crain, W. M. and A. Zardkoohi (1978). 'A Test of the Property Rights Theory of the Firm: Water Utilities in the United States', *Journal of Law and Economics.*

Davies, D. G. (1971). 'The Efficiency of Public versus Private Firms: the Case of Australia's Two Airlines', *Journal of Law and Economics*.

De Alessi, L. (1977). 'Ownership and Peak Load Pricing in the Electric Power Industry', *Quarterly Review of Economics and Business*.

Demsetz, H. (1968). 'Why Regulate Utilities?', *Journal of Law and Economics*.

Ekern, S. and R. Wilson (1974). 'On the Theory of the Firm in an Economy with Incomplete Markets', *Bell Journal of Economics*.

Feigenbaum, S. and R. Teeples (1983). 'Public versus Private Water Delivery: a Hedonic Cost Approach', *Review of Economics and Statistics*.

Finsinger, J. (1984). 'The Performance of Public Enterprises in Insurance Markets', in M. Marchand, P. Pestieau and H. Tulkens (eds.). *The Performance of Public Enterprises: Concepts and Measurement*, North-Holland, Amsterdam.

Frech, H. E. (1976). 'The Property Rights Theory of the Firm: Empirical Results from a National Experiment', *Journal of Political Economy*.

Gilbert, R. J. and D. Newbery (1982). 'Pre-emptive Patenting and the Persistence of Monopoly', *American Economic Review*.

Grossman, S. and O. D. Hart (1980). 'Takeover Bids, the Free-Rider Problem and the Theory of the Corporation', *Bell Journal of Economics*.

Hammond, E. M., D. R. Helm and D. J. Thompson (1985). 'British Gas: Options for Privatization', *Fiscal Studies*.

Hart, O. D. (1983). 'The Market Mechanism as an Incentive Scheme', *Bell Journal of Economics*.

Harris, C. J. and J. S. Vickers (1985). 'Patent Races and the Persistence of Monopoly', *Journal of Industrial Economics*.

Hayek, F. A. (1945). 'The Use of Knowledge in Society', *American Economic Review*.

Hirsch, W. (1965). 'Cost Functions of Government Service: Refuse Collection', *Review of Economics and Statistics*.

Holmstrom, B. (1982). 'Moral Hazard in Teams', *Bell Journal of Economics*.

Kitchen, H. M. (1976). 'A Statistical Estimation of an Operating Cost Function for Municipal Refuse Collection', *Public Finance Quarterly*.

Kreps, D. M. and R. Wilson (1982). 'Reputation and Imperfect Information', *Journal of Economic Theory*.

Mann, P. and J. Miksell (1976). 'Ownership and Water System Operation'. *Waterworks Bulletin*.

Meyer, R. A. (1975). 'Publicly Owned versus Privately Owned Utilities: a Policy Choice', *Review of Economics and Statistics*.

Millward, R. (1982). 'The Comparative Performance of Public and Private Ownership', in E. Roll (ed.) *The Mixed Economy*, Macmillan, London.

Neuberg, L. G. (1977). 'Two Issues in the Managerial Ownership of Electric Power Distribution Systems', *Bell Journal of Economics*.

Nordhaus, W. D. (1969), *Invention, Growth and Welfare*, MIT Press, Cambridge.

Pashigian, B. P. (1976). 'Consequences and Causes of Public Ownership of Urban Transit Facilities', *Journal of Political Economy*.

Peltzman, S. (1971). 'Pricing in Public and Private Enterprises and Electric Utilities in the United States', *Journal of Law and Economics*.

Peltzman, S. (1976). 'Towards a More General Theory of Regulation', *Journal of Law and Economics*.

Pescatrice, D. R. and J. M. Trapani (1980). 'The Performance and Objectives of Public and Private Utilities Operating in the United States', *Journal of Public Economics*.

Pier, W. J., R. B. Vernon and J. H. Hicks (1974). 'An Empirical Comparison of Government and Private Production Efficiency', *National Tax Journal*.

Pommerehne, W. W. (1977). 'Public versus Private Production Efficiency in Switzerland: a Theoretical and Empirical Comparison', *Urban Affairs Annual Review*.

Posner, R. (1971). 'Taxation by Regulation', *Bell Journal of Economics*.

Pryke, R. (1982). 'The Comparative Performance of Public and Private Enterprise', *Fiscal Studies*.

Rowley, C. K. and G. K. Yarrow (1981). 'Property Rights, Regulation and Public Enterprise: the Case of the British Steel Industry 1957–75', *International Review of Law and Economics*.

Savas, E. S. (1974). 'Municipal Monopolies versus Competition in the Delivery of Urban Services', *Urban Affairs Annual Review*.

Savas, E. S. (1977). 'An Empirical Study of Competition in Municipal Service Delivery', *Public Administration Review*.

Shavell, S. (1979). 'Risk Sharing and Incentives in the Principal and Agent Relationship', *Bell Journal of Economics*.

Shleifer, A. (1985). 'A Theory of Yardstick Competition', *Rand Journal of Economics*.

Singh, A. (1975). 'Takeovers, Economic Natural Selection and the Theory of the Firm', *Economic Journal*.

Smith, A. (1776). *Wealth of Nations*.

Spann, R. M. (1974). 'Rate of Return Regulation and Efficiency in Production: an Empirical Test of the Averch-Johnson Thesis', *Bell Journal of Economics*.

Stigler, G. (1971). 'The Theory of Economic Regulation', *Bell Journal of Economics*.

Vickers, J. S. (1985). 'Strategic Competition among the Few – Some Recent Developments in Oligopoly Theory', *Oxford Review of Economic Policy*.

Vickers, J. S. and G. K. Yarrow (1985). *Privatization and the Natural Monopolies*, Public Policy Centre, London.

Williamson, O. E. (1975). *Markets and Hierarchies: Analysis and Antitrust Implications*, The Free Press, New York.

Williamson, O. E. (1976). 'Franchising Bidding for Natural Monopolies – In General and with Respect to CATV', *Bell Journal of Economics*.

Wilson, G. W. and J. M. Jadlow (1982). 'Competition, Profit Incentives, and Technical Efficiency in the Provision of Nuclear Medicine Services', *Bell Journal of Economics*.

Yarrow, G. K. (1985). 'Shareholder Protection, Compulsory Acquisition and the Efficiency of the Takeover Process', *Journal of Industrial Economics*.

Yunker, J. A. (1975). 'The Economic Performance of Public and Private Enterprise: the Case of US Electric Utilities', *Journal of Economics and Business*.

Economic Policy   April 1986   Printed in Great Britain

██████████

SUMMARY

Curing hyperinflation

Michael Bruno

In the summer of 1985 the Israeli government introduced an economic programme aimed at reducing inflation from nearly 500% per annum. This paper sets forth the theoretical background to the plan and assesses progress so far.

The astronomical inflation rate was the consequence of two features of the Israeli economy: a large budget deficit, and the full accommodation of inflation in monetary aggregates. Progress has been made at reducing the deficit and the indexation of liquid assets has been ended.

Rather than fix a target for the rate of growth of the money supply, the authorities have opted for an exchange rate target on the grounds that the public's desired holdings of cash and bank deposits are likely to be very unstable in such an environment.

However, the choice of one nominal anchor for the price level is insufficient. A reduction in inflation is likely to lead to disparate movements in wages and prices because wage and price setting decisions are not synchronized in the economy. This is likely to lead to increased unemployment. To avoid this the authorities have negotiated wage and price controls through an agreed social contract.

A programme which involves a rapid adjustment from a very high to a low inflation rate is likely to be more credible politically than one that requires only gradual adjustment. So far the programme seems to have been successful with inflation falling to under 3% per month by the end of 1985 accompanied by only a modest rise in unemployment.

Sharp disinflation strategy: Israel 1985

Michael Bruno

Hebrew University of Jerusalem

1. Introduction

By mid-1985 Israel's economic crisis reached a new high. Earlier partial attempts at stabilization had failed. In spite of a recent improvement in the trade balance, Israel was losing foreign exchange reserves very rapidly, and inflation was up to monthly rates of 10–25%. On July 1 the government adopted a comprehensive emergency programme for stabilization and recovery which has had dramatic consequences, at least in the very short run. Within a few months inflation went down to 1–2% a month, foreign exchange reserves have rapidly increased and in spite of rather harsh contractionary fiscal and monetary policy measures average unemployment did not rise by more than two percentage points above the pre-July level. This paper deals with the background to the acute crisis of the Israeli economy, the conceptual underpinnings of the stabilization plan and with the first six months of its implementation.

2. The nature of the economic crisis in the past decade

The prolonged economic crisis manifested itself in three major areas: stagnation in real growth of output and productivity for almost an entire decade; rising private and public consumption in face of stagnant output leading to a reduction in investment, growing foreign debt, and ever increasing balance-of-payments difficulties which recently

* An earlier and abridged Hebrew version of this article appeared in *Riva'on Lekalkala* (Economic Quarterly) in October 1985. I benefited from many useful discussions with Eitan Berglas, Nissan Liviatan, Stanley Fischer, Mordecai Fraenkel, and Emanuel Sharon, and am also grateful to David Brodet, Moshe Kotzer, and Avinoam Ron. Avi Ben-Bassat, Daniel Gottlieb, Ruth Lowenthal, Sylvia Piterman, Zalman Shiffer and Charles Wyplosz offered helpful comments on earlier drafts of this article. Full responsibility for the contents is entirely the author's and the paper does not necessarily reflect the views of any governmental or other institution.

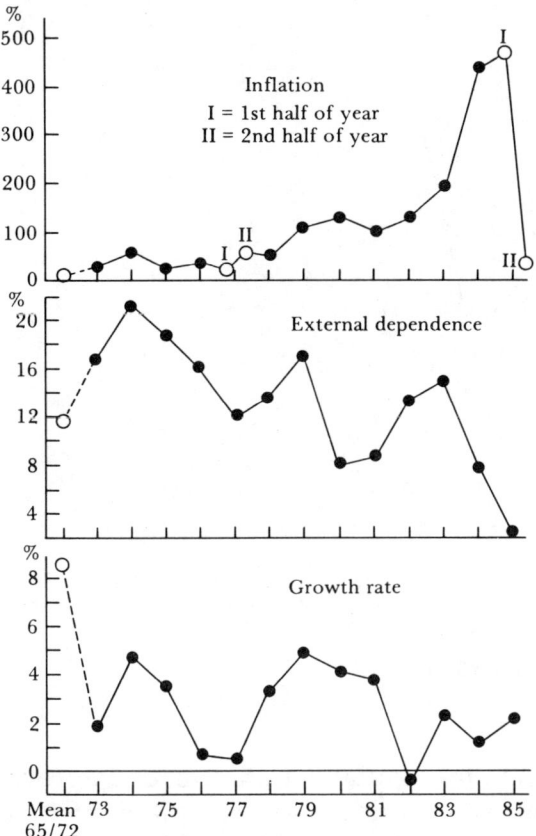

Figure 1. Inflation, external dependence and growth

bordered on a serious liquidity crisis; and step-wise acceleration of inflation in which each price shock due to external causes or deliberate government action (such as devaluations or other government-induced price hikes) translated into a permanently higher inflation-rate plateau.

Figure 1 summarizes the developments in these main areas over the past twenty years. The middle panel measures the civilian external deficit (imports of goods and services excluding direct defence imports *minus* exports of goods and services) as a percentage of gross national product. The upper panel gives annual inflation in terms of the consumer price index. The lower panel gives the rate of growth in terms of dòmestic product in the business sector. The figures portray the sharp transition from the period of relative prosperity, 1965–72, to the crisis of 1973–75 (rising fuel prices and the Yom Kippur war) as a steep decline in the rate of growth (from an annual average of 8.72% in 1965–72 to 2–4% and less in recent years). Finance Minister Rabinowitz's

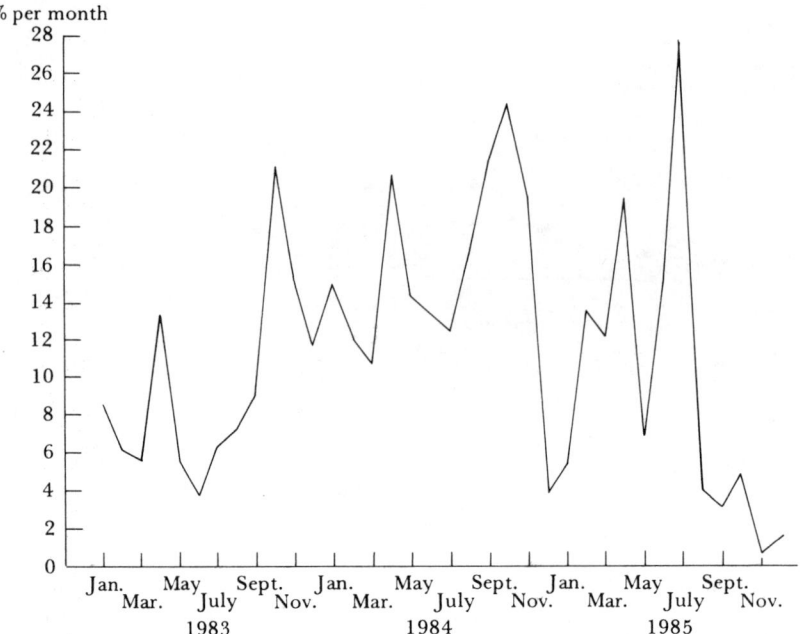

% per month

Figure 2. Monthly inflation rates, 1983–85

1975–77 stabilization programme brought about a dramatic improvement in the balance of payments and considerable restraint of inflation in 1977 (point 77I in figure 1 refers to January–May 1977), but at the cost of a further slowdown in growth. Nonetheless, it left behind a persistent structural problem: the large size of the public sector (its share rose from 20 to 30% of the labour force over the past decade), and in particular the size of the public sector deficit relative to GDP, which peaked at 17%. (For a macroeconomic analysis of these problems, see Bruno, 1984a).

Throughout the past decade the cycles of deterioration and improvement in the current account of the balance of payments can be related to the succession of Finance Ministers: an improvement during Rabinowitz's term of office (1975–77), deterioration under Ehrlich (1977–79), temporary improvement with Hurwitz (1979–80), considerable deterioration and slowdown of growth under Aridor (1981–83), and a notable correction towards the end of Cohen-Orgad's term of office and under the new National Unity government with finance minister Moda'i (1984 to the present). Improvements in the balance of payments were usually accompanied by an acceleration in the rate of inflation, as they were secured through subsidy cuts, indirect taxes and exchange-rate depreciations: for example a 9% devaluation and subsidy

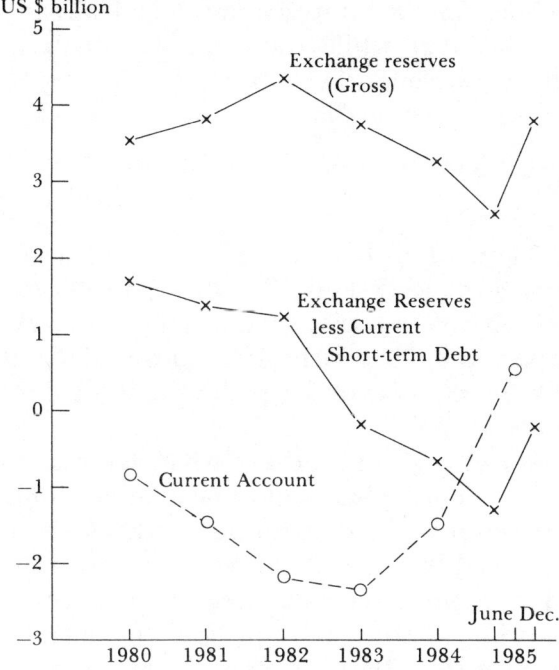

Figure 3. Current account, exchange reserves and current short-term debt

cuts were introduced upon the entry of the Unity government (note the leap in inflation during the period August–October 1984 in Figure 2). I shall say more on these price shocks and inflationary inertia in the subsequent discussion.

Over the past two years it has become evident that balance-of-payments and foreign reserve difficulties may arise from the capital account, even when the current account improves. In part, at least, these problems stem from loss of public confidence in the government's ability to control the economic system, leading to massive private purchases of foreign currency and capital flight. Figure 3 presents Israel's official foreign-currency reserves together with the current repayable debt (which includes short-term credit and medium- and long-term credit due within a year, *less* exporters' credit). The figure also gives the import surplus, excluding direct defence imports. Two central points stand out. First, the deterioration in the economy's foreign liquidity position started while official reserves were still increasing (1980–82); in 1983–84 the current debt gradually exceeded foreign reserves, frequently the signal that a liquidity crisis is imminent. Second, this deterioration persisted in spite of the improvement in the current account during 1984 and the first half of 1985. (The figure presents the surplus for 1985 as a whole, but an improvement had already occurred in the first half of this year while the liquidity situation, reflected in the net current debt, worsened).

3. Theoretical background: real and nominal factors in the inflationary process

The inflationary process (see Figure 1) is best described as a series of jumps in the inflation rate (1973–74, 1977II, 1979, 1983–84) followed by periods of relatively stable high inflation plateaux, the most remarkable of which is the four year period 1979–83 (the 1983 jump occurred in the last quarter, after a bank share crisis and large devaluation). This pattern may be explained in two ways.

First, we may consider the series of 'flats' and ask what determines the steady state inflation rate and hence what could make an economy shift from one steady state to another. Concentrating on that part of the budget deficit which is financed by the inflationary erosion of the money stock (the inflation tax), a shift in steady state inflation could occur for any one of the following reasons: (a) a permanent increase in the government deficit, relative to GDP, causing an increase in the required inflation tax, and thus an increase in the inflation rate; (b) a permanent reduction in the growth rate of the economy, causing a fall in the noninflationary transaction demand for money, thus requiring more inflation to acquire the same inflation revenue; or (c) a fall in the demand for base money due to institutional changes, such as the appearance of new, inflation-proof, substitutes for money. As the public moves out of money holdings higher inflation is required to finance the same given budget deficit.

Argument (a) can at best account for a rise in Israel's inflation rate in the early 1970s but not in subsequent periods: the step-wise leaps in inflation from 30–40% in 1973–76 to nearly 500% annually in 1984–85 occurred while the budget deficit, though large, was more or less stable at 12–15% of GDP. Argument (b), the drop in the growth rate, could be invoked to account for the step rise in inflation after 1972 (see Melnick and Sokoler, 1984) and argument (c) could be applied to the large step after 1978, as the financial opening up reform[1] introduced a new foreign-exchange-linked money substitute ('PATAM' accounts)

---

[1] In October 1977 a major reform measure ('Mahapach') was undertaken by Ehrlich, Finance Minister of the incoming Likud government. Controls on capital flows were lifted, a new foreign-exchange-linked, highly liquid domestic bank deposit ('PATAM') was introduced, and the exchange rate regime moved (temporarily) from a crawling peg to a float. All of this was accompanied by a large devaluation at full employment and no budget cut.

which increased very rapidly, while the demand for base money plummeted.

A second somewhat complementary line of argument relates the step-wise nature of the inflationary process to price level shocks, which account for the jumps. Coupled with full monetary accommodation, these explain why a price level shock translates into a jump in the *rate* of inflation. The price shocks may be entirely exogenous (e.g. oil and raw material price increases in 1973 and 1979 or the shock introduced with the October 1977 reform) or may be induced by balance of payments difficulties leading to devaluations and price increasing fiscal measures such as subsidy cuts, as in 1974, 1983, 1984.[2]

Monetary accommodation has taken the form of automatic indexing of liquid financial assets such as PATAM accounts, price guarantees on outstanding government bonds and for a time (up to 1983) government supported commercial bank shares. Such accommodation was further enhanced by an exchange-rate adjustment policy which roughly followed a purchasing power parity rule, and by the cost of living arrangements (COLA) which had been well established for a long time. Wages do not appear to have contributed to an acceleration of inflation: Israel has known decades of COLA agreements when inflation was no more than 5–7% annually and increases in wages usually followed price changes rather than vice versa. Nonetheless the COLA agreements, and in particular the shortening of the indexation lag, from a year to six months, then to three months and most recently to one month, have contributed to the persistence of high inflation 'flats' after price level shocks. Then, on top of all these components of inflationary inertia comes the reinforcing role of expectations fed by the accommodating fiscal and monetary policies.

Why then has inflation almost always only gone up and not down? One reason may be that positive and negative price shocks are not symmetric in their effects on the dynamics of inflation. When the general thrust of fiscal and monetary policy is expansionary, a temporary unexpected downward shift in the inflation rate will not lead to a downward revision of expectations. Such asymmetries imply that a sequence of positive and negative shocks of zero mean impart an upward thrust to the inflation rate.[3]

---

[2] For an analysis of the relationship between balance-of-payments problems and jumps in inflation see Liviatan and Piterman (1984); for a general characterization of the inflationary process in 1970–1984 see Shiffer (1982), and Bruno and Fischer (1984).

[3] For a formal representation of the inflationary dynamics see Bruno and Fischer, (1984). The asymmetry argument could be applied to the failure of Finance Minister Aridor's attempt to extricate the economy from inflation by reducing the cost of imports and slowing down the rate of devaluation; the worsening balance of payments situation ultimately led to a large devaluation and another price jump in October 1983.

Finally, what is the main role of the government budget under this
'shocks and accommodation' view of the inflationary process? Obviously
the role of the budget deficit is not merely confined to the direct pressure
of aggregate demand on market prices. In fact, the apparent lack of
correlation between the size of deficits and the accelerating inflation
'steps' (which has sometimes led to a wrong diagnosis) might suggest
that this relationship is of no importance whatsoever. The principal
mechanisms are more indirect. First, a budget deficit contributes directly
to a deficit in the balance of payments, as the government's negative
savings widen the gap between savings and investment. The need to
respond to a deterioration in the balance of payments and an increase
in foreign debt requires measures that by their very nature tend to
raise prices (this is the main argument raised by Liviatan and Piterman,
1984). The other indirect effect of a deficit is reflected in the large
internal national debt accumulated over time. The need to recycle this
debt, which is among the highest in the world in relative terms (150%
of GDP) and especially the liquid part of that debt, has limited the
government's freedom of action in both fiscal and monetary policy.
Hence, the prevention of an increase in the internal and external debt
had to constitute a key element in a programme designed to stabilize
the economy.

To sum up, the various arguments all converge to the view that the
inflationary process and the balance-of-payments difficulties originated
from two major sources. First a large real government deficit persistently
increased the internal and external debt. Second, the loss of a monetary
anchor meant an accommodation to inflation through the automatic
supply of linked liquid assets and an almost automatic adjustment of
the exchange rate. Since, however, the various nominal magnitudes
(money and exchange rates, as well as wages) are never perfectly
synchronized, asymmetries in adjustment to price shocks imparted an
upward bias to the inflationary outcome.

The implication is that it does not suffice to deal with only one of the
two major causes, but rather a necessary condition for achieving
economic stability is to tackle both of them simultaneously. Adherents
of a standard economic approach to inflation would have no difficulty
in believing that a drastic reduction in the budget deficit is necessary
for stabilization (though here, too, some dissenting voices have recently
been heard in Israel, owing to the apparent lack of correlation mentioned above). It is harder to convince followers of the conservative
approach that the inflation of the past decade also incorporated a very
powerful nominal inertia component, namely the need to synchronize
wages, prices, credit, and exchange rates across various economic sectors. It is entirely conceivable that the real budget deficit could be

substantially reduced by some drastic government action, while inflation persists by sheer inertia because the nominal aggregates in the economy are not properly synchronized. A stabilization programme that fails to come to grips with this problem of synchronization is bound to fail, at least in combating inflation. Our argument is that such failure will rapidly manifest itself also in real terms, because unsynchronized changes in nominal magnitudes will bring about serious changes in relative prices (real wages, real credit, real exchange rates) which lead to deep unemployment, a drain on foreign reserves, or both.

Another question related to these issues, and one that has occupied economists in Israel in recent years, is whether it is possible to extricate the economy from high inflation gradually. Adherents of the gradualist approach could find support in the claim that before attempting stabilization one should cut the budget, and that this step should precede the implementation of any social contract ('package deal' in local parlance) designed to cope with incomes policy and the synchronization problem. The counterargument maintains that the inflationary process is a vicious circle in which the budget deficit, inflation, and cessation of growth reinforce one another (see, e.g., the breakdown of the tax system in 1984 and the decline in productivity throughout the past decade). Moreover, a gradual, perfectly synchronized reduction in inflation is a practical impossibility because of inertia, natural leads and lags, etc.[4]

There is no doubt that synchronization around a 'zero' rate (a complete freeze on exchange rates, credit, wages, and prices) is far simpler for the public to grasp: consumers may monitor increases in price levels of goods but are less inclined to compute rates of change. But the clinching argument against gradualism and in favour of drastic action is a political consideration. Even a strong government is not likely to be capable of more than one determined effort centring on an 'emergency' plan. One may add considerations related to public confidence and government credibility and reputation, and these too are more in tune with the case for a sharp and comprehensive programme for ridding the economy of inflation in which the Prime Minister and Finance Minister mobilize the political system and the public for a concerted effort to restore control over the economic system. Strange as it may seem at first glance, the avoidance of deep and persistent unemployment is more likely under a programme that attempts to eradicate inflation sharply and decisively, since, with a strong impact

---

[4] It is not quite clear whether the 'Aridor Experiment' of 1982–3 is a good example: on the one hand, the reduced pace of devaluations was not accompanied by a similar slowdown in the rate of wage and price increases; but on the other hand, there was also no monetary restraint. At any rate, the second and third 'package deals' of early 1985 attest to the difficulty entailed in attempting to synchronize rates of change, quite apart from the lack of accompanying budget cuts.

on the public's expectations, strict limitations on credit and demand need not be expected to last more than six to twelve months. As matters turned out, the debate between these conflicting approaches was not settled on a theoretical level[5], as the pace of events in the first half of 1985 in both inflation and foreign currency movements thwarted the gradualist line and eventually dictated a drastic move.

4. Formation and main points of the economic programme

Although the broad terms of reference of the economic programme were laid out in earlier discussions and deliberations, its detailed preparation started only in the beginning of June 1985. The professional team[6] appointed jointly by the Minister of Finance and the Prime Minister was given three weeks in which to submit the programme to the government on June 30, 1985. The team relied mainly on studies conducted at the Ministry of Finance, the Bank of Israel, and the Ministry of Commerce and Industry.

The team's work proceeded against a background of a growing crisis in foreign currency outflow and loss of control over the inflationary process. An attempt was made to learn the lessons of various tripartite package-deal agreements that formed the basis of stabilization policy during the period October 1983–May 1985. Inflation was getting out of hand, and the new budget that had just been approved was already in jeopardy through rising commodity subsidies and submission to pressure from the expenditure side, and the continued improvement in the external trade account (which had already begun in 1984) was matched by considerable foreign currency outflow. The 3-month tripartite agreement on a wage–price freeze, the first 'package deal' of November 1984, seemed like a considerable political-social success in rapidly curbing price increases. But the absence of an accompanying cut in the budget, the continuation of (delayed) COLA adjustments in wages (thus

---

[5] Alternative ways out of the inflationary process were discussed in a series of staff seminars held at the Hebrew University at the end of 1983 and throughout 1984, as well as in various studies prepared at the Bank of Israel Research Department. An article by Liviatan (1984) on the dollarization plan and a memorandum by the present author with an alternative proposal for monetary reform (1984b) represented two suggestions for drastic action. Learning the experience of the great European hyperinflations (see Sargent, 1982), and in particular that of Germany in 1923, was very helpful. A study by Sokoler, Piterman and Fraenkel (1984), detailing a plan prepared by the Bank of Israel, preferred implementation in stages.

[6] The team, headed by Emanuel Sharon, Director General of the Finance Ministry, included Eitan Berglas (Tel Aviv University), Michael Bruno (The Hebrew University of Jerusalem), Mordecai Fraenkel (Head of the Bank of Israel's Research Department) and Amnon Neubach (the Prime Minister's Economic Advisor). Nissan Liviatan (The Hebrew University) was an active participant in various internal discussions prior to the team's appointment. An earlier team which included Yoram Ben-Porath, Haim Ben-Shahar, and David Golan, submitted the broad outline of a very similar plan to the Prime Minister in July 1984.

raising real wages), and in particular the continuation of devaluations and rising import prices made it necessary to introduce a one-time price level correction ('seam' in local parlance) between this agreement and the next, in effect 'blowing up' the package deal in January 1985. The next two package deals largely failed because they attempted unsuccessfully to control *rates* of price increases rather than freezing the price *level* as had been done in the first package deal.

To sum up, as far as the budget, the balance of payments, and certainly the inflationary process were concerned, the period immediately preceding the new economic plan was ripe both in terms of background conditions and in terms of the need felt for a drastic new tack. The aim of the new economic stabilization programme was to reduce inflation at once from a monthly rate of around 15–20% to virtually nil. Given some inertia and tail-end effects, this would in effect imply a reduction of inflation at first to no more than 2–3% a month and, within a few months, to even lower rates. The programme was also designed to permit a significant improvement in the balance of payments.

In line with our analysis of the origins of the crisis, such a programme would have to be comprehensive and drastic in its effects on public expectations and confidence. It would have to simultaneously tackle the real source of difficulty, namely the government budget, as well as establish a nominal anchor or, rather, several synchronized nominal anchors. A reduction of the budget deficit by $1.5 billion (7.5% of GDP) below the 1984 budget was announced. Simultaneously, the Israel shekel was devalued by about 20% together with partial reduction of existing import duties and export subsidies. Simultaneously the government declared its intention to freeze all shekel-denominated aggregates: wages, prices, exchange rates, and credit (after an initial adjustment). The peg of the exchange rate was made dependent on preserving the required level of nominal wages. The latter, including the temporary cessation of the COLA agreement, remained to be determined through negotiations with the Federation of Labour and the employers. The Bank of Israel undertook to restrict the nominal size of bank credit, and the Ministry of Commerce and Industry remained responsible for price controls. The government also announced its intention to limit the *nominal* budget level planned for July–September 1985. As for the capital market, the operative principle here was clearly to ensure the preservation of long-term (indexed) saving while at the same time reducing the liquidity of linked assets, in a clear departure from the previous regime. Current PATAM (dollar-linked) deposits would henceforth be 'one-way' only: withdrawals were permitted, but deposits would be accepted only for periods exceeding a year. Furthermore, the government would gradually make all its bonds fully tradable (with the exception of pension funds), so as to widen the base for open market operations. The time span set for the stabilization programme was a year, whose first three months were declared as an economic emergency period. In what follows I shall dwell in greater detail on several elements of the programme.

4.1. Pruning the public sector

At the core of the 'real' part of the programme, initially, was the desire to reduce the budget deficit up to the point at which 'the government's internal and external debt would no longer grow in absolute real magnitude' so that subsequent GDP growth would entail a gradual reduction in the debt/GDP ratio. This would have required a cut of \$2.0–2.5 billion (10% of GDP) in the budget relative to 1984. A top-level decision barring substantial cuts in (among other things) defence expenditures brought the planned reduction of the deficit to \$1.5 billion, with the hope that complementary cuts would be introduced in the 1986 budget. The reductions included a cut in subsidies to basic commodities and additional direct and indirect taxes with only 20% of the total cut coming from reduced real government activity. The limited size of reduction in expenditures introduced a constraint on another central aspect of the programme, namely, the ability to moderate the erosion of net wages by tax concessions (see below). As we shall see, the government's real excess demand in 1985 dropped by more than the planned cut, and it is very likely that the government's internal and external debt will not have grown in the budget year ending March 1986. In addition, emergency aid from the US government of \$750 million (3.0–3.5% of GDP) in both 1985 and 1986 will help bridge over the stabilization period without the full budget cuts required to achieve long-term balance (the domestic deficit including interest payments and subsidies to credit in 1984 was \$3.6 billion, or about 16% of GNP).

A second important element in reducing the size of the public sector was the decision to cut manpower by 3% (some 10,000 persons, counting also local government and other publicly-financed institutions). This step was not, in itself, of any immediate major budgetary significance as it calls for expenditures on severance pay, etc. Its importance lay mainly in signalling the government's intentions concerning the structural change required in the economy.

4.2. Devaluation

In addition to a devaluation of about 6% towards the end of June 1985, the Israel shekel was devalued by 18.8% on the day the programme was introduced and set at ISh.1,500 per dollar. In a pure change of numeraire, a shift from Old Shekels to New Shekels (1 New Shekel = 1,000 Old Shekels) was announced in August 1985 and fully implemented on January 1, 1986, when the exchange rate became INsh.1.5 = $1. As part of the partial unification of effective exchange rates in the trade accounts, the VAT was reduced by 2%, the excise duty on fuel was lowered, and import deposits were reduced. Subsidized shekel credit for exports was abolished, as was the special subsidy for preserving the profitability of exports; the existing export exchange-rate insurance was replaced by an equivalent arrangement gauranteeing an effective 11% subsidy for value added in exports. This arrangement no longer depends on changes in the consumer price index in relation to the exchange rate which was an integral part of the insurance scheme, and thus eliminates a distortion that had increased inflationary pressures in recent years.

The devaluation was less than the amount required to permit the total abolition of export subsidies[7] so as to limit the size of the price shock immediately upon implementation of the programme. A price shock of at least 15% was inevitable, due to the devaluation, the subsidy cuts, and the partial increase in controlled price ceilings. Going beyond that was considered too dangerous because of the implied size of real wage erosion.

4.3. Stabilization of the exchange rate and the setting of nominal anchors

As we have seen, an important part of the plan to achieve rapid price stabilization is the determination of one or more nominal anchors and the need to secure them in social agreements and appropriate policy measures. The quantity of money (M_1 or M_2) often serves as such an anchor, and its preservation by the central bank ensures stable prices. Under conditions of rapid inflation, and especially in the transition to disinflation, the demand for means of payment is extremely unstable (the demand for money can be expected to increase substantially, but one cannot tell by how much) and therefore cannot serve as an anchor. It is thus preferable to rely on the overall volume of bank credit, which is closely related to nominal GDP. However, control over the level of credit in Israel is indirect (in the recent past the Bank of Israel controlled the price of credit rather than its quantity), and it would have been hazardous to rely solely on credit for this purpose. Given the importance of the cost side in the inflationary process of recent years, the best

---

[7] Such abolition, combined with a desire to preserve the profitability of exports, would have required a devaluation of around 30%. The smaller size of devaluation therefore substantially limited the scope of effective exchange rate unification in both imports and exports.

combination of central nominal anchors appeared to be the dollar exchange rate and the nominal wage. The dollar exchange rate has for a long time served as a widely quoted price index, at a time when the regular CPI index was published only monthly and with a considerable time lag. Setting the exchange rate in dollar terms[8] in the early stages of stabilization was therefore deemed extremely important. On the other hand, the programme did not call for a continued real appreciation. Specifically, it would have been inconceivable to fix the exchange rate for prolonged periods unless nominal wages were also frozen, because the dollar wage (the nominal wage divided by the exchange rate) is a central factor in determining the cost and profitability of exports. Hence the freeze in the exchange rate was made conditional upon the stability of nominal wage costs (beyond an initial compensation, see below).[9] Price controls, which completed the system of nominal anchors for the duration of the stabilization period were one of the conditions stipulated by the federation of labour unions for a package-deal agreement.[10] After several months have elapsed, gradual decontrol was to be considered and this process has in fact started in January 1986.

4.4 Wage and incomes policy

Formal wage indexation agreements are helpful in avoiding undue erosion of real wages during high inflation processes, but are anathema to a sharp disinflation effort. Even with the minimal wage adjustment lag of one month of recent past, a sharp deceleration in inflation would be thwarted by the immediate steep rise in the real wage in the first month or two of stabilization. There was no escape, therefore, from a temporary suspension of the COLA agreement and at least a temporary reduction in the real wage. On the assumption that net real take home pay prior to the programme had already been eroded to the 'right' level, all that the plan had to stipulate was that the further

---

[8] Foreign trade stability would call for linking the shekel to a basket of currencies reflecting the composition of Israel's trade. Once the first stabilization phase is over, it will therefore make sense to link the (new) shekel to such a basket.

[9] The bilateral monopoly of a labour federation fixing the nominal wage and the government fixing the exchange rate, with each made conditional on the other, raises some interesting game-theoretic credibility considerations, recently discussed by Horn and Persson (1985).

[10] If general equilibrium determines relative prices in the economy, anchoring *one* of the nominal variables (such as the exchange rate, wages, credit, or prices) then suffices to determine the nominal levels of all other variables in equilibrium. But what we have here is a disequilibrium situation. The notion of 'multiple anchors' is suggested by analogy, securing a ship with several lines so as to distribute the strain in case of rough weather, with at least one of the lines taking the pressure at any point in time. Should one of the lines fail, the others can take up the strain, but it is nonetheless important to coordinate the lengths of the different lines ahead of time. (The analogy is based on a discussion with Mordecai Fraenkel some two years ago.)

reduction in the net real wage be temporary and could be corrected at the end of the 1985 budget year in March 1986. Given the relatively strong position of the trade union federation (Histadrut) in the wage bargaining process, and the relatively weak starting point of a government that has to deliver price stability from a base of rather poor past performance, it was clear that the workers would ask for initial compensation as well as some kind of additional insurance in return for a three months suspension of the COLA agreement. Consequently, an immediate wage compensation of 14% of the gross wage was offered. Finally, on July 15, after some tough bargaining, a wage agreement was signed between workers and employers in the private sector[11] that included the following items. First, an extra 14% of the July wage, payable on August 1. Second, a once-off 12% increase on September 1. Third, projected wage increases of 4, 4, and 3.5% on January 1, February 1, and March 1, respectively. (Employers in the industrial sector undertook to absorb these increments within the existing price ceilings and the agreed-upon export subsidies.) Fourth, the COLA arrangement (80% of last month's rise in the consumer price index) would be renewed on December 1 (November's wage) according to the price rise in October, with a minimum inflation threshold of 4% (instead of the 12% threshold before the stabilization period).

The extension of this arrangement to the public sector was eventually secured by the Histadrut from the government during September in return for the postponement of certain previously agreed wage increases, due in October 1985, until after March 1986. Clearly the succession of projected monthly wage increases at the end of six months, and in particular the renewal of monthly COLA adjustment with a very low threshold, seemed very problematic but were, presumably, the insurance costs required for achievement of the crucial temporary suspension. The impact of these arrangements on real wage behaviour will be discussed below (see also Figure 5).

The public debate over wage policy brought up many issues pertaining to social justice and the sharing of the burden. The main declared objective of the stabilization programme was the elimination of inflation, the most serious economic and social distortion in the economy. For example, it had eroded the tax paid by the self-employed more than that paid by wage earners and thus had a relatively more damaging effect on the disposable income of wage earners, in addition to any tax

---

[11] In Israel the government is formally not a partner to the COLA agreement, which is traditionally signed by the employers' association and the Histadrut and then adopted by the government in the public sector. This may explain why the contract had some obvious drawbacks for stabilization policy (see below).

evasion consideration. Beyond that, the programme did not propose to improve the income distribution. It attempted to reduce as much as possible the impact of price increases of basic commodities on low income brackets through compensation via the social security system. It also included a tax on luxury housing in addition to an extra property tax on vehicles and equipment imposed earlier.[12]

Finally, it seemed clear from the outset that the stabilization programme would cause a rise in unemployment, at least temporarily. The objective was to prevent unemployment from exceeding a level of 8–9%, from an initial level of approximately 5%.

5. Early developments

Six months may be too short a period to evaluate the disinflation programme merely on the basis of immediate actual price performance but a glance at the key price indicators in Table 1 already shows a considerable measure of success, with consumer price inflation down from 14–15% to an average monthly rate of 2.6% (and wholesale prices to a rate of 2%). Once special seasonal elements are taken into account the monthly rate is about 1–2%. This is also the rate projected for the early months of 1986. However, a longer period has to elapse before one knows whether the sharp deceleration in inflation will indeed persist. At this stage, we can only evaluate the key background variables that should support the sharp disinflation effort.

A central ingredient determining the success of a stabilization programme is the public's attitude toward it. This attitude can be measured by opinion polls, which indicated an improvement from the beginning of July into August: A poll taken by 'Dahaf' for the 'Yedi'ot Aharonot' newspaper shows an increase in the number of respondents in favour of the programme from 45% at the beginning of July to 64% at the beginning of August, whereas the number of those opposing it declined from 51 to 31% in the same period ('Yedi'ot Aharonot,' August 9, 1985). The first weeks of July were marked by considerable confusion. The vehement debates between the Histadrut and the government, the strikes, and the lack of clarity as to the government's intentions, cast the very beginning of the programme in doubt. The wage agreement eventually signed in the private sector on July 15 served as an important signal in the process of creating a nominal anchor for the price system. Public debates, grassroots pressure on the trade unions, and a general

---

[12] One major proposal of a general capital levy (including financial capital) had to be shelved early on because of a Law for the Protection of Savings that the Knesset had adopted prior to the July 1984 elections, a law that could only be revoked by a 2/3 majority.

Table 1. Key indicators, 1980–84 and 1985, before and after stabilization (Monthly % rates of change)

	Mean 1980–84	1984 (During year)	1985 January–July	1985 August–December
Prices, exchange rates and wages				
Consumer prices	8.7	15.2	14.0	2.6
Wholesale prices (manufacturing)	8.9	13.3	12.4	2.0
$ exchange rate (official)	8.8	15.9	13.6	0.0
Black market $ rate	—	16.1	13.3	0.0
Nominal wage	9.0	16.5	11.0	2.1
Interest rate (end-of-period level)	—	16.1	20.3	5.4
Money and credit				
Means of payment (M_1)	8.0	13.4	10.6	11.9
Quasi-money (M_3)	10.7	15.9	13.0	3.0
Total bank credit	9.1	16.8	13.9	3.9
Budget deficit (% of GDP)	10.2	15.0	12.0	4.0
Unemployment rate (%)	4.9	5.9	6.0	7.5
Balance-of-payments, basic balance ($m)	−210	−480	+340	

Source: Central Bureau of Statistics and Bank of Israel.
Notes: Quasi-money includes liquid assets and PATAM. For the budget deficit, unemployment and the balance of payments the first column shows data for the mean of 1980–83. 1985 data for the budget deficit are for subperiods January–June and July–December.

feeling that the Unity Government should be given another chance, may all have helped to bring the wage agreement about. The fact that the exchange rate remained stable during the early weeks of the programme (as did the black market rate, see Table 1) and that foreign exchange reserves started rising are not surprising, as both were expected immediately after a sizable devaluation and a price freeze, but that, too, helped. An interesting measure of public confidence is represented by expectations of inflation as indicated in the indexed bond market. This indicator revealed a gradual decline in expected inflation. For example, according to these calculations, the monthly price increase forecast three months ahead dropped from about 18% in June to 11–12% in July–August and gradually declined in the course of the following months to 1.7% by the end of 1985 (see Table 3, column (8)). Hence, the credibility of the programme grew in its first months of operation.

We now turn to the real economy, first and foremost the implementation of the budget. Figure 4 shows data on the government's revenues

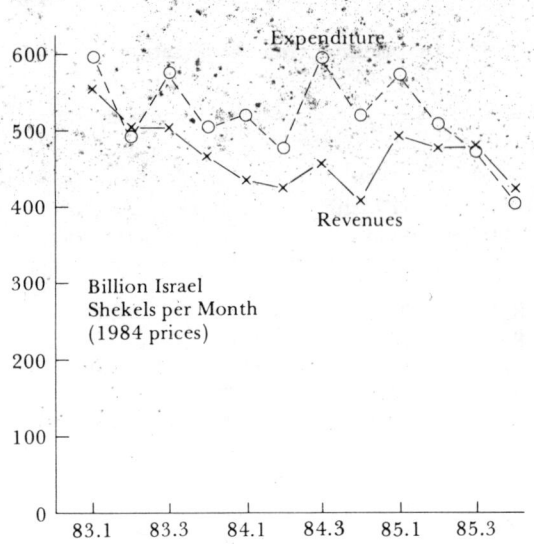

Figure 4. Real expenditure and revenues of the public sector, 1983Q1 to 1985Q4

and expenditures, in constant prices, from the first quarter of 1983 to the fourth quarter of 1985. These data, unlike the data of table 1, do not include interest payments. Note the decline in real spending (including subsidies) in the more recent period and the systematic decrease in the deficit until it turns into a slight surplus by the third quarter of 1985.

The deficit in the first eight months of the 1985 budget year was smaller than expected. In fact, if the first two thirds of the budget year 1985 were representative of the year as a whole, the reduction of the deficit (including interest payments) compared with 1984 would reach $1.8 billion instead of the planned $1.5 billion. This would mean (see Table 1) that the deficit as a share of GNP dropped from 15% in 1984, or around 10–12% on a longer-term average, to only 6% in 1985 (4% in the months July–December). In Figure 4, comparing the developments so far in the budget year 1985 with the corresponding quarters of 1984, we see that the improvement in April–June was due entirely to an increase in taxes and not to a reduction in spending, whereas the further improvement since the implementation of the programme (July–September) stems in increasing part from the expenditure side. This reduction was brought about mainly through subsidy cuts and only in small part by cutbacks in real government activity. It is too early to tell whether the government will manage to reduce its activity during the rest of the budget year and in the next (1986) budget. At any rate one should emphasize that, at least so far, budgetary restraint did support the attempt to effect rapid stabilization of prices and exchange rates.

This brings me to the second facet of the real system – the balance of payments. Here, no less than for the budget, the picture for 1985 as a whole shows substantial improvement, and not only in terms of the import surplus. The current account as a whole (including unilateral transfers) got 'into the black' for the first time for many years.[13] The improvement in liquidity for the end of 1985 can be observed in Figure 3: reserves rose considerably while the current debt levelled off. This improvement is related to the continued decline in imports, a further though not dramatic increase in exports, and the $750 million emergency grant from the US government. The import surplus developments clearly continue trends that started before the emergency plan was implemented. The programme can, in the short run, reinforce these trends, especially in restraining imports, but its major immediate effect has been on the capital account, in arresting the wave of speculative foreign currency purchases (in July-August the private sector even started selling foreign currency; overall repatriation of private capital in the second half of 1985 may have been of the order $500 million). The main point is that the balance-of-payment developments strongly support the possibility of continued exchange-rate stabilization.

Finally, Table 2 indicates a high real exchange rate (in terms of relative wholesale prices) not only relative to the dollar but also vis-à-vis a basket of European currencies, in a process that has been going on for over a year. The average index of the real exchange rate vis-à-vis a basket of five major countries for the third and fourth quarters of 1985 was close to the highest levels ever achieved since 1972, which is related in the last two quarters of 1985 to the pegging of the shekel to a depreciating dollar. Naturally, this index may suffer a setback if the price level in Israel continues to rise relative to the rate of inflation in competing countries while the nominal exchange rate remains unchanged. But considerable 'breathing space' has been gained, which makes it possible to place the main emphasis in exchange-rate policy on stabilization of the price level.

Let me now turn to monetary considerations. The shift from rapid inflation and a high rate of devaluation to a stable exchange rate is very dramatic and usually fraught with great difficulties, especially in an economy that has widely used dollar-linked along with nominal and real shekel assets. The effective monthly rate of interest on dollar assets was 17% (in shekel terms) just before the programme was introduced,

---

[13] The preliminary estimates for 1985 put the net current account (including unilateral transfers) at a surplus of close to $600 million in 1985 compared with deficits of $1,500 million and $2,300 million in 1984 and 1983, respectively. Even without the unilateral transfers this would constitute a further improvement of over a billion dollars in 1985.

**Table 2. Relative wholesale prices of selected trading
partners, 1977–85
(Indices, 1972 = 100)**

		USA	European basket	Basket of five currencies
1977		91	96	94
1981		107	105	106
1982		105	95	99
1983		101	86	81
1984	1	106	87	93
	2	107	87	94
	3	108	82	91
	4	111	81	92
1985	1	120	83	96
	2	124	94	104
	3	128	106	114
	4	119	106	111

Source: Bank of Israel Research Department.
Notes: Data refer to manufacturing wholesale prices relative to Israeli index multiplied by representative exchange
rate. The 'basket of five' refers to the US, UK, Germany,
France, and the Netherlands weighted by Israel's trade
with these countries.

dropping the following day to 3%; the monthly shekel borrowing rate
was 18–20%, and 11–14% on time deposits (see Table 3, columns (9)
and (10)). A sharp change in inflationary expectations caused the real
rate of interest to leap upward. Concern was voiced in public about
'the danger of a monetary flood that would sweep away the economic
programme' owing to the different liquidity ratios applying to dollar
as against shekel deposits in commercial banks. The data presented in
Table 3 reveal that the monetary system stood firm throughout the first
six months of stabilization. As expected, there was an immediate steep
drop in PATAM deposits, which has moderated since August, and a
dramatic increase in short-term shekel deposits and the quantity of
money. Total liquid assets declined by 11% in real terms in July,
remained more or less stable in August, and dropped again in September. The slowdown in nominal credit, both 'directed' and free (columns
(1)–(3)) was in line with the aims of the stabilization programme. Total
bank credit in the economy decreased in real terms by 9% in July, rose
slightly in August, and did not change much in September–December.
During the first six months of the programme the marginal borrowing
rate declined in stages, reaching 5% in December, while the deposit
rate sank to 2% per month. Even with inflationary expectations of 1–2%

Table 3. Bank credit, liquid assets, and interest rates: April–December 1985
(Monthly rates of change)

	Credit			Means of payment and shekel time deposits (4)	PATAM (in $) (5)	Total liquid assets (6)	Inflation rate		Interest rate (monthly)	
	Free[a] (1)	Directed (2)	Total (3)				Actual (7)	Expected[b] (8)	Bank lending (9)	Time deposits (10)
Relative weight, end of 1984	(49)	(51)	(100)	(18)	(82)	(100)				
April	11	17	14	20	−2	11	19.4	11.3	18.4	11.1
May	17	8	13	4	0	9	6.8	10.3	18.8	11.3
June	18	16	17	7	−1	16	14.9	18.1	20.4	14.4
July	13	23	18	64	−14	17	27.5	10.9	20.3	11.2
August	13	1	8	14	−3	4	3.9	11.7	15.7	6.7
September	10	−1	5	14	−2	4	3.0	7.9	12.2	4.9
October	4	2	3	9	−4	2	4.7	6.0	9.2	3.9
November	2	−1	1	11	−2	4	0.5	3.9	6.9	2.7
December	5	−1	3	0	−2	−1	1.3	2.2	5.4	2.3

Source: Bank of Israel Research Department.
Notes: (a) Excluding fuel, shipping and aircraft, and savings accounts. (b) Yariv (1985), average expected inflation over next three months, based on the market for indexed bonds.

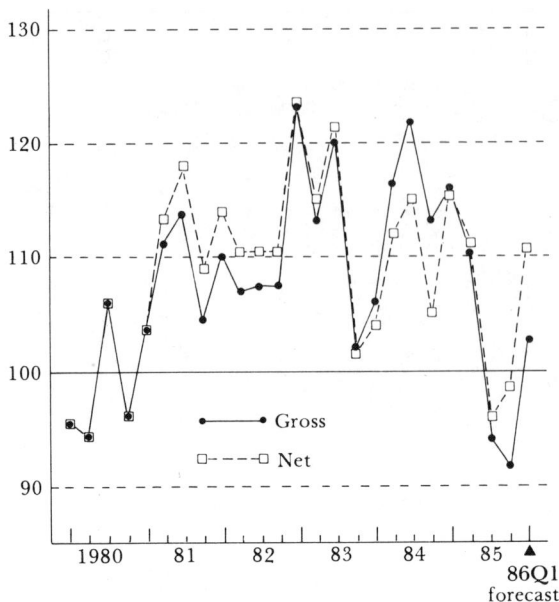

Figure 5. Gross and net real wage movements, 1980Q1–1986Q1
(Indices: 1980 = 100)

a month, the real borrowing interest rate remained substantially higher than the level that would encourage production and employment. But the speed at which this pressure is relieved must take into account the continued effort to stabilize the exchange rate. Extremely high real interest rates in the early stages of stabilization are a familiar phenomenon encountered in the historical experience of many countries (see, for example, the developments in Germany in 1923 as described in Dornbusch (1986) and similar events in present-day Argentina).

Finally, one should mention the problem of real wage erosion that elicited considerable debate when the stabilization programme was announced. Figure 5 describes the evolution of gross and net wages in constant prices over the budget years 1980 to 1984, and includes a forecast for the end of the 1985 budget year (April 1986). Several facts stand out. First, in 1984 real gross wages were about 16% higher than in 1980 although product per employee had not risen and may even have declined. Second, immediately before the programme was put into effect gross wages had already been eroded slightly compared with the average for 1984. A further 15% erosion in 1985 should have restored real gross wages in the economy as a whole to approximately their 1980 level, which is believed to accord with the economy's equilibrium conditions with respect to both productivity and the trade balance. Finally, erosion of gross wages in the course of the stabilization programme was compensated for by inflation adjustment of the tax brackets and the sharp slowdown in inflation, so that by the end of the budget year net wages are expected to have regained their prestablization level, i.e., 10% higher than in 1980. The real erosion between June and October and onward is smaller because we are comparing a high inflation month (June), when wages were eroded, to low inflation months.[14]

6. Problems and open questions

The developments in the first six months after its implementation provide support to the stabilization programme in the coming months and its ability to achieve its major objectives. But one should also emphasize the difficulties and dangers ahead. First, the danger of deviations from the budget. Subsidies have indeed been cut, but the scope for reductions in real government activity is still not clear. Demands for expansion of the budget by ministries that fail to carry out the cuts required, and by firms in financial straits seeking government assistance, are not likely to decrease. Similarly a fierce internal debate has erupted concerning the 1986 budget. It is too early to say whether it will support a permanent reduction in the rate of inflation, which requires a sizeable further reduction in government expenditures.

A potentially serious problem could arise because of growing unemployment. The rate of unemployment by the end of 1985 was estimated at 7–8%. A rise in unemployment is inevitable in a stabilization programme of the sort presented here but could take on proportions leading in the case of Israel (with a long high-employment tradition) to a social and political reaction that might thwart the successful completion of the programme. The sooner it is felt that the economy has really moved onto a new path of relative price stability, the easier it is to relax the constraints and to permit a gradual revival of economic activity. The question of wage increases agreed upon for the beginning of 1986 is relevant in this context. Although the employers undertook to absorb the wage increases, the very fact that wages were to increase by 4% a month during three consecutive months (on top of the COL allowance

---

[14] This is a 'tail-end effect', found by dividing nominal wages by average monthly prices although wages are paid at the end of the month. This effect reduces the erosion of real wages (or overstates its increase) in times of accelerated inflation and exaggerates it during the transition to stability. Correcting for this bias reduces the wage erosion relative to the inflationary base period by 5–8% (estimates by S. Amir, Bank of Israel).

for October, which was paid on December 1, when the October index fortuitously exceeded the 4% threshold) could bear with it the seeds of renewed inflation. As wage contract negotiations are scheduled to resume in April 1986, a critical factor will be the government's ability to throw into the bargain further tax concessions, which in turn depends upon the government's success at curbing its own spending.

The system still lacks the robustness that can prevent the translation of price level shocks into renewed accelerated inflation. One important further step in this connection could be the total abolition of all subsidies for basic commodities, and their substitution by a system of direct agricultural support. This could immunize the system against government induced price shocks of the type that characterized the inflationary process in the past. Since the inflationary process was deeply rooted, the process of price increases could also be renewed as a result of errors in judgement on the part of some sector or other, or a fortuitous price increase that exceeds the 4% threshold for COL allowances. For this reason it was considered important to exercise caution and discretion in the gradual removal of price controls. While the prices of many tradable goods can, in principle, be controlled via the market by exposure to competing imports, this is not true in the case of non-tradable goods and services, especially when markets are far from competitive.

Another issue that requires a great deal of caution is the easing of credit restrictions and reductions in interest rates. A high rate of interest which helps maintain the stability of exchange rates may also reduce output and employment. How fast the interest rate may be reduced depends on how rapidly inflationary expectations decline which, in turn, depends on budget and wage developments. Importantly, the greater the restraint in government spending, the easier it is to relax restrictive monetary policies.

Finally there is the longer term issue: when will the economy start growing again? Price stabilization is a necessary precondition for the programme's third objective of renewed economic growth. As growth resumes, the need for more investment may well lead to several years of trade deficit. But such a temporary increase in external dependence, which will now reflect a position of strength as it is designed to finance productive investment, differs entirely from the state of disinvestment that has plagued the economy for close to ten years. At the time of writing, however, the main hurdle, that of extricating the economy from the vicious circle of inflation and balance-of-payments crises, still requires most attention. Restoration of control over economic policy enables greater leeway, but does not, in itself, gaurantee safe passage to journey's end.

Discussion

Patrick Minford
University of Liverpool

This interesting account by Michael Bruno of the latest stabilization package in Israel is a paper produced in the heat of crisis by a major participant. As such it is unusual and welcome. I say 'latest' because since 1975 there appear to have been a succession of these packages. Like Italian governments they come and go, promising Israelis a permanent environment of transitory stabilization programmes.

To those who believe – along the lines of the evidence given in 1980 by Professor Frank Hahn to the UK House of Commons Treasury and Civil Service Committee – that inflation should be 'built in' to an economy rather than reduced/eliminated, the Israeli experience should be a cautionary tale. Such an attitude of benign neglect characterized Israeli policy until only a few years ago. I well remember a report on Israel by Anatole Kaletsky in the Financial Times in the early 1980s in which he quoted a leading Israeli Minister as saying, 'Yes, inflation is I admit 100%. But *real* inflation is only 11%'!

A striking feature of hyperinflation which we do not properly understand (at least I don't) is how tenacious people are in continuing to use non-indexed money; this seems to be true in Israel too in spite of dollar-based alternatives. Is it perhaps because its substitutes are even riskier to use (dollar deposit sharks? banks which may disappear?) especially for ordinary people and small firms? At any rate, it is because it is so hard to substitute for non-indexed money in practice (contrary to the build-it-in-via-indexed-accounting school) that inflation is so devastating to any economy, as Israel so clearly shows.

There are two main aspects to the Bruno *et al.* stabilization package of 1985. It plumps for immediacy (or 'cold turkey') as opposed to gradualism; and for an interventionist monetary/fiscal plan rather than a free market one. This curious combination of features indicates that an eclectic model (of which more anon) underlies the package.

The need for immediacy is based by Bruno on credibility; in fact he points out that the government had no effective choice, as the situation was so out of hand that only drastic measures had any hope of success. In this he is surely right; though the very recent literature on credibility does not yet tell us quite why this should be so, it seems obvious enough that the worse the initial situation the more likely it will seem that gradualist measures would be reversed or swept away. Presumably the reasoning would go: gradualist measures will offend powerful vested interests anyway and yet will not produce enough visible improvements to consolidate general public support. As well be hung by vested interests for a sheep as a lamb, and hope the sheep will impress the public. In this reasoning, Bruno is clearly appealing to a rational expectations element in his model.

Now consider his interventionist desire for price, income and exchange controls (including cost-of-living-clause overrides) to 'buttress' his monetary contraction (via an exchange rate rule) and his government deficit reduction. In Britain we had this 'belt and braces' approach from Chancellor Denis Healey in his 1976–79 stabilization programme; it contrasts of course with the later programme of Mrs. Thatcher in which decontrol of goods, labour and financial markets simultaneously accompanied an otherwise similarly conceived fiscal/monetary contraction. Another contrast between these two philosophies is in the way in which the fiscal deficit is to be cut back; at least in principle (if not always in practice) the free market approach envisages the desirability of cutting public expenditures, if possible enough to bring taxes down too for incentive reasons. That idea is quite absent from the Bruno plan where taxes must rise and stay up, while only a few politically less sensitive expenditures are to be cut.

I would certainly back Bruno on the need for parallel cuts in government deficits, on the same credibility grounds as those he gives for immediacy. For how is the government to persuade people it will not succumb to the pressures of vested interests for monetization if it cannot show the strength to beat the vested interests that oppose cuts in spending or higher taxes? Again the reasoning seems secure enough though we have no good models of political behaviour to base it on.

But from there I part company. No doubt the interventionist, even socialist, flavour of the package is necessitated by the predilections of the principal politicians; indeed Bruno seems to take this for granted. But that these politicians are misguided and court great difficulties, I am in little doubt.

Leave aside the issue of loss of freedom by ordinary citizens and firms. Though this is something I care deeply about, as economists perhaps we should not dwell on it, as being 'ideological'.

Turn then to the erosion of incentives. That there is a supply problem in Israel is not documented in this paper but it seems very likely at the levels of taxation and public spending prevailing in Israel. The Bruno plan does not address it; in fact it must worsen it by raising taxes.

Finally, there is the political aspect of controls. They must surely increase the likelihood of public coalitions against the package, for to the general unpleasantness of the monetary freeze is added the micro distortions of controls. Those groups that feel their relative wage or product price has been held below the market rate will react with fury and justice, after the initial euphoria and solidarity have evaporated;

in a corporatist economy like Israel's a disaffected union or producer group will have substantial market power. They will have a strong incentive to use it, since their individual action will not as such destroy the monetary plan to which they subscribe but will gain their individual advantage. They will 'free ride' on the corporatist consensus. Yet once one does, others will follow to protect themselves.

Those who impose controls – and Bruno is no exception – always do so as a 'temporary' measure intending to dismantle them before they cause serious micro damage or provoke the protests just described. But they are then caught in the dilemma that it is never the right time to dismantle a control, because any concession to one group will be a price rise for others. The controls not subject to this problem are permanent controls but they require full socialist planning from which Bruno and his colleagues naturally shrink.

These problems were well illustrated by the difficulties experienced with Mr. Healey's 'belt and braces', culminating in the famous 'winter of discontent' in 1978–79 with undug graves and rubbish piling up in the streets. For all the generalized unpopularity of Mrs. Thatcher's stabilization policies, the absence of controls meant that no single group had the incentive to try and overthrow the policies. What serious strikes there were – the steelworkers in 1980, the miners in 1983 – were against pruning of nationalized industries not against wage/price controls; accordingly they had no popular legitimacy.

Bruno's Figure 1 is a neat summary of recent Israeli economic history. It looks as if there were distinct phases of Israeli policy: up to 1972 when government deficits were moderate and able to be financed by substantial foreign borrowing, and 1977–85 when the excess of foreign debt forced reliance on domestic monetary financing with accelerating inflation. Growth suffered most seriously after inflation had seriously accelerated. But during the bond-financed phase and the early inflationary period (1977–81), growth was maintained at reasonable rates. I would have expected the real exchange rate to be strong in the bond-financed phase and to weaken sharply from 1977. Presumably too, much of the inflation in its early stages was unanticipated and so helped to sustain growth. All this is consistent with an open economy rational expectations model in which supply depends on the terms of trade and unanticipated inflation; and I was sorry not to see Bruno discuss it in these terms, or indeed in any but purely descriptive terms.

Bruno dismisses the direct control of money as inadequate ('money is unsuitable as a nominal anchor') because its demand is unstable in the transition from hyperinflation. Instead his technical prescription for monetary control is fixed exchange rates, 'buttressed' by wage/price controls. Let us ignore the solecism involved in 'fixing' (at least) *two* nominal variables, exchange rate and wages; Bruno is in fact proposing to fix *one* nominal variable, namely the exchange rate, and then manipulate a whole range of *relative* prices, a description which, had he adopted it, might have warned him more clearly of the dangers already discussed.

The problem with fixing the exchange rate in this type of crisis situation is that it does not put direct pressure on the non-traded sector, it only does so indirectly via expectations if people believe the exchange rate will not be changed accommodatively; yet this condition is hard to satisfy immediately without *other* actions demonstrating 'toughness', etc. This is presumably why Bruno *et al.* reach for a wage/price policy with all its problems. But if *money* is controlled directly, it puts direct pressure on all sectors, traded and non-traded; furthermore, the pressure is self-reinforcing because as inflation is slowed, demand for money rises increasing deflationary pressure. The 'instability' (not a correct description) of money demand in disinflation is a positive advantage to the disinflating government.

In sum, while this paper in its original form was clearly written for a popular audience and so understandably stripped of model and hard analytics, nevertheless I was disappointed with its lack of a clearly set out implicit model. In so far as one gets glimpses of an underlying framework, it appears to be an eclectic early-70s-vintage neo-Keynesian affair with a dash of 'cost-push' and rational expectations added to taste; not a stucture that is either intellectually coherent or very persuasive. No doubt that is why the policies it produces fill me with foreboding for the economic future of Israel.

General Discussion

Gerhard Fels argued that inflationary periods were usually associated with an inappropriate wage and price structure. An inflationary stabilization programme was unlikely to be successful unless it was accompanied by measures to ensure the final system of relative prices was consistent with full employment and balance of payments equilibrium. In a totally indexed economy it would be difficult to bring about the necessary realignment of prices. Historical experience suggested that the successful counter-inflationary programmes were those that achieved this. There was more involved than a simple nominal change in the units of measurement of prices.

Bruno's approach was that of an 'eclectic Neo-Keynesian' according to Paul Krugman. He welcomed this as a retreat from some of the models of the seventies which had heavily emphasized the role of expectations. These models suggested that it was relatively costless to disinflate, purely by announcing a lower rate of monetary growth.

Recent experience suggested this was not a good model for the industrial countries. He felt there were two reasons why these models had been misleading. First, people had to be aware of the problem and its causes; it was not clear that private agents were in fact aware of the link between monetary policy and inflation. Second, the credibility of the commitment to a lower rate of monetary growth was a crucial factor. Sargent's work on the ending of four hyperinflations had found that it was, indeed, relatively costless to disinflate in a high inflation economy. This was because, firstly, in such an economy people were acutely aware of the problem and its causes and, secondly, a feeling of desperation was likely to lend credibility to the announcement of a disinflationary programme. Unfortunately, this suggested that the easiest way to disinflate in a low inflation economy was to first accelerate into hyperinflation!

Mike Wickens questioned the absence of money as a central feature of Bruno's analysis. According to Bruno high government spending had produced a current account deficit inducing a depreciation of the exchange rate in turn raising inflation. The control of credit played some role but it was not clear how this linked in with the behaviour of the money supply. Bruno said that this de-emphasis of money reflected the fact that the Bank of Israel was not an independent institution and, historically at least, monetary policy had been accommodatory and was not seen as an independent stabilization tool.

References

Bruno, M. (1984a). 'External Shocks and Domestic Response: Israel's Macroeconomic Performance, 1965–1982', Falk Institute Discussion Paper No. 84.01, Jerusalem.
—— (1984b). 'An Anchor for Economic Stability', unpublished manuscript, Hebrew University, Jerusalem.
Bruno, M. and S. Fischer (1984). 'The Inflationary Process in Israel: Shocks and Accommodation', Falk Institute Discussion Paper No. 84.06, Jerusalem.
Dornbusch, R. (1986). 'Stopping Hyperinflation: Lessons from the German Experience in the 1920's', forthcoming in J. Bossons and S. Fischer (eds.) *Essays in Honour of Franco Modigliani*, MIT Press, Cambridge, Mass.
Fraenkel, M., M. Sokoler and S. Piterman (1984). 'Principles of a Plan for Rapid Disinflation'. *Riva'on Lekalkala* (Economic Quarterly), (Hebrew).
Horn, H. and T. Persson (1985). 'Exchange Rate Policy, Wage Formation and Credibility', Institute for International Economic Studies, Seminar Paper No. 325, Stockholm.
Liviatan, N. (1984). 'The Dollarization Plan', *Riva'on Lekalkala* (Economic Quarterly), (Hebrew).
Liviatan, N. and S. Piterman (1984). 'Acceleration of Inflation and Balance of Payments Crises: Israel 1973–1984', Bank of Israel Research Department, Discussion Paper No. 84.04, Jerusalem.
Melnick, R. and M. Sokoler (1984). 'The Government's Revenue from Money Creation and the Inflationary Effects of a Decline in the Rate of Growth of GNP', *Journal of Monetary Economics.*
Sargent, T. (1982). 'The Ends of Four Big Inflations', in R. E. Hall (ed.) *Inflation: Causes and Effects*, University of Chicago Press, Chicago.
Shiffer, Z. F. (1982). 'Money and Inflation in Israel: The Transition of an Economy to High Inflation', *Review of the Federal Reserve Bank of St. Louis.*
Yariv, D. (1985). 'Estimates of Inflationary Expectations, 1984–85', Bank of Israel Research Department, unpublished manuscript (Hebrew), Jerusalem.

Economic Policy   April 1986   Printed in Great Britain

SUMMARY

Protection and the LDCs

Gordon A. Hughes and David M. G. Newbery

Conventional wisdom suggests that non-tariff barriers erected by the industrialized countries have harmed the developing countries. However closer investigation suggests that the main sufferers have not been the primary targets of these protectionist measures, the Newly Industrialized Countries such as Hong Kong, Singapore and Taiwan. Producers in these countries redirected their exports towards markets in other Less Developed Countries. They also switched production into more advanced products in order to circumvent protectionist measures.

At the same time the New Exporting Countries such as Malaysia and the Philippines have been able to take advantage of reduced competition in developed country markets to increase their market share. In addition multinational corporations, attracted by low labour costs have located in these countries, transferring technology and expertise from the developed economies.

The major sufferers have been the poorest developing countries such as India and Pakistan. They were less able to adapt than the more sophisticated and agile exporters of the Far East.

Protection and developing countries' exports of manufactures

Gordon A. Hughes
University of Edinburgh
and
David M. G. Newbery
University of Cambridge

1. Introduction

It is widely believed that since the mid-1970s the developed countries have increased tariff and non-tariff barriers to imports from the less developed countries (LDCs). Furthermore, the most powerful protectionist measures have been adopted for manufactured goods, the sector in which LDC exports had been growing most rapidly. Our aim is to document these claims and to analyse their effects on the LDCs. We shall argue that it is hard to detect a significant effect on the total exports of manufactures by LDCs. Rather, the new protectionism may have induced a reallocation of exports from one group of LDCs to another.

Prior to 1973 world income had grown at an unprecedented rate, and world trade had grown even more quickly as trade restrictions had gradually been dismantled. Trade between developed countries had outpaced the exports from LDCs, but this largely reflected the greater importance of manufactures in developed country trade. World trade in manufactures grew at 8.9% per annum between 1960 and 1975 whereas total merchandise trade had grown at 7.1% per annum.[1] However LDC exports of manufactures grew at 12.3% per annum compared to 5.9% per annum for total LDC merchandise exports. Thus the dynamic element in world trade during this period was manufactures and here LDCs, starting from a low base, experienced more rapid growth than the industrial countries.

Deflationary policies adopted by many industrial countries in the aftermath of the 1973–74 and 1979–80 oil price shocks lowered rates of growth of both income and trade. In the recessions of 1974–75 and 1981–82 the total GDP of the industrial countries fell, non-oil primary

---

[1] *World Development Report 1978*, Table 13. These figures thus approximately describe pre-oil shock growth rates. All figures for growth rates in this paper are real growth rates.

Table 1. Annual growth rates of manufactured exports
(% p.a. at 1970 prices)

| | Export growth rates to | | | |
| | Developed market economies | | LDCs | |
Exports from	1965–73	1973–80	1965–73	1973–80
Developed market economies	11.4	4.3	8.1	9.0
LDCs	20.9	8.5	13.2	13.0

Source: UN *Yearbook of International Trade Statistics*, 1981.

commodity prices fell sharply, and the total volume of world imports contracted. Thus the industrialized countries experienced the deflationary impact of the two oil shocks as the developing countries were becoming increasingly important exporters of manufactures. These manufactured exports were of relatively labour-intensive goods[2] in which LDCs have an obvious comparative advantage. In the period before 1973 when the industrial countries experienced tight labour markets, imports of labour-intensive goods allowed them to reallocate labour to higher valued alternative forms of employment and thus to raise the level and rate of growth of output. Since 1973 the industrial countries have experienced both slower growth and rising unemployment. In such an environment the rapidly growing trade in labour-intensive goods was perceived as a threat to employment rather than an opportunity to benefit from international trade. As unemployment increased and traditional industries experienced major structural changes, so the calls for protection grew louder. A variety of 'voluntary export restraints' and 'orderly marketing arrangements' were instituted to protect domestic production in different developed countries. Clothing and textile imports from LDCs were particularly affected by this trend towards protectionism as the Multifibre Arrangement first consolidated and then strengthened a range of non-tariff barriers limiting such trade.

Table 1 shows the dramatic fall in the growth rates of exports of manufactured goods to developed market economies after the first oil shock. In the earlier period, manufactured exports from LDCs to developed market economies grew faster than to other LDCs, but after

[2] See Balassa (1983) for evidence on the labour intensity of LDC exports. This is not to deny that there were many other reasons for comparative advantage, such as access to cheap raw materials. See the detailed studies in Cable (1983).

1973 this pattern was reversed, so that an increasing share of LDC manufactured exports now go to LDCs, most notably to the Middle Eastern OPEC countries. This may be due in part to increased protection by industrial countries, and in part to the rapid growth in manufactured imports by the OPEC countries.

It is important to try to document the extent to which protection has recently increased. In the first half of the post-War period, world trade was stimulated by the lowering of tariff barriers as a result of a series of GATT negotiations, though the tariff reductions were primarily concentrated on items of interest to the developed countries. Tariff barriers against trade in manufactured goods were further reduced in the early 1980s as a result of the Tokyo Round negotiations. Balassa and Balassa (1984) report GATT calculations concerning average tariff levels before the implementation of the Tokyo Round reductions for a variety of manufacturing sectors. Trade-weighted average tariff rates on all manufactures ranged from 7% for the US to 10% for Japan, but using weights reflecting LDC exports, the US average increased to 11.4% while the averages for the EEC and Japan were between 9 and 10%. Sectoral tariff averages for all developed countries were as high as 20.6% for finished manufactures of textiles and clothing, 14.7% for semi-finished textiles and clothing, and 11.5% for finished manufactures of leather, footwear, rubber and travel goods, whereas for wood and paper products the averages were no higher than 7%, and for chemicals, machinery and transport equipment they were between 7.8 and 10.5%. Thus the tariff structure of the developed countries tends to discriminate against finished products from simple, labour-intensive industries and in favour of trade in raw materials and semi-processed natural resources. The Tokyo Round reductions tend to exacerbate this discrimination, though at lower overall tariff levels, since the largest tariff reductions apply to raw materials and sophisticated industrial goods. To a very limited extent this discrimination against LDC exports of manufactured goods is offset by the provisions of the Generalized System of Preferences (GSP) which, in theory, provides tariff preferences for developing country exporters. In practice, the developed countries have introduced the GSP in a very restrictive manner, excluding many products of potential interest to LDC exporters as well as placing severe limits on the volume of trade eligible for preferential tariffs.

It is conventional wisdom that non-tariff barriers against LDC exports of manufactured goods have increased significantly since the mid-1970s. However, in practice it is extremely difficult to measure the severity of such barriers and the extent of recent changes in them. A major study is currently under way at the World Bank (see, for example, Winters, 1985). In the absence of detailed results we can only rely upon more impressionistic evidence and previous studies of trade barriers. The most important non-tariff barriers are the whole range of quotas and other restrictions on textile and clothing exports imposed under the Multifibre Arrangement (MFA). The background and effects of the successive MFAs have been discussed at length by many authors (see, for example, Wolf, 1983, and Silberston, 1984). Between 1974 and 1976 restrictions on LDC textile exports were modest, EEC imports being allowed to increase by approximately 25% per annum in volume terms, but the second phase MFA which came into effect in 1977 drastically reduced the allowable rate of increase in imports to between 4 and 6% per annum in volume terms. Subsequent renewals have tightened the restrictions yet further so that the scope for new exporters, especially with respect to low quality textiles or clothing, is extremely limited. To some degree the sophisticated exporters have been able to sidestep the quotas, which operate in terms of pieces of clothing or lengths of textile materials, by increasing their value-added per quota unit, but there is pressure to stop such substitution and in any case it offers little prospect of further growth to the poorest exporters.

More generally, work by Page (1980, 1981) on the extent of 'managed' trade suggests that there was a major increase in the extent of non-tariff barriers among the OECD countries between 1974 and 1979. She finds that the proportion of OECD manufactured imports that was managed, i.e. subject to some form of non-tariff restrictions, increased from 4% in 1974 to 17% in 1979–80. Since 1980 the indicators examined by Balassa and Balassa (1984) suggest that there has been little further tightening in the overall restrictiveness of OECD non-tariff barriers. Indeed the US eliminated a number of barriers affecting exports of footwear and consumer electronics from South Korea and Taiwan in the early 1980s. Apart from textiles and clothing the products most severely affected by non-tariff barriers were identified by Page as cement, iron and steel, ships and footwear. All of these are items for which LDC exporters were becoming important competitors in world markets. Overall, Page concluded that by 1979, 34% of LDC manufactured exports to the OECD were subject to some kind of non-tariff barrier, though it should be remembered that textiles and clothing account for a very large fraction of this managed trade.

Faced with such widespread evidence of increased protectionism and public pressure for further restrictions on developing country trade in many OECD countries, it is easy to become pessimistic about the prospects for the future growth of LDC exports. Since rapid growth in such exports is essential in achieving any solution of the Third World debt problem, the implications of present trends appear to cast a large shadow over the future stability of the international financial and trading system.

Such fears would, however, rest upon an over-simple interpretation of the effects of the trade policies of the industrial countries. The fact that protection may have increased in various sectors during the past decade does not by itself imply that the export prospects facing LDCs have dramatically deteriorated. Before any such conclusion is warranted it is necessary first to look at the effect of protection on LDC manufactured exports, and then to try to assess how vulnerable these exports might be to future restrictions.

Before we examine the evolution of LDC exports of manufactured exports over the past 20 years in more detail, it is useful to discuss the principal elements of the dynamics of LDC exports and the possible effects of increased protectionism. The issues involved are too complex to yield simple testable hypotheses, but they do provide a better framework for interpreting the data and making forecasts about future developments.

2. Principles of LDC export growth

2.1. Demand and supply factors

One distinctive feature of the 1970s was the fall in manufactured export growth rates in the Newly Industrialized Countries (NICs) and a rise in the manufactured export growth rates of a second tier of medium middle income countries which we shall call the New Exporting Countries (NECs). Can this be explained by the particular form that protectionism often took – that of export quotas limiting access and the growth rates of exports of particular commodities by particular countries? This section examines the possible effects of quotas on the NICs, and the diffusion of exporting expertise among the NECs.

In order to measure the effect of protection on manufactured exports of the LDCs, one needs a theory of the effect of protection on international trade, or, equivalently, a model to predict what might have happened in the absence of protection. The problem is that over the period in question a great deal changed apart from the level of protection, and disentangling the effects is a formidable task. Nor is international trade theory of much direct help, for that is an essentially static theory not well adapted for the analysis of growth and change. Instead, what seems to be needed is an eclectic synthesis of growth theory, theories of development, and trade theory. The following elements, or 'stylized facts', would seem to be important. It is useful to distinguish between factors which affect the potential supply of exports from LDCs, and those which affect the demand for these exports.

Four stylized facts characterize the supply side. First, manufactured goods are typically produced in private enterprises. This may not be true for heavy industries like steel production or shipbuilding, but it is a characteristic of textile production, light engineering, and especially of the faster growing products of international trade. Second, efficient production of manufactured goods requires experience or expertise. Experience or 'learning-by-doing' (Arrow, 1962) increases with cumulative production or investment (the two being essentially indistinguishable). Expertise may be provided by multinational companies. Third, there is a maximum rate of growth of production of a single management team (Penrose, 1959). Fourth, labour costs per unit of product depend on wage rates and labour productivity, the latter rising with learning. Both differ across countries.

When brought together, these four stylized facts direct attention to the supply constraints which may slow down the growth process in LDCs. The first observation implies that capital accumulation, and hence both labour productivity and output growth, are driven by the rate of profit. In an early stage, wages are low and experience can be quickly acquired so that labour costs decline, profit rates rise and the rapid rate of capital accumulation further increases labour productivity. As long as wages remain low, high profit rates encourage savings and investment. During this period, the effective constraint on growth is the availability of management skills as pointed out in Marris (1964). As development proceeds, the demand for labour steadily increases, labour scarcities eventually develop, wages rise faster and labour costs stop falling and may rise. With a declining rate of profit, the binding constraint shifts from management skills to savings and capital accumulation.

Another element relevant to the supply of exports follows from the observation that exports are simply the difference between total domestic production and total domestic consumption. Starting from a situation where exports are low, but production is growing faster than consumption, it follows that the rate of growth of exports is initially very high. As capital accumulation and output growth falls and consumption accelerates, export growth steadily falls. Aggregating over all exporting firms, one might expect to see an early phase in which the number of exporting firms increases, and the number of foreign markets penetrated by each firm also grows. During this period the growth rate of total exports of manufactured goods may steadily increase. In the second stage as each firm increases the share of production which is exported, so the growth rate of its exports will fall towards the growth rate of production, and eventually the growth rate of total exports of manufactured goods will also fall.

The remaining supply consideration concerns the choice of product to be exported. Here traditional comparative advantage has a role to play, though with learning-by-doing and set-up costs, accident and history as well as factor supplies and transport costs will play a role in determining comparative advantage. Few of the other components of standard international trade theory seem relevant. In particular, it is hard to accept that factors are fully employed and perfectly mobile within the countries. Capital is imperfectly mobile both because much physical capital is product specific, and more important, because indigenous firms, especially small ones, are likely to have restricted access to capital markets. Multinationals, on the other hand, may well be able to escape the financing constraint, though not the natural limits on rates of expansion. Nor does it follow that countries with the lowest wage rates are automatically the most favoured as far as exporting manufactures is concerned – they may have low labour productivity, few managerial resources, and be severely capital constrained. Finally, there are mixed blessings in being a late starter. Certainly there is more technical progress waiting to be transferred, but learning-by-doing gives dynamic growth advantages to the early starter, so that latecomers have to chase the leaders down the learning curve.

The demand side factors are harder to identify, but two seem reasonable. First, breaking into a new export market involves fixed costs (of establishing contacts, a distribution network, and a reputation for reliability). Second, once these costs have been incurred, the long-run elasticity of demand facing any single firm (or country) is likely to be high (in the absence of quotas), and the export market effectively competitive. Table 9 shows that in 1981 the share of total manufactured imports from *all* LDCs by industrial countries was only 2% of their consumption, and was less than 4% for each two digit category except clothing (for which it was 14.4%). Obviously the share of even the largest single country in any market will be very much smaller. Of course it is possible that a country's market share of world consumption of a very narrowly defined commodity is quite high, but the more narrowly defined the commodity, the higher will be the own-price elasticity of aggregate demand, so it remains hard to reject the hypothesis of high demand elasticities facing individual firms or countries.

2.2. The likely effects of country and commodity specific quotas

Consider the likely effect of a quota which limits the sales of a particular commodity by a particular LDC to a particular importing industrial country (the Multifibre Arrangement is a suitable model here for a whole range of quotas and other non-tariff barriers). The exporting firm, faced with a binding constraint limiting sales in one country has three options: it can redirect sales to another market, it can reconfigure production to produce a similar, but currently less restricted commodity, or it can relocate in another LDC whose quota has not yet been reached. Each option involves set-up costs. Whilst relocating is likely to be the most expensive, it is not obvious *a priori* which of the other two options is likely to be cheaper or more profitable, and one might expect both types of response.

In the early phase of protection, where few goods are covered and few importers have yet imposed restrictions, the effect on total growth rates of manufactured exports might be slight because the returns to exporting a wide range of products should be high for moderately experienced exporting countries, like the NICs. If indeed these countries have reached a stage of development where growth rates are limited by technological gains and population growth, the set-up costs which affect profit rates will have no lasting effect beyond a temporary reduction in investment. On the other hand, for those LDCs still at the stage where the binding constraint is savings and capital accumulation, the fall in profit rates may well have a significant effect on export growth.

A subsequent phase of protection arises when more and more countries feel threatened by LDC manufactured exports, so the scope for redirecting sales of existing goods between countries diminishes, and the need for product change increases. But a change in product may stimulate a further restrictive response by the importing country, particularly if that country worries about its overall manufactured trade balance with LDCs (or specific countries). Thus we might expect that the initial effects of protection on LDC manufactured export growth rates would be relatively small, but that as time passes, they would become more severe. Eventually the option of moving production to another LDC, a New Exporting Country (NEC), may be the most attractive, and will be analysed in more detail in the next section. Of course, once this happens, the original host LDC will lose some of its dynamism on the supply side, though the loss to the original LDC will be offset by the gain in the new host LDC.

Thus import quotas may be expected to have three effects. First, although LDC export growth rates may fall at the detailed product level, there may be little apparent reduction in growth rates at the 2 digit level, let alone at the aggregate level. Second, there may be a switch in the pattern of destinations, with non-protected markets growing more quickly than protected markets. Third, with the switch of production from the NICs to the NECs, growth in the latter should, eventually, accelerate while growth in the former should decelerate. However these predictions are hard to test. Our preceding discussion of supply and demand suggests that, even in the absence of protection, the export growth rates of the NICs could not have been sustained, and that the NECs should in any case have grown faster during their

early phase of market penetration. Further whilst protection may have
been important, it was not the only force at work. Indeed a major
feature of the 1970s was that the oil price shock, which created a balance
of payments crisis in many industrialized countries and fuelled protectionist sentiments, also redistributed world purchasing power to the
members of OPEC, and created another market for the manufactured
exports of LDCs. It could therefore be hard to disentangle the effect
of the redistributed income pulling LDC exports into OPEC, and the
protectionist measures pushing LDC exports out of the industrialised
countries.

Thus far the argument has been simple, and to that extent hardly
worth formalising. However, when it comes to the decision to relocate
production to a different country, the various factors influencing the
decision are rather more complex, and worth exploring more carefully.
The next section describes a model whose formal structure is set out
in Appendix B.

2.3. Relocation of production and quotas

Multinational companies (MNCs) have limited managerial capacity,
which embodies expertise. If they locate in a NEC which had previously
lacked experience, they transfer technology and start the local process
of learning, and hence acquiring experience. As experience increases,
the country gradually develops the capacity to start its own locally owned
export production, and so becomes capable of earning rents on such
production. Initially, NECs have abundant labour of low productivity
supplied at a constant wage. Eventually, if they are successful and
graduate to NICs, the labour becomes more productive and its wage
rises. At this point the country captures rents in the form of higher
wages.

2.3.1. Technology transfer to NECs. Consider the investment decision of an
MNC in a particular NEC. The maximum initial level of production
possible in the NEC will be limited by, amongst other things, the size
and sophistication of the manufacturing sector, the availability of skilled
labour and transport infrastructure. From the MNC's viewpoint the
profitability of investing in a particular NEC will depend on the
maximum initial level of production, the size of the fixed costs, and the
opportunity cost of expertise per unit of initial capacity. If the maximum
initial level of production is below some critical level, then investment
will be unattractive.

Countries may thus be ranked in order of decreasing attractiveness
to MNCs, depending on the size, the price of the product, the supply

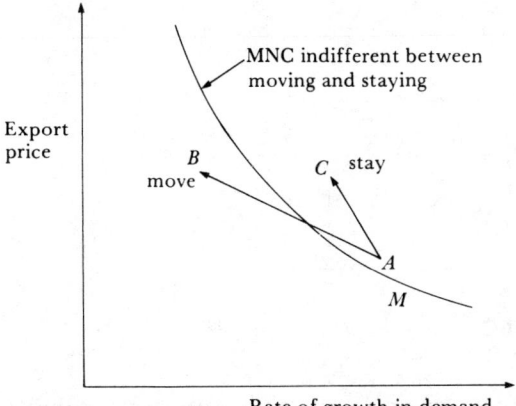

Figure 1. Effect of a quota on MNC's location decision

price of expertise, the productivity of labour, the wage rate and the extent and type of export linkages with other countries. Cheap labour is neither necessary nor sufficient for success in exporting manufactured goods in this model. The crucial variable which links the fate of the NECs and the NICs is the supply price of expertise, which will be affected by the industrialized countries' trade policy.

2.3.2. Relocation of MNCs from NICs to NECs. An MNC currently operating in a NIC can continue production, in which case its current management team remains tied to the NIC, or it can sell out to a local producer and transfer its expertise elsewhere. The supply price of expertise will thus depend on the profitability of remaining in the NIC, which in turn will depend on the price it earns for its exports, the rate of growth of demand for these exports, and country specific factors such as the wage rate, labour productivity, etc.

2.3.3. The effect of quota restrictions. Quotas have two effects on NICs: they reduce the rate of growth of demand, and possibly raise the market clearing price of exports. Lowering the growth rate will tend to encourage MNCs to move whilst raising the price (by the shadow price of the quota) will discourage movement. Figure 1 shows two possibilities. If the quota moves the firm from A to B, the MNC leaves, but if the movement is to C it stays.

But the quota will also affect the opportunity cost of experience. Because the costs of relocation may be large, the profitability of relocating in a NEC will increase with the initial size of the production scale. There is then a critical production level for any country, q^*, at which technology transfer will next occur. This critical level is also a measure

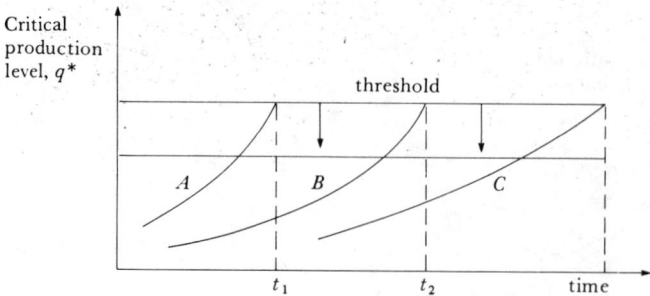

Figure 2. Graduation from LDC to NEC

of the MNC's opportunity cost of experience if, as it seems reasonable to assume, the 'quantity of expertise', e.g. the size of the management team, is proportional to the size of the initial scale of production. In Figure 2, this value of the critical production level defines the threshold at which developing countries graduate to become NECs, as a result of growth in GNP, increases in the size of the industrial sector, and improvements in the skill and commitment of the labour force. Country A reaches the threshold at time t_1, country B at t_2 etc.

Now we ask what happens to this critical level, q^*, as the quota is imposed. If the quota has no effect on the growth rate of NEC exports (which have not yet reached the limit set by the quota), then a fall in the allowed NIC export growth rate unambiguously lowers the threshold, and hence will cause a shift in MNC investment to potential NEC graduates. Quotas also tend to raise export prices. If the expertise required per unit of output in the NIC, and/or the fraction of the present discounted value of the firm realized upon sale to an indigenous firm, are high, then a rise in export prices will lower the threshold and cause MNCs to relocate to potential NEC graduates. Only if it is both expensive to leave the NIC, and if leaving would not release much managerial talent, will this effect be thwarted. Thus the formal analysis confirms the intuition that when quotas are targetted against NICs, the consequence is to increase the attraction of relocating production in the NECs.

2.4. Evidence for the theory

The theory predicts that MNCs located in developing countries subject to quotas may diversify into other LDCs in order to avoid these quotas, and as a result will increase the exports of the NECs. The evidence appears to support this theory, although most studies of MNCs stress that they invest abroad for a whole variety of reasons. One of the interesting developments in the last decade has been the rapid rise of

foreign direct investment by MNCs located in the NICs in other developing countries – a rise documented by Chen (1983), Lall and others
(1984), and Wells (1983), as well as by the UN Center for Transnational
Corporations.

Over the last decade, about 15% of foreign direct investment (FDI)
by MNCs in Indonesia came from the South Asian NICs, whilst the
figures for Malaysia were 37% and for Thailand were 19% (*CTC
Reporter*, 1984, Vol 17, pp. 32–35). Wells (1983, p. 10) lists the foreign
direct investment and number of subsidiaries of firms in fifteen developing countries for the period 1975–78, and finds that Hong Kong, India,
Argentina, Brazil and Korea accounted for three quarters of the total
number of subsidiaries in his data file (988 out of 1,312) though
Singapore and the Philippines also appear to be important sources of
FDI (measured by the total value of investment).

The argument also requires the MNCs to be highly export-oriented,
and here again there is extensive empirical support for the claim. The
share of exports to sales of MNCs has been growing rapidly, and
averages 18% for all developing countries in 1977, but over 60% in
Asian developing countries (UNCTC, 1985, Table 1.2). MNCs
accounted for more than one third of all manufactured exports in at
least six NICs (Argentina, Korea, Mexico, Brazil, Singapore and Hong
Kong) (UNCTC, 1983, p. 154).

The argument that at least some of this foreign investment by Third
World MNCs was designed to circumvent country-specific quotas is
advanced by Chen for Hong Kong firms investing in Indonesia in the
period 1967–70, though later the more important motive was apparently
to find an outlet for outdated machinery (Chen, 1983, pp. 174–5). This
'quota-hopping' motive was apparently important for Hong Kong textile and garments firms investing in Singapore in the 1960s. (Op. cit.,
pp. 182–3.) Chen surveyed the managers of Hong Kong MNCs and
presented them with a list of seventeen factors which might be reasons
for foreign direct investment: circumventing tariffs and quotas ranked
eleventh (op. cit., pp. 189–90), though they may have been more important earlier.

Wells (1983) claims that *most* offshore operations of firms from
developing countries were established when exports from the home
countries were threatened by quotas. He notes that Hong Kong textile
manufacturers first started investing in Singapore, then, in response to
the 1965–66 round of agreements, invested in Macao, Malaysia and
Thailand. As these were successively subject to controls by the main
importers, they relocated to Mauritius (Wells, 1983, pp. 73–4).

In conclusion, then, the theory and the evidence together suggest
that country-specific, commodity-specific quotas such as the MFA may

cause some MNCs to switch production to less restricted countries, and hence to increase the rate of growth of manufactured exports from these favoured NECs.

3. LDC exports of manufactured goods, 1963–85

In order to build up a fuller picture of the manufactured export performance of different countries we have collected detailed data on trade and national income from a sample of 49 developing countries.[3] The sample was chosen to include all developing countries for whom exports of manufactured goods comprised more than 10% of total exports in 1982 and all countries which had manufactured exports worth at least $50 million in 1982. Reasons of data availability meant that centrally planned economies (Afghanistan, Algeria, Angola, China, Cuba, Vietnam, Yemen PDR) had to be excluded, as were Bolivia, Ghana, Iran, Iraq, Lebanon, Sierra Leone, Zaire and Zimbabwe for similar reasons. Despite its disappearance from official international statistics after 1978 Taiwan has been included in the analysis since it is now the largest developing country exporter of manufactured goods. Another country which has, perhaps unusually, been included in the analysis is Spain. Up until 1982 the World Bank included Spain in its list of middle income developing countries since its GNP per capita was below that of Israel and little greater than those of Greece and Singapore. It was not a member of either the European Community or EFTA and its trading position at the beginning of the period was similar to that of other NICS – for example, in 1965 manufactured goods comprised only 40% of total exports – so that is seems appropriate to include it in the analysis.

The countries have been divided into four categories on the basis of their importance as exporters of manufactured goods, population and GNP per head. These categories were defined as follows.

The first group includes all of the NICs as conventionally defined, e.g. OECD (1979), with the exception of India, which is sometimes regarded as a NIC but seems more appropriately grouped with other large, poor countries. Exports from the NICs, especially from the subgroup of four Far Eastern countries, Hong Kong, Korea, Singapore and Taiwan, have been one prime target of the protectionist measures adopted by the developed countries during the past decade. Tariffs on manufactured goods might be expected to affect all LDC exporters equally, but the prevalence of selective quotas and voluntary export

---

[3] Details of data sources and trade figures by country are given in Appendix A.

restraints has allowed protectionist measures to be directed against the most successful and largest exporters.

The second group comprises countries with populations in excess of 10 million and incomes per capita in 1983 of at least $750. The combination of size and income means that these countries have substantial manufacturing sectors with the skills and infrastructure required to produce exportable manufactured goods. With a large enough manufacturing sector it is possible for new exporters of manufactured goods to diversify both in terms of products and country markets. This corresponds to the crucial condition for attracting MNCs and technology transfers, as argued in the previous section. For this reason we will refer to this group as new exporting countries, or NECs.

The third group consists of large/medium countries, i.e. populations in excess of 10 million, with incomes per capita below $750. In all of these countries the manufacturing sector accounts for a small proportion of GDP, though the absolute size of the manufacturing sector in a country such as India is, of course, very large. A relatively small manufacturing sector tends to be associated with limited infrastructure and concentration on fulfilling domestic market requirements, both of which restrict the rate of growth of manufactured exports, especially if quality and flexibility of market response are important. On the other hand, low levels of income per capita mean that real wage rates are low which should enable such countries to undercut producers of labour-intensive goods in richer countries. Because of these fears, countries such as India, Pakistan and Egypt have been excluded from some of the trade benefits offered under the Generalized System of Preferences and other preferential trading arrangements designed to help the poorest developing countries.

The final group comprises small countries with populations of less than 10 million. All of them are classed as middle income countries by the World Bank. Their size means that they are at a disadvantage when a large domestic market or other economies of scale are important in developing manufactured exports. However, it also means that rapid rates of growth of such exports would have had a negligible impact on developed countries, so that they had little to fear from export restrictions and, as middle income countries, they should have had the capacity to develop export-oriented manufacturing industries.

In discussing trends in the manufactured exports of these countries all growth rates refer to volume changes calculated by deflating values of manufactured exports by a common price index for trade in manufactured goods constructed by the World Bank with 1975 = 100. Aggregate growth rates of manufactured exports from the four groups of countries to all countries are given in Table 2. The share of the NICs in the total

Table 2. Aggregate growth rates of manufactured exports by LDC group, 1965–83 (% p.a.)

	NICs (1)	NECs (2)	Large/medium poor (3)	Small middle income (4)
1965–70	18.9	8.8	4.8	14.0
1970–73	20.2	29.9	7.1	13.7
1973–77	8.2	11.1	5.2	8.8
1977–80	10.5	18.3	0.2	6.0
1980–83	11.8	14.8	3.9	0.5
1965–73	19.4	16.2	5.7	13.9
1973–83	9.9	14.3	3.1	5.1
% share of LDC manufactured exports in sample countries				
1965	69.9	5.5	20.3	4.4
1983	84.8	7.9	5.0	2.3

Notes: (1) Argentina, Brazil, Greece, Hong Kong, Israel, Korea, Mexico, Portugal, Singapore, South Africa, Spain, Taiwan, Yugoslavia. (2) Chile, Colombia, Malaysia, Morocco, Nigeria, Peru, Philippines, Thailand, Turkey, Venezuela. (3) Bangladesh, Egypt, India, Indonesia, Kenya, Pakistan, Sri Lanka, Tanzania. (4) Cameroon, Costa Rica, Dominican Republic, Ecuador, El Salvador, Guatemala, Honduras, Ivory Coast, Jamaica, Jordan, Nicaragua, Papua New Guinea, Paraguay, Senegal, Syria, Trinidad and Tobago, Tunisia, Uruguay.

manufactured exports of the sample countries rose rapidly during 1965–73 and more slowly in the later period, while the share of the NECs fell initially and then grew rapidly during 1973–83. These changes were accompanied by a dramatic decline in the share of manufactured exports from the third group of poor countries – in particular India and Pakistan – who were large exporters of manufactured goods in the mid 1960s. As Table 1 indicated, the aggregate growth rate for all countries fell substantially after the first oil shock in 1973, though it is worth noting that the major contrast is between the years immediately preceding and following the oil shock, reflecting the general boom in the world economy during 1970–73 and the subsequent recession.

More detailed comparisons of growth rates by group and sub-period show that the NICs achieved a higher growth rate than the NECs during the latter half of the 1960s. This pattern was reversed in the 1970s and especially in the second half of the decade so that over the period 1973-83 the NECs achieved a growth rate half as high again as that of the NICs. On the other hand, the performance of the poor countries in group 3 was dismal in both periods, while the small, middle income countries in group 4, which had managed to achieve a high rate of growth of exports in the late 1960s, progressively fell behind the first two groups of countries during the 1970s – to the extent that their manufactured exports appear to have fallen during the early 1980s. While the NICs were overtaken by the NECs after 1970 in terms of their rate of growth of manufactured exports, they have nonetheless managed to sustain very respectable rates of growth. Apart from the impact of the post-1973 recession there is little sign that their performance has so far been seriously hampered by protectionist measures in the developed countries since their exports grew more rapidly during 1980–93 than in the preceding sub-periods.

There are three possible explanations for the reversal of the ranking of the NICs and NECs after 1970. First, the NICs had become sufficiently large exporters of manufactured goods in absolute terms by 1970 that it was no longer possible for them to continue to achieve growth rates very much higher than the overall growth of world trade in manufactured goods, whereas this did not affect the NECs. Second, protectionist moves in the industrial countries were indeed beginning to limit the export performance of the NICs at whom they were aimed, whereas the NECs, with a much lower share of manufactured exports, were not hampered in this way. Third, the NICs had been so successful in expanding their exports of manufactured goods that any surplus labour, or other resources, had been absorbed into employment with the effect that further growth pushed up real wages and hence reduced the competitive advantage of the NICs compared to both the industrial countries and the other middle income countries. In simple terms these explanations may be characterised as the world demand model, the protectionist model and the supply model. To decide which of them provides the most plausible explanation requires more detailed evidence of the kind examined below, but it seems probable that all three factors contributed to the change.

The experience of the group of poor countries in increasing their exports of manufactured goods over the period 1965–83 was most disappointing. Individual countries (e.g. Indonesia) achieved very rapid rates of growth but only from tiny initial levels, and as a whole the countries in this group performed substantially worse than both other developing countries and the general level of world trade in manufactured goods. The group of small, middle income countries performed substantially better than the large, poor countries, but their growth rates were consistently below those of NECs during the 1970s. This can hardly be ascribed to the impact of protectionism since this should have favoured the smaller countries. Hence, we conclude that supply considerations must be the major explanation of the difference between the performance of the countries in groups 2 and 4, since most of the usual supply factors – economies of scale, availability of technical,

Table 3. Manufactured export performance by LDC group, 1965–83

| | Number of countries by group | | | | |
	NICs (1)	NECs (2)	Large/ medium poor (3)	Small middle income (4)	Manufactured export growth (% p.a.)
1965–73					
High growth	6	4	2	4	> 18.5
Medium growth	5	3	0	8	13.0–18.5
Low growth	2	4	5	5	< 13.0
1973–83					
High growth	4	8	2	2	> 11.4
Medium growth	6	2	1	8	3.1–10.8
Low growth	3	1	5	7	< 3.0

Note: For each period the high, medium and low growth categories were constructed by ranking all of the sample countries in terms of their average rates of growth of manufactured exports over the period and defining the categories as consisting of the top, middle and lower third of countries in this ranking.

financial and marketing skills, size of home market, etc. – favour the countries in group 2.

Because the groups were very far from being homogeneous in their growth performance, aggregate growth rates can give a somewhat misleading picture. To counter this, Table 3 gives a cross classification of countries by growth performance and group. Since it is possible for countries to achieve very high growth rates starting from low bases and because we are most interested in the ranking of different groups of countries, the table divides countries into three categories of export performance (high, medium, low) which, for each sub-period include the top third, middle third and bottom third of the sample ranked according to their growth rates of manufactured exports. The table demonstrates in a striking manner the substantial dispersion of performance within each group of countries, and this is supported by the high coefficients of variation for the mean growth rate in each group. (The χ^2 test statistics for the hypothesis of identical distributions across groups are 9.1 and 15.9 for 1965-73 and 1973-83 respectively. The former is not significant at the 5% level, but the latter is significant at the $2\frac{1}{2}$% level.) The hypothesis that the distribution of growth rates is the same for the four country groups is clearly rejected for the later period. These figures confirm that after 1973 the successful countries in terms of manufactured export growth were predominantly the NECs whereas up to 1973 the NICs provided the largest share of high performers. Other cross-tabulations show that in the period 1965-70 the high growth countries were mostly either NICs or small, middle income countries while by the 1980s the NICs were again doing well, with five high growth countries by comparison with four from the NECs. This resurgence by the NICs and the relatively poor performance of the small, middle income countries would seem to suggest that, once the NICs had been able to diversify away from their original pattern of manufactured exports, protectionist measures by industrial countries had little effect on the overall growth of manufactured exports from the larger countries with more highly developed manufacturing sectors.

In view of the disparities within the four groups, the sample countries have been divided into ten groups reflecting geographical as well as economic differences. The aggregate growth rates of manufactured exports for each of these groups are shown in Table 4. The four Far Eastern NICs have substantially outstripped the European and Other NICs in their manufactured export performance over the period 1965–83 as a whole and over most of the sub-periods. Only in the most recent sub-period was their performance bettered by the other NICs who were, in part, making up for ground lost in the earlier sub-periods and were under great pressure to increase exports because all of the countries in this group face major problems in servicing their international debt. Manufactured exports from the European NICs, which have encountered very limited protectionist barriers, have grown steadily – except for the 1980–83 subperiod – but consistently at a lower rate than for the Far Eastern NICs which have experienced more severe protectionist pressures.

Trade barriers do, however, seem to have affected the Far Eastern NICs relative to the ASEAN NECs[4]. These two groups of countries correspond most closely to the model outlined in the latter part of the previous section because geographical and cultural considerations play a relatively minor role in influencing multinational investment and trade performance for the different countries. There have been some moves to increase the barriers facing manufactured exports from the ASEAN NECS (e.g. the imposition by the UK of restrictive quotas on textile imports from Indonesia) but in general they have been much less seriously affected in recent years by such barriers than have the Far Eastern NICs. Thus, the sustained higher growth rates for the ASEAN NECs than for the Far Eastern NICs since 1970 suggest that protection has certainly hindered the latter group's export performance

---

[4] Note that Indonesia has been included among the ASEAN NECs in this context as, despite being an oil producer and classified as a large poor country in the principal grouping, it has tried hard to promote manufactured exports since 1978 and, though poorer and less developed in its manufacturing sector, it shares many characteristics with other ASEAN countries.

Table 4. Comparison of rates of growth of manufactured exports for the NICs and Other LDCs (% p.a.)

Group	1965–70	1970–73	1973–77	1977–80	1980–83
Far East NICs: Hong Kong, Korea, Singapore, Taiwan	21.1	25.6	9.9	12.5	12.7
European NICs: Greece, Israel, Portugal, Spain, Yugoslavia	15.1	15.4	7.1	10.5	4.0
Other NICs: Argentina, Brazil, Mexico, South Africa	21.6	16.4	5.3	4.2	21.4
ASEAN NECs: Indonesia, Malaysia, Philippines, Thailand	6.0	36.6	12.9	21.1	18.0
North Africa/Middle East: Jordan, Morocco, Syria, Tunisia, Turkey	14.3	29.8	11.5	11.7	26.2
Latin America: Chile, Colombia, Paraguay, Peru, Uruguay	18.9	15.4	13.4	17.7	−10.6
South Asia: Bangladesh, India, Pakistan, Sri Lanka	4.1	7.9	5.3	0.4	2.4
Tropical Africa: Cameroon, Ivory Coast, Kenya, Senegal, Tanzania	19.4	7.3	0.9	1.7	6.6
Central America/Caribbean	10.3	20.0	5.9	2.2	−8.1
Oil Producers: Ecuador, Egypt, Nigeria, Trinidad, Venezuela	5.4	0.1	2.0	−1.8	4.4

despite the impressive rates of growth that the countries have achieved. This picture is reinforced by the relatively good performance of the group of NECs from North Africa and the Middle East (Jordan, Syria and Tunisia would have been classified as NECs in the earlier tables but for their small size) which have also experienced few protectionist barriers.

While these comparisons indicate that protection had had some effect, especially on the Far Eastern NICs, Table 4 shows decisively that protection is far from being a satisfactory explanation of the main discrepancies between the export performance of different groups of countries. The difference between the Far Eastern and European NICs would seem to be a consequence of both demand and supply factors. The latter group export primarily to rich European countries while the former depend heavily on the US market. Changes in the relative rates of growth of imports into the two markets would explain the narrowing of the gap between the export growth rates of the two groups over 1973–77 and its widening in 1980–83, but supply factors must explain the average gap itself. Another illustration of this point is the discrepancy between the North African and Middle Eastern countries and those from Tropical Africa. Both groups rely primarily on markets in Europe and the Middle East, while post-colonial and other traditional links have meant that they have not suffered seriously from protectionist measures, in fact the two North African countries and Turkey have encountered more severe trade barriers than the Tropical African countries. Yet the manufactured export performance of the Tropical African countries has been very poor, except for a brief period after independence, presumably because of the small and unsophisticated nature of their manufacturing sectors.

The other groups of countries which have performed poorly in these terms include the oil producers, which is hardly surprising in view of the common 'Dutch disease' syndrome experienced by oil exporters with rising real exchange rates and a shift away from manufacturing to non-traded goods and services. The poor South Asian countries have also experienced low rates of growth of their manufactured exports. This may partly be due to protectionist barriers affecting textile exports in particular, but supply factors, including inflexibility in economic policy concerning trade and industry, must have played a significant role.

The group of Latin American countries managed to sustain growth rates above the aggregate level during 1973–80 but then apparently suffered a major reverse in the 1980s. This was not the result of a decline in one or two countries alone since it occurred in all countries except Colombia, which achieved a marginally positive growth rate. The reason for this decline seems to have been high domestic demand combined with overvalued exchange rates, both sustained by relatively heavy foreign borrowing. Some of the same factors affected the Central American and Caribbean countries over the same period, though rather less severely. In view of their small size and easy access to the US market, the failure of these countries to achieve higher rates of growth of manufactured exports is clearly rather discouraging for their prospects of development in future.

The overall conclusion to be drawn from these comparisons is that protection did restrict the export performance of the Far Eastern NICs after 1973. Even so, they managed to achieve satisfactory growth rates throughout the period and protection seems to play little role in explaining the major differences between the performance of other groups of countries.

In order to identify any other factors which might explain differences in the manufactured export performance of developing countries we have examined a number of economic characteristics of the sample countries discussed above.[5] These were divided into the three growth categories for the two periods 1965–73 and 1973–83 as described above and then we tested for significant differences between the mean values of the variables for the countries in the three growth categories. The results of the analysis of variance are shown in Table 5. Despite the apparently large differences between the category means for some variables, the formal tests indicate that few of the differences are statistically significant because of the large amount of within-group variation. (The general absence of significant differences between the growth categories is confirmed by the results of non-parametric tests of the same hypotheses using the Kruskal-Wallis chi-square test statistic which have not been reported in the table.) For the 1965-73 period, only the growth rate of manufacturing output differs significantly across the manufactured export growth categories, with a strong positive correlation between the two growth rates. A similar pattern is observed for 1973–83 but the correlation is much weaker and the differences between growth categories are not statistically significant. These observations indicate that the point after which the growth rate of manufactured exports decelerates, as the manufacturing sector grows relative to total GDP, varies substantially across countries and is influenced by supply factors that we have been unable to investigate. Nonetheless, the fact that the average GDP per person for the medium growth category is significantly higher than for the other two categories in the later period suggests that centripetal tendencies, whether on the demand or the supply side, do eventually operate and bring about a deceleration in the export growth of the most successful countries.

4. The composition and direction of manufactured exports

Protection is typically targeted at particular commodities. Hence the natural way to investigate the impact of protectionist measures is to compare the rates of growth of different commodities to see what effect, if any, the measures had. Indeed, as Hughes and Krueger (1984) argue, it is difficult to see how else to measure the impact of non-tariff

---

[5] The data were compiled from the World Bank Tables data tape (1985 version) supplemented by figures obtained from statistical yearbooks of various countries to fill in the gaps.

Table 5. Economic characteristics of developing countries by export growth categories, 1965–83

Variable[a]	Average values by manufactured export growth category			
	High growth	Medium growth	Low growth	*F* value[b]
1965–73[c]				
GDP per person ($)	507	581	446	0.47
Manufacturing output per person ($)	110	110	88	0.24
Total population (million)	19.6	9.7	50.3	1.44
Manufactured exports as % of total exports	13.1	19.8	20.0	0.59
Manufactured exports as % of GDP	1.4	7.4	2.9	2.35
Manufacturing output as % of GDP	18.4	16.7	17.0	0.34
% Annual growth of manufacturing output 1965–73	10.2	8.4	5.9	4.78
1973–83[d]				
GDP per person ($)	532	977	528	3.74
Manufacturing output per person ($)	119	206	108	2.41
Total population (million)	33.2	13.1	53.8	0.94
Manufactured exports as % of total exports	23.3	33.1	29.2	0.64
Manufactured exports as % of GDP	8.0	8.4	4.2	0.62
Manufacturing output as % of GDP	19.6	19.3	16.6	1.03
% Annual growth of manufacturing output 1973–83	6.1	3.9	3.5	2.03
%Annual growth of manufactured exports 1965–73[e]	13.4	14.9	16.3	0.11
% Annual growth of manufacturing output 1965–73[e]	10.2	7.1	7.0	3.12

Notes: (a) All dollar values were obtained by converting local current price values to constant 1973 prices and using the 1973 official dollar exchange rates. (b) Test of the hypothesis of equal means with 2, 45 df. The 5% significance value of this *F* distribution is 3.23, the 1% significance value is 5.18. (c) The variables, other than growth rates, are for 1965. (d) The variables, other than growth rates, are for 1973. (e) The country classification by growth rate is different in 1965–73 and 1973–83.

barriers. There are two problems with this approach – one surmountable, the other less so. The first difficulty is that we at present have data only for the decade 1970–80, and, as table 2 makes very clear, growth rates differed substantially between the three sub-periods, being much higher during 1970–73 than later in the decade. Since protectionist measures increased in severity towards the end of the decade, it becomes important to examine rates of growth by sub-period. The problem then is that small errors in measured levels of exports magnify into large errors in the growth rates, and it becomes very difficult to detect

Table 6. Growth rates of manufactured exports by LDC group and industrial origin, 1970–80
(% p.a.)

	NICs	NECs	Large/ Medium, poor	Small, middle income	All LDCs
Food, drink, tobacco	5.1	4.1	1.6	1.6	4.2
Textiles, clothing	10.8	20.1	3.6	8.4	9.9
Wood products	7.3	9.8	26.9	5.2	8.2
Paper products	10.0	10.6	1.2	7.4	9.7
Chemicals	13.3	10.2	15.4	7.0	11.8
Non-metallic minerals	17.3	11.6	3.6	6.1	15.1
Basic metals	8.9	0.8	3.8	7.0	5.1
Metal products	15.5	25.1	8.6	6.5	15.4
Misc. manufactures	18.7	23.6	5.1	9.6	18.6
All manufactures	12.0	7.4	5.7	5.2	10.3

Note: Manufactured goods are here defined as those originating from enterprises classified under ISIC 31–39.

significant trends, or changes in trends, from the intrinsic noise in the data. The second problem is that it is hard to construct a counterfactual. Even if observed growth rates were high, might they not have been higher without protection?

Despite these limitations, the data on the composition of manufactured exports and growth rates for different industries in Table 6 (see also Appendix A) reveal some interesting patterns. Before discussing them it is important to stress the differences between this data and the figures underpinning the analysis of the previous section. Here, manufactured exports encompass all items produced by enterprises classified under ISIC sectors 31 to 39, whereas the previous figures related to goods classed under SITC categories 5 to 8 excluding 68 (non-ferrous metals). The SITC definition is much narrower since it excludes almost all items produced under ISIC 31 (food, drink and tobacco) plus a major part of ISIC 37 (basic metals). The differences are important because at first glance it appears that the results in the tables conflict with the previous analysis with respect to the relative performance of the NICs and the NECs. However, the low rate of growth of manufactured exports from the NECs is a consequence of the inclusion of processed foods and smelted non-ferrous metals, which together accounted for over one-half of manufactured exports on the broader definition in 1970, but which grew very slowly during the 1970s.

The NICs dominated the exports of almost all categories of manufactures in 1970 except basic metals because of the role of countries such as Chile, Malaysia, Peru and Thailand as exporters of copper, tin and other metals. The other notable feature of the composition of manufactured exports in 1970 was the 18% share of the South Asian countries in textile exports as compared with their share of less than 7% for other sectors. The textile sector shows very striking differences in export growth rates between the various LDC groupings. The NECs achieved a growth rate more than double that for all countries together (due primarily to the very rapid growth of textile exports from the ASEAN countries) whereas the growth rate for South Asia was just over a third of the aggregate value. Since the ASEAN countries and the NECs both started from a much lower base than the NICs and the poor countries, this appears to represent strong *prima facie* evidence for the restrictive impact of protectionist measures which were concentrated on textiles, clothing and footwear covered by ISIC sector 32.

The more detailed figures in Table A2 do not support a simple view of the restrictive impact of protection on LDC textile exports. Such protection was directed primarily against the large exporters which included both the Far Eastern NICs and the poor South Asian countries. The growth rates show that the NICs as a group achieved a growth rate for textile exports above that for all of the countries combined. The Far Eastern NICs in particular achieved a higher growth rate of textile exports than did the other NICs, so that their share of LDC exports of textiles and clothing increased over the decade despite protectionist barriers, though it is also true that textiles declined slightly as a share of their total manufactured exports. The European NICs suffered relatively little from protectionist measures but were able only to achieve a growth rate of 8.1% of textile exports by comparison with 12.1% for the Far Eastern NICs. Hughes and Krueger (1984) investigated the behaviour of exports from different developing countries to the USA, the EEC and Japan at the three digit level within category 32, and found that the four Far Eastern NICs *increased* their share of imports of each category (clothing, textiles and footwear) in most years in the USA, experienced ceilings on their import shares into the EEC after 1976, and lost shares in Japan after 1976. Part of the explanation for this continued dynamism in the face of protection appears to be that these countries were able to switch to more favourable export markets and to raise the quality and hence value of their textile exports.

While the Far Eastern NICs were able, to some degree, to surmount the trade barriers resulting from textile sector protectionism, it is clear that other countries suffered more severely. In 1970 the poor South Asian countries accounted for 18.4% of exports of textiles from the sample countries while the ASEAN NECs accounted for less than 1%. By 1970 the share of the South Asian countries was down to 10.8% while that of the ASEAN NECs was up to 4.1%. The ASEAN countries stand out in this case as achieving extraordinary rate of growth (over 30% p.a. for a decade) but the North African/Middle Eastern and Latin American NECs also increased their share of textile exports, again starting from very low bases. It seems, therefore, that the MFA permitted sophisticated exporters to sustain high growth rates by moving up-market in terms of quality and higher value-added terms but it penalised large exporters of lower quality, labour-intensive textiles who lacked the skills and capital to adapt, along the lines presented in Section 2.

In addition to textiles, the NECs were particularly successful in expanding their exports of metal products and miscellaneous manufactures. Protection may have encouraged diversification away from the Far Eastern NICs to the ASEAN NECs, as seems to have happened to textiles. The Far Eastern NICs achieved a growth rate of 20.4% over the decade but began to experience non-tariff barriers on their exports of consumer and other electronic goods. Multinational companies began to shift their assembly operations to some of the ASEAN countries with the result that the ASEAN NECs achieved an export growth rate of 31.6% for this sector over the decade, starting, of course, from a low base.

In addition to shifting the product mix of exports, developing countries have been able to mitigate the impact of protectionist measures by redirecting exports to different markets. A complete analysis of disaggregated trade data would be a substantial research project. However some inferences can be drawn from an analysis of the extent to which LDCs have shifted their aggregate manufactured exports between major trading blocs.

The increased revenue of oil-exporting countries and growth in the income of developing countries relative to the industrial countries have reduced the share of the industrial market economies as importers of manufactured goods during the 1970s. Thus, we need to focus on shifts in market shares relative to the average change. Unfortunately, detailed UN international trade data on the direction of trade is only available for some of the countries in our sample. Even then it is necessary to go back to 1980 in order to obtain a reasonable sample. As a first step we will compare rates of growth of LDC manufactured exports in total and to the OECD countries. The latter are derived from OECD import statistics which are, for most countries, valued on a cif basis rather than the fob valuations reported by the exporting country which form the basis of the UN statistics. This means that aggregate export values cannot be compared across the two sources – especially as certain special categories of trade are treated differently in each source – but growth rates should be less affected by such problems of comparability. Changes in publication arrangements mean that it is only possible to analyse

Table 7. Growth rates of manufactured exports to all markets and to OECD Countries, 1965–80
(% p.a.)

	1965–73		1973–80	
	Total exports	OECD imports	Total exports	OECD imports
Far Eastern NICs	22.8	26.9	11.0	9.4
European NICs	15.2	19.6	8.5	7.3
Other NICs	19.6	14.6	4.8	10.1
ASEAN NECs	16.6	20.6	16.3	19.5
North Africa and Middle East NECs	19.9	23.8	11.6	12.2
Latin American NECs	17.6	11.9	15.2	8.7
South Asia	5.5	7.1	3.5	4.9
Tropical Africa	14.7	5.3	1.3	3.5
Central America and Caribbean	13.8	22.1	4.3	−2.6
Oil producers	3.4	7.0	0.3	7.4
All LDCs	17.0	19.5	8.9	9.0

Notes: (a) Membership of the groups is given in Table 4. (b) Imports into the OECD from these countries; the basis of valuation of these imports is given in Table A2.

OECD imports from all of the sample countries up to 1980. Table 7 therefore shows growth rates of manufactured exports to all markets and to the OECD countries for 1965–73 and 1973–80 for the 10 categories of LDCs examined in Table 4.

During the period 1965–73 total OECD imports from the sample countries grew more rapidly than total exports, whereas during 1973–80 the two growth rates were equal. For the Far Eastern and European NICs the relative decline in the growth rate of OECD imports in the latter period was much more marked than for all countries. As a result their exports to non-OECD countries were growing much faster than their exports to the OECD countries during 1973–80. On the other hand the ASEAN and North African/Middle Eastern NECs continued to achieve faster growth of exports to the OECD than to other markets during the later period. The other NICs were relatively more successful in exporting to non-OECD countries in the early period, as also were the Latin American NECs, but this pattern reversed in the later period. Overall, it seems that it was the first two groups of NICs which were best able to take advantage of the relative growth of non-OECD markets after 1973, whereas the most successful NECs depended heavily upon continued growth of their exports to the OECD countries.

To extend this analysis of market shares, we have collected more detailed information on the direction of manufactured export trade in

1973 and 1980 for the major LDC exporters of manufactured goods. This data covers 20 of the top 26 exporting countries plus Jordan which completes the North Africa/Middle East category. The percentage composition of export markets in each year for four of the LDC categories plus all of the countries together is shown in Table 8. The figures show that in 1973 manufactured exports from the Far Eastern NICs went predominantly to the developed market economies – 79% of the total. As a result of diversification of export markets after 1973 this share had fallen to 66% in 1980. Within these totals the proportion going to the European developed market economies increased from 31% to 37%, while the share of the other developed market economies – mainly Japan – fell by the same amount. The European NICs also reduced their dependence on the developed market economies from 67% to 60%, while the share of European markets increased both absolutely and relative to the rest of the developed world. In contrast to these trends in the NICs, the share of ASEAN NEC manufactured exports going to the OECD countries stayed constant, though this was accompanied by a shift towards European markets and away from Japan and other markets. In general LDC exporters of manufactured goods seem to have become more dependent on the European market while Japan has become relatively much less important as an importer of LDC manufactures.

Apart from the relative shift away from OECD markets, the major change in market composition has been the growth in the proportion of exports going to the Middle East, as one would expect given the large transfer of income to Middle Eastern oil producers following the 1973 oil shock. All of the LDC categories took advantage of this shift in demand but the major beneficiaries seem to have been the Far Eastern NICs and the NECs in North Africa and the Middle East. That the latter group benefited from this change is not surprising, but the performance of the Far Eastern NICs reinforces previous comments about their adaptibility in the face of changing market circumstances.

5. Conclusions and policy implications

The main conclusion which can be drawn from the observed experience of the period from 1973 to 1983 is that the NICs were able to sustain high rates of growth of manufactured exports despite protectionist moves. There is some evidence that protection forced the largest four (Far Eastern) NICs to switch some of their exports from industrial countries to other destinations, perhaps thereby allowing other developing countries to enjoy high rates of growth of exports to industrial countries, or perhaps displacing them from other markets. The second

Table 8. Market composition of manufactured exports

	% of Manufactured Exports going to:							
	Developed market economies			Developing market economies				Centrally planned economies
	North America	Europe	Other	South and Central America	Asia	Middle East[d]	Other	
1973								
Far Eastern NICs[a]	37.5	24.3	17.2	1.5	14.7	2.0	2.5	0.2
European NICs	14.2	50.1	3.0	5.9	3.1	3.7	8.6	11.3
ASEAN NECs	25.4	18.9	17.6	0.2	33.8	1.8	1.7	0.6
North Africa and Middle East NECs[b]	4.7	60.4	2.5	2.1	2.7	10.4	11.3	5.9
All countries[c]	24.7	34.9	10.1	7.5	9.7	2.9	5.0	5.2
1980								
Far Eastern NICs	31.5	24.3	10.4	3.0	17.5	7.2	4.6	1.5
European NICs	7.8	49.6	2.2	7.2	2.4	8.2	9.3	13.3
ASEAN NECs	26.3	24.4	10.6	0.6	32.0	4.0	1.2	0.9
North Africa and Middle East NECs	1.0	61.9	0.1	1.6	8.1	16.5	5.3	5.6
All countries	20.0	34.0	6.5	9.1	10.8	7.2	6.3	6.1

Notes: (a) Excluding Taiwan. (b) Excluding Syria. (c) The countries in the four categories plus Argentina, Brazil, Colombia, Pakistan and Peru. (d) This includes capital surplus, oil exporters such as Saudi Arabia and the Gulf states.

conclusion is that there is a group of medium middle income countries (the NECs) which has enjoyed higher export growth than the NICs during this period, though the large poor traditional exporters and the small middle income exporters have performed relatively poorly. Supply factors are the obvious explanation for the different performances of the non-NICs, whilst protection and demand factors are arguably important explanations for the decline in NIC export growth rates to industrial countries after 1977.

This raises the interesting possibility that protection may have assisted the second rank exporters, both by restraining the market shares of the most successful NICs, and by raising the profitability of exporting manufactures for those countries well placed to benefit. The reason for the increased profitability is that quotas and other export constraints, unlike tariffs, raise the price level in the importing country and generate rent for countries lucky enough to receive a quota or be exempt from the restrictions.

Hughes and Krueger (1984) have raised a number of interesting questions. Would Korea have moved up-market in textiles more rapidly or more slowly in the absence of the MFA? Would Mauritius have entered the international textile market sooner or later in the absence of the MFA? Did VERs (Voluntary Export Restraints) keep the NICs of the Far East exporting the same commodities longer than they otherwise would have? In Section 2 we presented a simple model which can address some, though not all of these questions. The model can account for the observed phenomenon that it is not sufficient to have low labour costs in order to be a successful exporter. The model also shows that while the effect of quotas on the NICs may raise or lower the profitability of continued exporting, and so by itself does not give unambiguous predictions. When the alternative of moving to NEC was initially present and almost attractive, the quota will make the NEC unambiguously more attractive. This accords with the acceleration in the diversification away from NICs and towards the next rank countries, the NECs.

The incentives to export in the 1970s were several and powerful – the increase in oil prices forced oil importing LDCs to increase exports to finance their oil imports, whilst the IMF and the World Bank continued to press for outward looking or export oriented development strategies. The success stories of the NICs began to be more widely appreciated, and to be imitated elsewhere. Some of the NECs were very successful; some of the older exporters of manufactures, such as India and Pakistan, were less so; and the evidence suggests that supply factors, rather than demand conditions, were the main determinant of export success, except for the leading NICs.

Table 9. Developed country trade in manufactured goods with LDCs, 1973–81 (expressed as % of size of domestic market in developed countries)

	Exports to LDCs relative to DC production			Imports from LDCs relative to DC consumption		
	Average	Marginal		Average	Marginal	
	1981	1973–78	1978–81	1981	1973–78	1978–81
Iron and Steel	6.5	7.3	17.5	1.0	0.7	4.8
Chemicals	4.9	5.9	5.8	0.7	0.7	1.0
Other semi-manufactures	3.0	6.5	5.2	1.5	3.4	1.1
Engineering products	8.7	11.2	15.9	1.5	1.6	3.8
Textiles	5.0	5.6	17.2	3.0	6.1	6.3
Clothing	2.6	3.2	12.2	14.4	19.6	41.5
Other consumer goods	3.3	3.6	7.8	3.3	3.5	7.5
Total manufacturing	6.4	8.5	11.3	2.0	2.4	3.8

Source: Balassa (1983, table 4).
Notes: Columns labelled 'average' give LDC share as a percentage. Columns labelled 'marginal' give increase in LDC trade as a percentage of increase in the domestic market in DCs.

If protectionism appears to have had little effect on aggregate developing country performance, there is now considerable evidence that it has visited high costs on the industrial countries. Detailed studies of different industries in a wide range of industrial countries suggest that protection is a very costly and relatively ineffective way of protecting workers in the declining industries, at best slowing the inevitable adjustment somewhat (Cable, 1983). In some cases protection encouraged the substitution of labour saving equipment in the industrial countries which resulted in a large fall in the labour force, whilst in other cases employment fell as the industries continued their inevitable decline.

Table 9, which is taken directly from Balassa (1983), places LDC manufactured exports to industrial countries in perspective, though it is taken from a different source and is not directly comparable with the earlier tables.

First, except for clothing, exports from industrial countries are still large relative to imports from developing countries for most manufactured goods. Second, although imports from LDCs have been growing fast, they still represent a small share of apparent consumption in the industrial countries. Third, the share of imports from LDCs in incremental consumption in industrial countries ($\Delta M/\Delta C$) increased in all categories except 'other semi-manufactures' in the period 1978–81 compared to 1973–78. Part of the explanation for the fall in the growth rate of manufactures from LDCs must therefore be the recession in the industrialized countries, which may be temporary (though the protectionist measures which it precipitated may not be so easily reversed). Fourth, the incremental shares of imports from LDCs are small for all categories except clothing, which rose from 19.6% to 41.5% in the second sub-period. Even without protection, one would expect demand factors to cause a fall in clothing import growth rates.

Thus protection directed against LDCs has relatively little effect in aggregate, is directed at a problem which looks quantitatively small, and yet is costly, both to the industrial countries, and to the poorer developing countries which have been most adversely affected. Moreover, protection cannot protect export markets, which, as Table 9 shows, remain quantitatively important for most manufactured products. Although employment fell in import competing industries, the industrial countries retain a surplus in trade in manufactured goods with developing countries, and the employment gains resulting from the increase in developed country exports to LDCs appear to have exceeded the employment losses by a substantial amount. For example, Balassa estimates the net employment gains to the industrialized countries in 1981 to be 1.47 million (Balassa, 1983, Table 6), with only clothing experiencing a fall in employment. Given the excess capacity in the industrialized countries in the later part of the period, the exports to LDCs made possible by their imports would enable a balanced budget multiplier process to increase GDP in the developed countries. To illustrate this, Cable and Weale (1983) studied the effects of eliminating UK trade barriers against LDC exports of manufactured goods using the Cambridge Growth Project multisectoral model. They concluded that this would lead to a significant overall increase in the real level of GDP and in employment. It follows that growth in manufactured trade was comparatively advantageous, and despite costly attempts to limit its effects, it appears to have allowed the successful exporting LDCs to weather the oil shocks remarkably well, whilst mitigating the recession in the developed countries.

Quite apart from the detrimental effects of protectionism on standards of living and employment in the developed countries, it has apparently had a rather perverse effect on the distribution of income among developing countries. As we have seen, countries such as the Far Eastern NICs have been able to respond to trade barriers by concentrating on new markets and new products and have thus sustained reasonably high rates of export growth. On the other hand exporters such as the poor South Asian countries have found it much more difficult to adapt in the same way. In part this may be a consequence of inadequate policies, but their task is certainly made more difficult by the shortages of skills, infrastructure and marketing experience which are a feature of countries with unsophisticated manufacturing sectors. Hence, the cost of the trade barriers falls disproportionately on the poorest countries rather than on the countries against which the barriers were originally directed.

The policy implications of this study follow directly. Protectionism has not been very effective at reducing imports into the developed economies, and to the extent that it was successful, it probably reduced developed country exports of manufactured goods by as much, or more, than it reduced imports. It harmed the poorest developing countries disproportionately. On both efficiency and equity grounds, therefore, there is a powerful case for removing trade barriers directed against developing countries. If all industrial countries acted together, all would gain from the stimulus given to their exports, as well as from the reduction in the threat to financial stability caused by LDC debt. But even if coordinated action is not feasible, the various studies and simulations for the UK suggest that it is still in its interests unilaterally to dismantle these trade barriers, and the same is almost certainly true for most other industrial countries.

Discussion

Ravi Kanbur
World Bank and University of Essex

The object of this paper is to analyze the performance of LDC manufactured exports, and in particular to locate the role of protectionist measures in the DCs as a determinant of this performance. The way an economist would think of export performance would be in terms of supply side factors and demand side factors – protectionist measures would be one of the several possible demand side factors. Ideally, what one would like is to estimate structural equations capturing these different factors and hence to assess their quantitative impact. The high degree of simultaneity and interaction, and the fact that a number of different exogenous factors such as OPEC I and OPEC II have clouded the historical picture somewhat, would seem to recommend an explicitly econometric approach. This is *not* the approach the authors have taken. The authors' method is 'tabular' rather than econometric.

Much of my unease with the conclusions of this paper is that although they seem to make sense in terms of my intuitions about the world economy, I do not have a sense of the statistical significance of the different factors which are argued to affect LDC manufactured export performance. I certainly do not have a feel for their relative quantitative importance, and, as we shall see, these magnitudes could well be crucial from a policy point of view. However, in what follows I take the authors' approach as given, and examine what we can get out of it.

Table 4 contains the gist of the story. There is of course a reduction of growth rates, by and large, as one moves from left to right. But what is interesting is the performance of the different groups relative to each other. In particular, the Far Eastern NICs did better than the NECs pre 1970, but the position was reversed post 1970. What is the story behind this remarkable turnaround? Before 1970 the NICs were doing extraordinarily well. The standard explanation for this is their outward looking policies (note that this does not necessarily mean that they were free market policies), which are contrasted with the import substitution policies followed by the South Asian countries – both groups of countries having comparative advantage in labour intensive manufactures. The authors do not provide a story as to the poor performance of the NECs relative to the NICs in this period, but they do put forward three possible reasons for the reversal of the NIC/NEC ranking post 1970:

(i) The NICs were running out of surplus labour, i.e. the balance of comparative advantage was changing against manufactured exports.

(ii) The NICs became large relative to total world exports, i.e. they started moving down the world demand curve.

(iii) The NIC's demand curve shifted to the left (or at least did not shift to the right as fast as it was doing before) because of protectionist measures in the industrial countries. The NECs rushed in to fill the gap.

As noted earlier, the main problem is that in the absence of an econometric analysis it is not clear if any one or all of these explanations are statistically significant. One does not have a feel for the importance of the comparative advantage argument versus the demand curve argument. However, it could be argued that the authors' objective is to focus on protectionism and to establish its effects.

Given this, I would have liked to have seen a closer link between the timing of protectionist measures and the shift in the relative performance of NICs versus NECs. Also, the exact nature of these measures is important. Tariffs are commodity specific, while voluntary export restraints are country *and* commodity specific. If the bulk of protectionist measures were commodity specific then it is difficult to see how the NECs could rush in to fill the gap left by the NICs in those commodities. Since 'The degree of protectionism' is the key independent variable in the authors' analysis, I would have liked to have seen much more on its quantification and documentation, sub-period by sub-period, to match up with the sort of relative export performance figures presented in Table 4.

The quantification of the three factors behind the relative slowing down of the NICs is important precisely because the policy conclusions that follow from each are so different. If the slowdown is attributed largely to a disappearance of surplus labour the conclusion is that this is a natural stage in development and in the shifting balance of comparative advantage. If the 'end of surplus labour' stage has not been reached and demand side factors dominate, we have to ask what the consequences are of urging, as international agencies are doing these days, *all* cheap labour economies to export manufactures. The systemic effects of this warn us to be careful in accepting any such panacea. Relatedly, if protection is important, what are LDCs to do? If they expand beyond a point in manufactures, they face restrictions. What does comparative advantage mean in such a situation?

Thus the policy conclusions of a study such as this are extremely important, and I end by calling upon the authors and others to do a more systematic and detailed quantification of LDC manufactured export performance.

Paul Krugman
Massachusetts Institute of Technology

This paper contains a surprising mix of approaches. Most of the paper is what might be called a data survey: evidence on the growth of LDC manufactures is presented in a way that is certainly not dictated by any explicit theory, and is even relatively free from implicit theorizing. In the midst of this atheoretic empirical survey, however, is a quite exotic model, with at least three unconventional and controversial assumptions. The mix is disconcerting, which is not necessarily a bad thing; but I am not convinced that it is productive in this case.

Let me begin with the data survey. The authors attempt to shed light on the effects of protection by presenting a number of tables that compare growth rates of exports across groups of countries, industries and time periods. This presentation is somewhat difficult to follow, largely because the authors show a peculiar fastidiousness about aggregating their data to make their points. What they offer are not two by two or three by three tabulations, but large tables with many entries. Presumably one is supposed to scan across these large tables and arrive at a sense of what is going on; this is an art which I guess I have not fully mastered.

What the authors find, if I understand their argument correctly, are three main facts. First, LDC manufactures exports as a whole have not slowed their growth to the extent that a direct examination of OECD restrictions might have led one to expect. Second, there has nonetheless been some replacement of OECD imports from the NICs by imports from a second-tier group, the NECs. Third, the NICs have to some extent substituted around trade barriers by shifting to other lines of production and third world markets.

These facts are not crystal clear in the data presented, but I have no doubt that they are correct. The reason is that it is hard to imagine a model that would not predict these results from the kind of increased protection that we have seen – namely, restrictions aimed at specific exporters of specific goods. Consider a world in which there are four trade flows: NICs to OECD, NICs to third world, NECs to OECD, NECs to third world. Surely almost any model (except possibly for one with very strongly decreasing costs) would lead one to believe that these four flows are substitutes. Restrict NIC–OECD trade in manufactures and the other three flows will increase. The result will then be that overall OECD imports and overall NIC exports fall less than the direct restrictiveness of the quotas would suggest, while NEC exports rise and NIC exports are diverted. So Hughes and Newbery's conclusions must be right, whatever the data says.

To reach this conclusion a very conventional model will suffice – say, a common or garden variety supply and demand model with transport costs. What the authors suggest instead is an unusual model. This model has three features that I would not have expected. First, it assumes from the start that changes in the origin of manufactures exports result from locational shifts by multinational firms. Second, firms are assumed to need to finance growth from profits, giving the model a Kaldorian flavour. Third, there are assumed to be learning effects that are both firm specific and to some extent country specific. The resulting model of the firm is not easy to work with, and in fact the authors stop short of attempting to go from a description of the firm to a description of the market. That is, the approach is not even partial equilibrium.

Now unconventionality in modelling is a virtue – but only if it is aimed at explaining something that conventional analysis cannot. What is troubling here is that the various non-neoclassical features of the model do not seem to be doing any work for us. In fact, by focussing on an exotic model the authors seem to be led astray from simple insights that conventional models would make clear. For example, the authors at one point say that trade restrictions, while they did not much restrict LDC exports, were highly costly to the industrial countries. A conventional model, whatever its limitations, would have made clear that this is not a reasonable assertion: either import restrictions were binding or they were not.

Does this mean that we should be content to address the issue of OECD protection with standard competitive models? Surely not. The nexus between rapid growth and manufactures exports for a few lucky LDCs is one of the key riddles of economic development, and we will never understand it with conventional trade models. To assess the impact of OECD protection on the continuance of this economic miracle will also therefore require innovative analysis. The question is how to get there. The mix of data survey and theory in this paper was, I believe, intended to provide a set of 'stylized facts' and a model that gains credence by its ability to explain them. This is in general an approach of which I highly approve. It only works, however, if the stylized facts are surprising, and the model both resolves our puzzlement and has interesting further implications. Unfortunately the facts the authors uncover are not surprising, and therefore the model's ability to explain them does not make it more convincing. In any case the model itself does not have obvious further implications. In the end we have a useful data survey, but are still waiting for a good story about what it all means.

General Discussion

Giorgio Basevi believed it was necessary to look not only at the effects of protectionism on the flow of goods between countries but also on movements of factors of production. Capital would flow into the developing countries from the industrialized countries to take advantage of cheap labour. At the same time labour migration would occur in the opposite direction as workers in the LDCs were attracted by higher wages in the developed economies. Heightened protectionism would reduce the flow of capital to the LDCs and at the same time increase labour migration into the developed economies.

Gerhard Fels thought the continued growth of NIC and NEC exports in spite of VERs and other forms of protectionism in large part reflected the policing difficulties experienced by the bureaucracies charged with administering them. As a result there was almost a 'shadow economy' in international trade. Nevertheless it was difficult to assess the impact of protection because of the absence of a suitable counterfactual. Would the NICs have switched from textiles to electronics in the absence of protectionist measures by the developed countries? VERs also created uncertainty – how had this affected investment?

Patrick Minford was unconvinced that VERs on the NICs imposed significant costs. There was a wide range of alternative product lines which firms could move into in the face of protectionist measures as well as relocating in the NECs. Although there would always be distortionary costs imposed by protectionist measures they could be relatively trivial if these alternative product lines were very close substitutes for protected goods.

Charles Wyplosz pointed out that it was difficult for every country to experience export-led growth simultaneously. He argued that selective protectionist measures could be seen as a way of fostering new industries in the developing countries. These countries did not possess sufficiently large home markets to promote industrial development and access to foreign markets was essential. Placing VERs on the NICs had allowed the next generation of developing countries, the NECs, to industrialize. Placing VERs on the NECs in turn might then allow the next group of developing countries to industrialize successfully and so on.

Appendix A. Data on LDC exports of manufactured goods

The primary source of data used in this study is the UN trade database maintained by the UN Statistical Office from which statistics published in the UN *Yearbook of International Trade Statistics* (annual), IMF *Direction of Trade Yearbook* (annual), IMF International Financial Statistics *Supplement on Trade Statistics* (1982) and *World Development Report* (annual) appendices are obtained. The figures refer to the fob value of exports by SITC classification as reported by the exporting country. Differences between countries and over time in the basis for reporting export values are inevitable in a data source of this kind, with the result that different institutions seek to correct for non-comparabilities in their own ways which leads to difficulties in reconciling estimates of, say, trade growth rates. The major problems which we have identified concern: (a) the classification of precious metals and diamonds – this obviously affects South Africa most of all; (b) the treatment of exports from duty-free export processing zones – these are very important in Mexico and are the source of the major discrepancy between the OECD import statistics, which include such exports as Mexican exports, and the UN export figures which exclude this trade; (c) differences in the classification of goods by importing and exporting countries which are the cause of discrepancies between the reported value of exports to OECD countries and imports into the OECD as reported by the OECD – which uses import data reported by the importing country.

The compilation and publication of UN trade statistics is a lengthy process and the *Yearbook of International Trade Statistics* for 1983 had not been published by the time that this paper went to press. Hence, for 1983 we have used provisional or estimated figures based on published material relating to total exports for each country in 1983 and, when better data was not available, the share of manufactures in total

Table A1. Exports of manufactured goods at 1970 prices
($ billion)

	To developed market economies			To LCDs		
	1965	1973	1980	1965	1973	1980
From developed market economies	68.15	101.22	216.20	21.79	40.88	74.19
From LDCs	2.39	10.93	19.32	1.79	4.84	11.42
Share of LDC imports in increased imports (%)	8.4	13.2		14.0	16.4	

Source: UN *Yearbook of International Trade Statistics*, 1981.
Notes: The growth rate estimates are sensitive to the method of price deflation used. For this table the data is primarily obtained from Special Table D in the source which gives trade flows and unit value indices (1970 = 100) for each matrix element (i.e. from country group to country, by SITC, by year). The UN grouping of developing market economies includes certain OPEC countries such as Libya, Kuwait, Qatar, Saudi Arabia which are excluded from the developing country category by other sources. Manufactured goods are those classified under SITC categories 5–8 excluding 68 (non-ferrous metals).

exports in 1982. This is likely to understate rates of growth to 1983 since for most countries the share of manufactured goods in total exports has been growing since 1980. Trade data for Taiwan since 1976, which is not included in any UN publications, were obtained from the *Monthly Statistics of Exports and Imports of the Republic of China* (various issues). Odd gaps in data series have been filled by the use of country sources, the World Bank database, and miscellaneous international sources. Further details concerning the data used in this paper will be provided by the authors in response to specific requests for information.

Various studies have used different definitions of manufactured goods. Here we have, as far as possible, adopted the definition used by the UN – viz. all goods classified under SITC categories 5 to 8 with the exception of category 68 (non-ferrous metals). The analysis of trade by industrial origin in Section 4 is based on the ISIC classification and there is no simple relationship between SITC and ISIC categories. The ISIC definition of manufactured goods – those covered by categories 31 to 39 – is much broader than the SITC definition, so that care is required in comparing manufactured export performance measured according to the different definitions.

Table A2. Shares and growth rates of manufactured exports by LDC category and industrial origin, 1970–80

| | Industrial Origin (ISIC) | | | | | | | | | |
	Food, drink, tobacco 31	Textiles, clothing 32	Wood products 33	Paper products 34	Chemicals 35	Non-metal minerals 36	Basic metals 37	Metal products 38	Misc. 39	All industries
% Composition of Total Manufactured Exports for All Countries, 1970										
Far Eastern NICs	1.5	8.4	1.2	0.2	2.9	0.2	0.4	4.7	3.8	23.2
European NICs	4.0	3.9	0.8	0.8	2.7	0.4	2.1	5.3	0.4	20.5
Other NICs	7.8	1.2	0.5	0.6	2.4	0.2	3.4	2.8	1.1	20.0
ASEAN NECs	2.9	0.1	0.7	0.0	0.7	0.1	1.8	0.2	0.2	6.7
North Africa and Middle East NECs	0.7	0.3	0.0	0.1	0.2	0.0	0.1	0.1	0.0	1.6
Latin America NECs	2.5	0.3	0.1	0.2	0.2	0.0	5.3	0.1	0.0	8.8
South Asia	1.1	3.5	0.0	0.0	0.3	0.1	0.6	0.7	0.2	6.5
Tropical Africa	0.9	0.1	0.1	0.0	0.4	0.0	0.1	0.2	0.0	1.8
Central America and Caribbean	1.5	0.4	0.1	0.1	1.0	0.0	0.1	0.2	0.0	3.5
Oil Producers	1.1	0.8	0.0	0.0	4.9	0.0	0.3	0.2	0.1	7.3
All Countries	24.0	19.1	3.6	2.0	15.7	1.1	14.3	14.4	5.9	100.0

% Annual Growth Rates of Manufactured Exports, 1970–80

Far Eastern NICs	10.5	12.1	9.5	16.1	17.2	21.6	23.4	20.4	9.9	14.8
European NICs	2.6	7.4	5.8	8.7	12.9	16.8	9.6	11.5	6.6	9.2
Other NICs	4.9	11.0	3.3	8.9	6.9	13.1	4.1	11.5	32.7	10.8
ASEAN NECs	8.8	30.4	11.9	7.9	13.7	10.5	7.3	31.6	23.9	12.7
North Africa and Middle East NECs	0.5	17.4	12.7	3.4	20.4	12.6	2.1	16.9	3.3	11.0
Latin America NECs	−3.4	14.6	13.7	11.9	19.8	14.4	−1.9	16.6	27.0	1.7
South Asia	3.4	4.2	13.2	0.5	12.1	4.7	−13.7	8.1	5.0	4.3
Tropical Africa	1.9	5.4	5.1	5.8	12.6	4.0	−5.9	3.1	17.4	5.3
Central America and Caribbean	0.6	2.4	−1.6	8.2	3.6	4.7	20.6	4.2	10.2	3.0
Oil producers	−2.2	−3.6	6.0	4.7	8.5	3.3	9.2	6.6	11.0	6.4
All Countries	4.2	9.9	8.2	9.7	11.8	15.1	5.1	15.4	18.6	10.3

Note: Manufactured goods are here defined as those originating from enterprises classified under ISIC 31–39.

Appendix B. Model of the effect of quotas

Technology Transfer to NECs

Consider the investment decision of an MNC in a particular NEC. The maximum initial level of production will be limited by, amongst other things, the size and complexity of the manufacturing sector, the availability of skilled labour, transport infrastructure, etc. The following variables can now be defined:

q maximum initial production scale (units p.a)
p world price (marginal production is exported)
v capital-gross output ratio (value terms)
s fraction of revenue reinvested
g maximum feasible rate of growth of production
w wage rate, constant
ϕ labour required/unit output
r discount rate, $r > g$
K_t capital stock at t
F set up cost for exporting
z opportunity cost of expertise per unit of initial capacity

Learning-by-doing implies that ϕ is a function of cumulative total production, or, more simply, of cumulative investment, K. Let

$$\phi = aK^{-\mu} = aK_0^{-\mu} e^{-\mu g t}, \quad \mu > 0. \tag{B1}$$

Profits available for repatriation at t are

$$((1-s)p - w\phi_t)q_t. \tag{B2}$$

Investment out of retentions in steady growth is

$$\dot{K} = spq_t = \frac{spK}{v} = gK, \tag{B3}$$

so

$$sp = vg. \tag{B4}$$

The present discounted net value of investment in the NEC is

$$V = \int_0^\infty [(1-s)p - w\phi]q_t e^{-rt} \, dt - K_0 - \dot{F}$$

$$= \frac{(p - vg)}{r - g} q - \frac{awK_0^{-\mu} q}{r - (1-\mu)g} - K_0 - F, \tag{B5}$$

$$V = \left(\frac{p - vg}{r - g} - \frac{awK_0^{-\mu}}{r - (1-\mu)g} - v \right) q - F, \tag{B6}$$

since $K_0 = vq$. Simplifying, this becomes

$$V = \psi(p)q - F, \tag{B7}$$

where

$$\psi(p) = \frac{p - rv}{r - g} - \frac{aw(vg)^{-\mu}}{r - (1 - \mu)g}. \tag{B8}$$

If one unit of managerial expertise is required per unit of initial capacity (and any overheads can be added to the fixed costs F) then the present value of rent per unit of expertise is

$$\frac{V}{q} = \psi(p) - \frac{F}{q}.$$

If the opportunity cost of expertise is z then it will be unattractive to invest in any country for which the maximum initial capacity, q, is smaller than q^*, where q^* solves

$$\psi(p) - \frac{F}{q^*} = z$$

or

$$q^* = \frac{F}{\psi(p) - z}. \tag{B9}$$

This value defines the critical production level at which developing countries graduate to become NECs, as shown in Figure 2 of Section 3.

Relocation of MNCs fron NICs to NECs

An MNC currently operating in a NIC can continue production, in which case its current management team remains tied to the NIC, or it can sell out to a local producer and transfer its expertise elsewhere. The following additional variables defined the model:

Q current output,
γ rate of growth of demand, $\gamma \leq g$,
λ expertise/unit of output, $\lambda < 1$,
W wage costs per unit of output, constant,
α discount factor when selling firm, $\alpha < 1$.

Wage costs are assumed constant because increases in productivity are assumed to be offset by increasing wage rates, reflecting the tight labour market conditions of the NICs. If the firm sells, the present value of the current capital stock, assuming no subsequent expansion, is $(p - W)Q/r$ but it is assumed that only a fraction of this, α, would be realised. The net advantage of staying rather than moving is

$$V^s = \frac{((1-s)p - W)Q}{r - \gamma} - \frac{\alpha(p - W)Q}{r} - \lambda Qz. \tag{B10}$$

But $sp = v\gamma$, so

$$V^s = \left(\frac{p - v\gamma - W}{r - \gamma} - \frac{\alpha(p - W)}{r} - \lambda z \right) Q. \tag{B11}$$

The effect of quota restrictions

Quotas have two effects on NICs – they reduce the rate of growth of demand, γ, and possibly raise the market clearing price, p. This effect on V^s can be found by differentiating:

$$\frac{\partial V^s}{\partial p} = \frac{r - \alpha(r - \gamma)}{r(r - \gamma)} > 0, \tag{B12}$$

$$\frac{\partial V^s}{\partial \gamma} = \frac{p - rv - W}{(r - \gamma)^2} > 0, \tag{B13}$$

(since $p - W > rV$ if further investment is to be justified).

Thus lowering the growth rate will tend to encourage MNCs to move (at constant z) whilst raising the price (by the shadow price of the quota) will discourage movement. Suppose before the quota the NMC were on the margin of indifference between staying and moving to a NEC of 'size' q (i.e. $vs = 0$). This gives an expression for the opportunity cost of experience, z, from (B11) and (B9):

$$z = \chi(p, \gamma) = \frac{V}{q} = \psi(p) - \frac{F}{q}, \tag{B14}$$

where

$$\chi(p, \gamma) = \frac{1}{\lambda} \left(\frac{p - v\gamma - W}{2 - \gamma} - \frac{\alpha(p - W)}{r} \right).$$

This can be solved for q:

$$q^* = \frac{F}{\psi - \chi}. \tag{B15}$$

For any set of parameters, particularly p and γ, equation (B15) defines the margin at which technological transfer will next occur.

Now we ask what happens to q^* as the quota is imposed. If the quota has no effect on the growth rate of NEC exports (which have not yet reached the limit set by the quota), then

$$\frac{\partial q^*}{\partial \gamma} = \frac{F}{(\psi - \chi)^2} \frac{\partial \chi}{\partial \gamma} = \frac{F}{(\psi - \chi)^2} \frac{1}{\lambda Q} \frac{\partial V^s}{\partial \gamma} > 0, \tag{B16}$$

so a fall in the allowed NIC export growth rate unambiguously lowers the threshold, and hence will cause a shift of MNC investment to potential NEC graduates.

The effect of a rise in the export price p is given by

$$\frac{\partial q^*}{\partial p} = \frac{F}{\lambda (\psi - \chi)^2} \left(\frac{\lambda}{r - g} + \frac{\alpha}{r} - \frac{1}{r - \gamma} \right). \tag{B17}$$

If λ and/or α are high (near 1), then this will be negative so a rise in p will lower the threshold and cause MNCs to relocate to potential NEC graduates. Only if λ and α are both small will this effect be thwarted – that is if it is expensive to leave (low α) and would not release much managerial talent (low λ).

References

Arrow, K. J. (1962), 'The Economic Implications of Learning by Doing', *Review of Economic Studies*.

Balassa, B. (1983). 'Trends in International Trade in Manufactured Goods and Structural Change in the Industrial Countries', paper given to the IEA 7th World Congress.

Balassa, B. and C. Balassa (1984). 'Industrial Protection in the Developed Countries', *The World Economy*.

Cable, V. (1983). *Protectionism and Industrial Decline*, Hodder and Stoughton/ODI, London.

Cable, V. and M. Weale (1983). 'Economic Costs of Sectoral Protection', *The World Economy*.

Chen, E. K. Y. (1983). *Multinational Corporations, Technology and Employment*, Macmillan Press, London.

Hughes, H. and A. Krueger (1984). 'Effects of Protection in Developed Countries on Developing Countries' Exports of Manufactures', Chap 11 in R. E. Baldwin and A. O. Krueger (eds) *The Structure and Evolution of Recent US Trade Policy*, NBER/University of Chicago Press, Chicago.

Lall, S. and others (1984). *The New Multinationals: the Spread of Third World Enterprise*, John Wiley and Sons, Chichester, England.

Marris, R. (1964). *The Economic Theory of 'Managerial' Capitalism* Macmillan, London.

OECD (1979). *The Impact of the Newly Industrialising Countries on Production and Trade in Manufactures*, OECD, Paris.

Page, S. (1980). 'The Increased Use of Trade Controls by the Industrialised Countries', *Inter-Economics*.

—— (1981), 'The Revival of Protectionism and Its Consequences for Europe', *Journal of Common Market Studies*.

Penrose, E. T. (1959). *The Theory of the Growth of the Firm*, Blackwell, Oxford.

Silberston, Z. A. (1984). *The Multifibre Arrangement and the UK Economy*, HMSO, London.

UN Center on Transnational Corporations (1983). *Transnational Corporations in World Development: Third Survey*, UN, New York.

—— (1984) *CTC Reporter*, Vol 17.

—— (1985). *Transnational Companies and International Trade: Selected Issues*, UN, New York.

Wells, L. T. (1983). *Third World Multinationals*, MIT Press, Cambridge, Mass.

Winters, L. A. (1985). 'Non-Tariff Barrier Negotiations between Developing and Industrial Countries: Coverage and Internalisation Ratios', DRD Discussion Paper 119, World Bank, Washington, DC.

Wolf, M. (1983). 'Managed Trade in Practice: Implications of the Textile Arrangements', Ch. 14 in W. Cline (ed) – *Trade Policy in the 1980s*, Institute for International Economics/MIT Press, Washington, DC.

World Bank. *World Development Report*, annual from 1978, OUP, New York.

Economic Policy   April 1986   Printed in Great Britain

■■■■

SUMMARY

The EMS and the Dollar

Francesco Giavazzi and Alberto Giovannini

This paper examines the behaviour of exchange rates prior to and since the inception of the European Monetary System (EMS). Movements in bilateral European exchange rates tend to be associated with fluctuations in the dollar. In particular the mark tends to appreciate against other European currencies when the dollar depreciates. Further, most realignments of currencies in the EMS have generally occurred after sharp movements in the dollar. Conventional explanations relying on portfolio diversification by investors do not seem to explain the facts fully. A more satisfactory explanation is provided by the existence of capital controls. These limit the mobility of assets and ensure an asymmetric response by European currencies to movements in the dollar. These capital controls are, in the absence of coordinated monetary policy, essential to the smooth working of the EMS. However at the same time they limit the scope for the further integration of European capital markets. Thus the EMS is not a step on the road to greater financial integration. Indeed it is a cul-de-sac.

The EMS and the Dollar

Francesco Giavazzi
University of Venice
and
Alberto Giovannini
Columbia Business School

1. Introduction and Summary

The quest for exchange rate stability among European currencies has been present since the Bretton Woods system started to collapse. After the limited and unsatisfactory experience of the 'snake', the European Monetary System (EMS) emerged in 1979 and its success has surprised most observers, as the system has survived its detractors and the unprecedented swings of the dollar. While plans are being put forward to enlarge the scope and the size of the EMS, the markets are asking whether it would survive a likely future dollar depreciation.

The objective of this paper is to offer an analysis of the factors which work against attempts to limit exchange rate flexibility in Europe. We are able to establish that asymmetric movements of European exchange rates are indeed an empirical regularity, and we analyze in detail potential explanations of this asymmetry.

The conclusion of this paper is that the present system, in order to survive, has generated mechanisms which prevent further monetary integration.

Section 2 provides evidence on asymmetric movements of nominal exchange rates. We look at movements of daily, monthly and quarterly exchange rates to determine whether the data are consistent with the common observation that fluctuations in European exchange rates are associated in a systematic way with the dollar. We do find that this is a feature of the data, and one which is highlighted in specific episodes

* We would like to thank Susan Collins, Rudiger Dornbusch, Jeffrey Frankel, Maurice Obstfeld, Marco Pagano and Herakles Polemarchakis for discussions, John Williamson and the members of the Economic Policy panel for comments, and Utpal Bhattacharya for excellent research assistance. This project was supported in part by a grant from Consiglio Nazionale Delle Ricerche, research programme on Structure and Evolution of the Italian Economy.

of abrupt changes in the dollar rate. EMS realignments also tend to coincide systematically with sudden reversals in the value of the dollar.

Turning to the possible explanations of these regularities, we ask whether the predictions of international asset market equilibrium models are consistent with the evidence. This question is addressed in Section 3, where we look at two such models: a general model of equilibrium asset holdings, and a model of capital controls. First we carry out a few experiments to see whether the data is broadly consistent with some of the implications of portfolio models. As the theory predicts, covariations of output, money supplies, and asset stocks indeed go some way in explaining the data over the period preceding the EMS. During the EMS period, however, simple portfolio models are unable to explain the facts.

Next we analyse the effects of capital controls. The starting point of our analysis is the observation that the most important effect of capital controls is to increase transactions costs in assets denominated in the currencies that are subject to such controls. We show that these costs have three important consequences. They limit the number of agents who actively trade for portfolio purposes in currencies subject to capital controls. They make a country's financial assets less substitutable for assets denominated in other currencies, thereby enhancing the effectiveness of sterilized foreign exchange market intervention. Finally, they make price responses to exogenous shocks asymmetric between those assets which are costly to trade and those which are not. This result suggests the potential advantages of modelling capital controls explicitly in order to explain the empirical covariations of exchange rates.

In Section 4, we describe the main implications for policy of the evidence in Section 2, and the analysis in Section 3. In a system of fixed but adjustable parities there is a potential for exchange rate instability because countries have an incentive to move the exchange rate in order to shift the burden of adjustment onto their neighbours. In the presence of regional divergences, the fragility of fixed parities further increases because, as shown by Mundell (1968), exchange rate changes are the easiest instrument to use for redistributing asymmetric shocks when short term international factor mobility is low. If exchange rate realignments have periodically to be expected, the possibility of speculative attacks compels countries to choose between the welfare losses of capital controls and the losses arising from volatility of short term domestic interest rates. This tradeoff has so far been solved by imposing international capital controls, which by themselves limit the possibility of further financial integration in Europe.

2. Asymmetric fluctuations of European exchange rates

2.1. European bilateral exchange rates and the dollar: 1973–85

Many observers suggest that fluctuations of European exchange rates are often associated in a systematic way with fluctuations of the dollar: when the dollar is 'strong' in foreign exchange markets, the German mark tends to be 'weak' vis-à-vis other European currencies.[1]

Before looking at the data it is useful to warn that this statement taken literally could be a tautology. If, for example, a depreciation of the dollar vis-à-vis the mark reflects a strengthening of the mark it is no surprise that the mark also appreciates relative to other European currencies. More formally, if the variances of changes in bilateral exchange rates of European currencies relative to the dollar are of comparable magnitude, the covariance between changes in the dollar/mark rate and changes in the price of marks in terms of other European currencies is always negative. Therefore this type of empirical regularity is not at all surprising.[2]

The interesting question is whether fluctuations in the value of the dollar measured in terms of a weighted average of foreign currencies are systematically associated with fluctuations of bilateral European rates. By computing correlations between changes in the effective dollar rate and changes in bilateral European rates we avoid the problem of using the mark as a common reference point.

We report data for six European currencies (French franc, Italian lira, Belgian franc, Dutch guilder, pound Sterling, Swiss franc) plus the Japanese yen and Canadian dollar. Our data set includes daily observations (New York noon time) of exchange rates. We use daily percent exchange rate changes, and their averages over longer time periods.

The choice of the weights used to compute effective exchange rate indices depends on the nature of the empirical phenomena we want to document. Whereas shifts in international competitiveness are perhaps best measured by using effectve exchange rate indices constructed with trade weights, like for example the Multilateral Exchange Rate Model (MERM) weights of the International Monetary Fund, the correlations

---

[1] See, among others, Masera (1981), Thygesen (1981), Baer (1982), Kaufman (1985), Russo (1984), Giavazzi and Giovannini (1985a), Frankel (1985a, b), Dennis and Nellis (1984), Padoa Schioppa (1985).

[2] Let dln (DM/\$) indicate the percent change of the price of 1 dollar in terms of marks. For any other currency J:

$$2 \operatorname{Cov}[\operatorname{dln}(J/DM), \operatorname{dln}(DM/\$)] = \operatorname{Var}[(\operatorname{dln}(J/\$)] - \operatorname{Var}[\operatorname{dln}(J/DM)] - \operatorname{Var}[\operatorname{dln}(DM/\$)].$$

If the variability of bilateral exchange rates vis-à-vis the dollar is of comparable magnitude, we would expect the right hand side of the above expression to be negative. This problem is mentioned in Frankel (1980).

we want to analyse are most likely produced by disturbances in asset markets. Thus we need weights which represent the relative importance of each currency in the world financial market. We decided to compute GNP weights, because the more natural monetary weights reflect in some cases just different definitions of the corresponding monetary aggregate adopted by different countries. A comparison of our index with the MERM index shows, for example, that the 1980 MERM weight of the Canadian dollar in the US dollar index is 18.5%, whereas the weight of the mark is only 13.6%; in contrast, those two currencies have weights equal to 7.5% and 19.2% respectively in our index.

Table 1A reports the estimated percent changes in bilateral rates vis-à-vis the mark associated with each per cent change in the dollar effective rate. The coefficients are obtained simply by regressing the percentage change in each bilateral rate in turn on the percentage change in the effective dollar rate. A minus sign indicates that when the effective dollar appreciates the mark depreciates vis-à-vis the currency considered.

The first two rows of the table show the experience before and during the EMS. From June 1973 to March 1979 asymmetric movements of the mark and other currencies relative to the dollar are quite large. For example, a one percent depreciation of the effective rate of the dollar is associated, on average, with a 0.6% depreciation of the lira relative to the mark, a 0.56% depreciation of the pound, and a 0.23 and 0.16% depreciation of the Belgian franc and the French franc, respectively. On the other hand the Swiss franc appreciates on average by 0.32%. At the two extremes of the spectrum are the Dutch guilder, which follows the mark most closely, and the Canadian dollar, whose price in marks displays the largest negative correlation with the effective dollar rate.

The second row of the table indicates that the start of the EMS represents an important break in the data. After March 1979 a change in the effective dollar rate is associated with smaller fluctuations of bilateral rates with the mark. This is true for the currencies participating in the EMS, but also for the pound, the Swiss franc, the yen, and the Canadian dollar.

The periods before and after March 1979 are characterized not only by the emergence of the European Monetary System, but also by different long-term movements of the dollar exchange rate. The EMS period includes a prolonged appreciation of the effective exchange rate of the dollar (November 1978 to August 1981). Before the EMS, instead, we observe a dramatic depreciation of the dollar (May 1977 to October 1978). This seems to suggest that after March 1979 it has been easier for the 'soft' currencies to move along with the mark (because this

Table 1A. The effective dollar and bilateral mark exchange rates: daily data

Dutch Guilder	Belgian Franc	French Franc	Italian Lira	Pound Sterling	Swiss Franc	Japanese Yen	Canadian Dollar
Before EMS (1 June 1973 to 9 March 1979)							
−0.09	−0.23	−0.16	−0.60	−0.56	0.32	−0.53	−1.40
EMS period (12 March 1979 to 15 October 1985)							
−0.07	−0.03*	−0.02	−0.12	−0.17	0.07	−0.27	−0.99
Dollar depreciating (13 May 1977 to 31 October 1978)							
−0.08	−0.10	−0.26	−0.69	−0.34	0.72	−0.17	−1.27
Dollar depreciating (19 March 1985 to 15 October 1985)							
−0.11	−0.19	−0.06*	0.00*	0.22	0.06*	−0.65	−1.10
Dollar appreciating (1 November 1978 to 5 August 1981)							
−0.02	−0.07	−0.08	−0.26	−0.29	0.23	−0.15	−1.10

Regression coefficients of percent changes in each currency's price of the mark on percent changes of the effective dollar index. A negative sign indicates that a dollar depreciation is associated with a depreciation vis-à-vis the mark. Regressions include a constant term. The data is described in the Data appendix. A * indicates that the estimated coefficient is insignificantly different from zero.

required a depreciation vis-à-vis the dollar) than before the EMS, when to follow the mark they should have appreciated relative to the dollar. A comparison of the two periods of dollar depreciation (one before the EMS, the other in 1985) sheds some light on this question. The data indicates that during the 1985 fall of the dollar asymmetries among European currencies decrease dramatically relative to the previous dollar depreciation experience. Therefore explanations of the asymmetric movement of European currencies which only rely on the trend of the effective dollar exchange rate are invalidated by the recent data.

Are the general patterns observed in the daily data reproduced over longer time periods? Table 1B presents the same evidence as in Table 1A using quarterly data. Results for the period preceding March 1979 indicate that asymmetries tend to fade away over longer time intervals.

2.2. Exchange rate crises in the EMS and the dollar

As Mussa (1979) pointed out, exchange rate dynamics are characterized by periods of quiescence followed by periods of turbulence, in which day-to-day movements are large and frequently in the same direction.

Studying movements of exchange rates during crises is interesting for at least three reasons. First, as Mussa (1979) suggested, it is unlikely that the crises are simply a statistical artefact associated with the stochastic properties of exchange rates. It is likely, instead, that they reflect instances when 'the market changes its mind'. Second, it is often argued that although 'fundamentals' play the essential role in EMS realign-

Table 1B. The effective dollar and bilateral mark exchange rates: quarterly data

Dutch Guilder	Belgian Franc	French Franc	Italian Lira	Pound Sterling	Swiss Franc	Japanese Yen	Canadian Dollar
Before EMS (1973Q3–1979Q1)							
−0.17†	−0.07	−0.18	−0.23	−0.16	0.16	−0.07	−1.40†
EMS period (1972Q2–1985Q3)							
0.05	0.04	0.04	−0.16†	−0.01	0.15	−0.28	−1.00†

See note to table 1A. A † indicates that the coefficient is significantly different from zero.

ments, the exact timing of realignments has often been determined by dollar crises.[3] Finally, it is possible that asymmetric exchange rate movements are in general more evident during periods of turbulence than during periods of calm.

To what extent are EMS crises associated with dollar crises? Figure 1 shows the effective dollar index over the EMS period and highlights the dates of the realignments. In each realignment the mark has been revalued relative to (subsets of) the other EMS currencies. An interesting regularity which emerges from Figure 1 is the fact that all but one[4] EMS realignments take place after a fall of the dollar, and are followed by a dollar recovery. This phenomenon is particularly evident in the 1983 and 1985 episodes, but is also present, though to a smaller degree, during the first half of the EMS experience.

Figure 1 naturally raises the important question of what determines EMS realignments. As we discuss below in Section 4, in order to identify the policy motivations for exchange rate realignments, we need to study the behaviour of real exchange rates, i.e the behaviour of aggregate relative price indices. Figure 1 can be used, however, to dispel the naive notion that sharp dollar fluctuations necessarily lead to an EMS realignment. The figure shows many instances where large dollar movements have not been followed by EMS realignments.

Nevertheless there are several examples, often reported by the financial press, when EMS strains developed in association with large

---

[3] The *Financial Times* of September 25, 1979 reported: 'The main reason for the strains is the big difference in the economic performance of the EMS participants . . . but the final twist has been provided by the renewed dollar crisis . . . pressures were so intense that a meeting of EEC ministers had to be arranged hurriedly for Sunday.'

[4] On February 22, 1982 the Belgian franc and the Danish krone were devalued with respect to all other EMS currencies. The realignment was then attributed to 'diminishing confidence in the future performance of the Belgian economy' (Horst Ungerer, 1983).

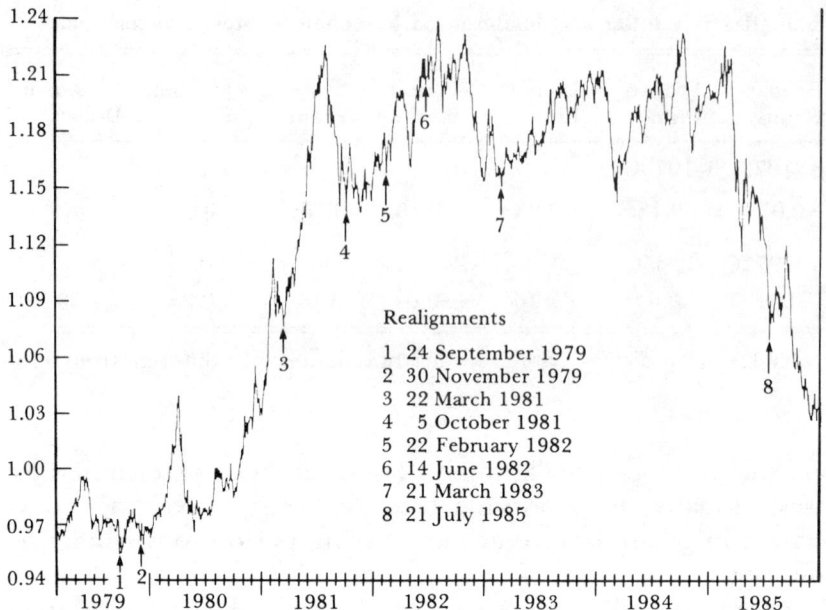

Figure 1. Effective dollar index (1980=1.00) and EMS realignments

movements of the dollar exchange rate. For example[5] a sharp and soon reversed dollar appreciation in April 1980 was accompanied by a sudden strengthening of the lira, the French franc and the Belgian franc with respect to the mark, which fell to the bottom of its fluctuation band. When the dollar surge reversed itself the lira and the French franc suffered sharp losses relative to the mark. This episode is interesting because it shows an instance when the dollar movement strengthened the lira and the French franc at a time when no significant change in underlying economic forces (fundamentals) was observed.

---

[5] For instance, the *Financial Times* reported, on the following dates: November 30, 1979; 'The crisis has crept up almost by stealth in the EMS over the past week – partly as a consequence of the sharp rise of the DM against the dollar in the wake of the monetary confrontation between the US and Iran. . . . The singling out of the Deutsche mark once again as the main international target for currency speculation when the dollar gets into trouble is likely to remain a source of strain in the EMS.' April 1, 1980: 'Dollar rises to two-year peak. . . . The DM weakens in the EMS. . . . The lira, recently weak in the EMS is now firmer against most EMS currencies . . . The French franc, firmer at the top of the EMS, improved again against the DM.' April 4, 1980: 'The DM required support against the French franc last week to keep it within the agreed EMS limits. The French franc at the top of the EMS gave assistance to its weakest partner.' March 19, 1981: 'The dollar lost ground rapidly in currency markets . . . European currencies continued to show strains within the EMS. The Lira eased to its divergence limit; the system suffered further pressure as the Belgian franc stood resolute outside its divergence limit.' March 20, 1981: 'The time is ripe for the long overdue, carefully rehearsed piece of theatre of DM revaluation . . . especially if it is accompanied by more signs from across the Atlantic that President Reagan's dollar levitation act is starting to lose its magic.'

2.3. Summary of the empirical regularities: what needs to be explained

In order to fix ideas, we conclude our survey of empirical regularities with a short summary of the most important findings.

The asymmetric movements of European exchange rates relative to the dollar which this section has attempted to document are indeed present in the data.

The daily data show that asymmetries among European currencies are more evident during the period preceding the EMS and during the first dollar depreciation period. These asymmetries tend to disappear in quarterly data.

Evidence for the 1985 dollar depreciation suggests that the observed asymmetries among European rates cannot be explained solely by trends in the dollar exchange rate.

Although on average asymmetric exchange rate movements have decreased during the European Monetary System, we find that several episodes of strain in the EMS are associated with a substantial weakening of the effective dollar rate.

In order to clarify the policy implications of the statistical regularities documented in this section we need to identify and assess possible causes of the observed exchange rate movements. We want to determine whether the empirical observations can be explained by two families of models: those that stress differences in international asset substitutability (portfolio models), and those that highlight differences of international capital mobility across assets denominated in various currencies. These models are described and evaluated in the next section.

3. International portfolio models: do they explain the evidence?

The short run nature of the nominal exchange rate asymmetries which we documented in Section 2 suggests potential explanations from the theory of international asset market equilibrium. Specifically, it seems reasonable to view such movements of exchange rates as the result of international portfolio reallocations.

In this section we investigate two possible explanations of the observed correlations, drawing on models of international asset market equilibrium. The first is based on a dynamic model of portfolio choice. The second uses a modified portfolio model which allows for the presence of capital controls. In this sense, the latter model allows both imperfect asset substitutability and imperfect capital mobility to affect exchange rate movements.

3.1. Evidence from portfolio models

Consider a hypothetical case where assets denominated in US dollars and pounds are very close substitutes in investors 'portfolios, while assets denominated in US dollars and marks are less close substitutes. In this world, an exogenous shock which affects relative prices gives rise to a potentially large portfolio reallocation between US dollars and pounds, whereas the relative demands for US dollars and marks change less. Exchange rate movements will have to reflect these portfolio reallocations accordingly.

How can we assess the relevance of the portfolio model in explaining the data? The straightforward answer to this question is a formal test of the restrictions that the international portfolio model imposes on the behaviour of exchange rates and interest rates. If these restrictions are incompatible with the data we would conclude that the observed empirical regularities are inconsistent with optimal portfolio diversification. The only task, at this point, would be to explain the source of asymmetries among European exchange rates, which are to be found in structural parameters, and in the exogenous shocks.

Notwithstanding the simple appeal of the assumptions behind portfolio models, it is remarkable that they have been tested so seldom in the international finance literature. On the few occasions when they have been tested they have usually been found wanting.[6] A possible explanation for these rejections lies in one of the assumptions under which these tests are carried out, namely that variances and covariances of rates of return are constant over time. There is increasing empirical evidence that this assumption is unwarranted.[7] Hence we cannot take these rejections as definite evidence against the model.

Rather than dropping portfolio models altogether therefore, we carry out a few illustrative calculations to see whether the data are broadly consistent with some of their implications. We consider the general equilibrium dynamic model studied by Lucas (1982), Svensson (1985), and Stockman and Svensson (1985), among others (for a survey, see Obstfeld and Stockman, 1985). The essential building blocks of the

---

[6] The capital asset pricing model of Kouri (1977) and Dornbusch (1982) has been tested by Frankel and Engel (1984); the dynamic asset pricing model of Lucas (1982) has been tested by Hansen and Hodrick (1983) and Hodrick and Srivastava (1984). All these authors report rejections. For a survey of portfolio models in international finance see Adler and Dumas (1983).

[7] Cumby and Obstfeld (1985) and Giovannini and Jorion (1985) find that the hypothesis that the conditional variance–covariance matrix of rates of return is constant over time is strongly rejected. In particular, as suggested by Giovannini and Jorion, it is apparent that for a large collection of assets, including foreign currency deposits and the stock market, conditional variances are correlated with nominal interest rates. This evidence points to nonstationarities as a possible reason for the rejections of the portfolio model.

model are described in Appendix B. According to the model, correlations of exchange rate changes are determined by the movements of money growth and output in the different countries, and the extent to which consumers regard the products of different countries as substitutes. For example, a higher correlation of monetary policy between Italy and the United States than between Germany and the United States would, other things equal, produce correlations between the effective rates of the dollar, and the lira/mark rate which are akin to the ones reported in Table 1A.

Using monthly data for money and industrial production as a proxy for GDP, for all the countries included in Table 1, we generate 'theoretical' correlations of changes in exchange rates, which are consistent with the implications of the model. These theoretical correlations are constructed assuming a plausible form for individual consumer preferences which allows for different substitutabilities of European goods on the one hand, and North American and Japanese goods on the other. For each period, Table 2 shows 'theoretical' regression coefficients in the first row, and actual regression coefficients for monthly data in the second row.

The table shows that in many cases the theoretical model can reproduce the signs of the empirical correlations. We find that, among EMS currencies, theoretical regression coefficients approximate the actual ones before March 1979, with the exception of the French franc.[8] After 1979, however, discrepancies between actual and theoretical correlations are quite noticeable, especially in the case of the Dutch guilder and the Belgian franc. In the case of the Canadian dollar the theoretical model approximates the actual correlations quite satisfactory in all sample periods. The opposite happens in the case of the Swiss franc: rather than generating small and positive correlations (as the actual ones), the theoretical portfolio model gives rise to large and negative regression coefficients.

In summary, our illustrative calculations suggest that the observed correlations, and the asymmetries among European currencies, can to some extent be approximated by the dynamic portfolio model during the period 1973–79: in other words, monetary shocks and their

---

[8] We also found that the assumption about higher substitutability among European goods produces results that are closer to the empirical observations. In the case where the elasticity of substitution is identical across countries, correlations tend to be smaller in absolute value, and in some cases change sign. The traditional specification of the monetarist model, which assumes purchasing power parity among all goods, also generates inconsistent results. The results are also inconsistent when output is irrelevant (the case of Cobb-Douglas utility), an indication that money supply covariances are by themselves insufficient to explain the covariance of exchange rate changes. The results of these experiments are available from the authors upon request.

Table 2. 'Theoretical' nominal exchange rate correlations from the dynamic portfolio model: monthly data

	Dutch Guilder	Belgian Franc	French Franc	Italian Lira	Pound Sterling	Swiss Franc	Japanese Yen	Canadian Dollar
Before EMS (June 1973–February 1979)								
Theoretical	−0.07	−0.31	0.28	−0.12	0.11	−0.52	−1.25	−1.37
Actual	−0.14	−0.12	−0.20	−0.52	−0.53	−0.05	−0.29	−1.40
EMS period (March 1979–October 1985)								
Theoretical	−0.86	−0.66	−0.11	−0.33	−0.47	−0.59	−0.58	−0.32
Actual	−0.01	−0.01	−0.03	−0.13	−0.24	−0.10	−0.13	−0.95
Dollar depreciating (May 1977–October 1978)								
Theoretical	−0.72	−0.74	−0.11	−0.07	0.02	−0.69	−0.60	−0.91
Actual	−0.12	−0.10	−0.26	−0.76	−0.50	−0.02	0.37	−1.40
Dollar appreciating (November 1978–July 1981)								
Theoretical	−0.14	0.28	0.01	−0.12	0.26	−0.08	−0.16	−0.81
Actual	0.01	0.01	−0.01	−0.04	0.00	−0.11	−0.05	−0.90

From the formulae in Appendix B, the first row of each subperiod shows the theoretical correlations, assuming that the intra-European substitution elasticity is equal to 2.0. The elasticity of substitution between European goods and goods produced by the rest of the world, and between American and Japanese goods are both assumed to be equal to 1.25. In the second row of each subperiod the table reports the actual correlations obtained from regressions using monthly data.

correlations with business cycles appear to explain some of the early exchange rate experience. During the EMS period the ability of the model to reproduce the empirical correlations decreases. This might be due to a more extensive use of (sterilized) foreign exchange market intervention by European partners, in order to maintain the exchange rate agreement.[9]

3.2. The role of capital controls

Instead of focussing on the correlations between demand and supplies of outside assets denominated in different currencies, there is an alternative way to interpret the results of Table 1. Assets which enter international portfolios differ according to the degree of capital mobility allowed by the country which issues them, so that some assets are more freely tradeable than others. In this setup there is a tendency for capital to flow more freely between, for example, dollar and Swiss franc assets than between dollar and lira assets given that capital controls insulate the Italian financial system from the rest of the world.

This view is not inconsistent with the data reported in Table 1. In the period preceding the EMS, Italy, the UK, and Japan were the countries where capital controls were most stringent, and their exchange rates against the mark appear to have the largest negative correlations with the dollar. This is what one would observe if shifts out of dollars

---

[9] In the spirit of Table 2, we also generated another set of 'theoretical' correlations from the *static* capital asset pricing model (CAPM). Our results were very unfavourable to the static CAPM. Frankel (1985b) reaches the same conclusion.

had only a small effect on the demand for assets denominated in lira, pounds, and yen. During the EMS period such a phenomenon would be less apparent because of the timing of the introduction and lifting of capital controls in France, Japan and the UK. It remains true, however, that the lira, which had capital controls throughout the period, still shows the largest negative correlation with the dollar. The results which show that dollar depreciations are systematically correlated with appreciations of the Swiss franc with respect to the mark, are also suggestive of the important role of Swiss franc assets as an alternative to dollar assets in international portfolios.

Below we sort out the evidence on capital controls and discuss their possible effects on European exchange rates.

3.2.1. Capital controls in Europe. European countries are characterized by a wide and bewildering variety of regulations concerning the international flow of financial capital. The usual motivation for introducing capital controls is to avoid the possibly negative effects on a country's balance of payments of the free flow of capital, and the repercussions of international disturbances on domestic interest rates. The links between domestic and foreign asset markets are usually severed in two ways. The first is to prohibit residents from investing abroad, either with the establishment of a quota, as in the case of France after 1981, and of the UK until 1979, or via prohibitive taxes, as in the case of Italy. Belgium imposes an implicit tax through a two tier market, where the 'financial' exchange rate is freely floating, and the 'commercial' exchange rate is pegged. The second is to prohibit foreign residents from borrowing at home, as in the case of France, Italy, and Denmark.

The effect of these restrictions is to discourage active arbitrage between the domestic and the offshore market. This is documented in Figure 2 which plots onshore and offshore interest rates on one-month deposits for France and Italy. Whereas in countries like the Netherlands, which is practically free of capital controls, onshore and offshore interest rates move very closely together, in France (especially after capital controls were made more stringent in the spring of 1981) and in Italy (throughout the period) we observe large deviations of offshore and onshore rates, especially at times of crises in the EMS. The data for France clearly shows the time of the March 1983 realignment. For these currencies, arbitrage between onshore and offshore markets is carried out mostly through trade credits: in periods of crisis trade credits do not provide sufficient funds to even out profit opportunities.[10]

---

[10] For a discussion of these effects see Giavazzi and Pagano (1985). Notice, moreover, that in the presence of capital controls the offshore market can grow almost exclusively through trade financing.

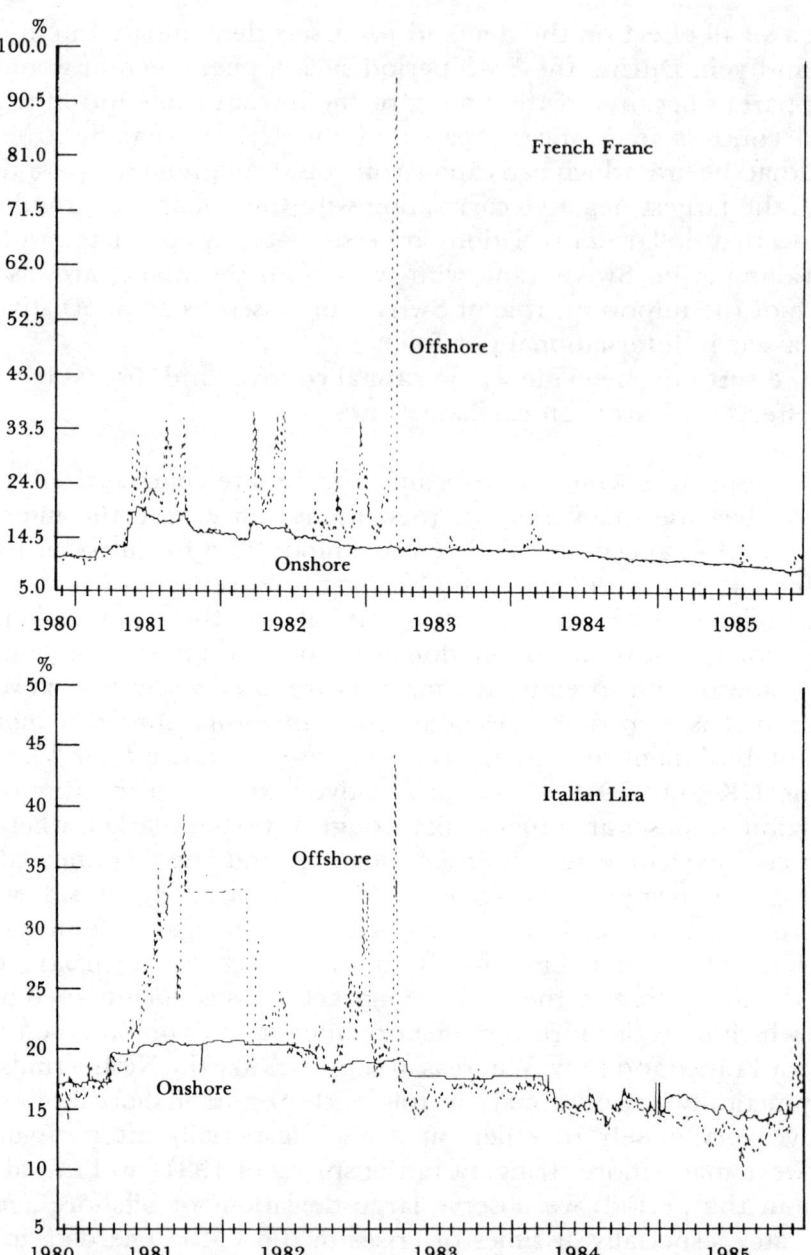

Figure 2. Onshore and offshore interest rates on one-month deposits

Table 3 below shows the Bank of International Settlements' estimates of the size of the offshore market of different currencies in December 1984, and compares them with relative GNP sizes of the corresponding countries. It is striking how closely the divergencies between market

Table 3. Offshore market size by currency of denomination (percentage share of total market size, December 1984)

American Dollar	German Mark	Swiss Franc	Japanese Yen	Pound Sterling	French Franc	Dutch Guilder	Italian Lira	European Currency Unit
Market share								
77.0	10.0	5.0	2.0	1.3	0.9	0.9	0.4	1.3
GNP share								
50.0	10.0	1.5	16.2	6.9	7.9	2.1	5.4	—

Source: Bank of International Settlements, *International Banking Developments*, for the Euromarket shares. GNP shares from World Bank, *World Development Report*, 1985. They are computed as the ratio of each country's GNP in US dollars to the total US dollar value of all eight countries' GNP.

sizes and GNP shares can be explained by the presence of capital controls.

3.2.2. The effects of capital controls on international portfolio diversification. Imperfections in international financial markets have traditionally been modelled (see Black, 1974, and Stultz, 1981) assuming that they are equivalent to a tax on holdings of foreign securities by domestic residents. In contrast here we assume that the most important effect of capital controls is to increase transactions costs in assets denominated in the currencies subject to such controls. These costs represent the obstacles that controls impose on free exchange of a country's financial assets for the purpose of international portfolio diversification.[11]

What are the effects of transactions costs in international portfolio diversification? They can be illustrated using a standard capital asset pricing model, modified for the presence of transactions costs.[12] The formal model is presented in Appendix C. Consider the case where capital controls impose two types of transactions costs: a lump-sum cost per transaction and a cost which is proportional to the volume of the transaction. Suppose, in addition, that these costs differ across different agents: international banks may face lower transactions costs than multinational corporations: residents of some countries may face lower transactions costs in assets of those countries. Investors have to decide whether the cost of trading in any given asset is worth the expected return to that asset. In this world each asset is held only by investors

---

[11] Discussing capital controls in Italy, Baffi (1978) suggests that one of their effects is to increase transactions costs in the foreign exchange market.

[12] The role of transactions costs in the CAPM is studied in Mayshar (1983), whose basic approach is followed here. Pagano (1985) illustrates a rational expectations version of that model.

who face relatively lower transactions costs in that asset. Therefore assets with relatively high lump-sum transactions costs will be traded in thin markets. This is the first important effect of capital controls. It appears to be consistent with the evidence on the size of international financial markets reported above.

The important implication of this result is that (sterilized) foreign exchange market operations which affect the relative supplies of assets denominated in different currencies should have larger effects on the price of assets with capital controls, and hence on their exchange rates. This result can be illustrated as follows. Consider for example a (sterilized) foreign exchange market operation which raises the supply of lira denominated assets. For every lira which is added to the market, the lira exchange rate moves more the smaller is the number of investors who hold lira assets. This result depends on market thinness, which is associated with lump-sum transactions costs. The existing literature on capital controls, as for example Aliber (1973), Claassen and Wyplosz (1982) and Obstfeld (1982), suggests that their presence makes assets less substitutable because the uncertainty about imposition of future controls increases the variance of the rate of return. Even if the probability of tighter capital controls in the future is zero, assets are less substitutable because of market thinness, endogenously generated by capital controls.

Finally the capital controls model is consistent with the empirical regularity documented in Section 2. Consider an increase in the expected return on both lira and mark denominated assets, both by the same amount. Because capital controls (and therefore transactions costs) make it more expensive to shift portfolios into liras than into marks the demand for lira assets increases less than the demand for mark assets. As a consequence the lira depreciates vis-à-vis the mark. The depreciation of the lira, which is accompanied by an increase in demand for European assets, is in this case associated with a depreciation of the effective rate of the dollar, as investors shift out of dollars into higher-yielding European assets. This result is more marked the higher are proportional transactions costs.

Although we believe this analysis shows the potential of this approach to modelling capital controls, unfortunately we cannot draw conclusions on the relative empirical performance of standard portfolio models, like that discussed in Section 3.1, and models of imperfect capital mobility like that discussed here. Such a comparison is difficult for two reasons; first, the two models are both consistent with some of the statistical regularities presented in Section 2. In other words, the models do not necessarily produce conflicting predictions. Second, the data needed for an empirical evaluation of the market thinness model, i.e.

on transactions costs in international financial markets, is hard to obtain, and difficult to interpret.[13]

4. Policy: are exchange rate fluctuations in Europe desirable?

Section 2 has documented the presence of fluctuations of European bilateral exchange rates vis-à-vis the mark which appear to be systematically associated with fluctuations of the dollar. Section 3 has pointed to two possible explanations of this empirical regularity: international portfolio behaviour and capital controls. As we have argued above, it is impossible to detect to what extent each story explains the observed asymmetries: probably both jointly operate given how widespread capital controls are in Europe.

In this final section we turn to the policy implications. The policy questions can be summarized as follows. First, to the extent that the international portfolio model suggests that monetary policies lie behind the fluctuations of bilateral exchange rates in Europe, are such policies desirable? By 'desirable' we mean: do such policies reflect the optimal coordinated response of European monetary authorities to external shocks, or are they the outcome of non-cooperative behaviour in Europe, for example efforts to run 'beggar-thy-neighbour' policies? Second, to the extent that the observed exchange rate fluctuations are generated by transactions costs that investors face when they try to get in and out of currencies which are subject to capital controls, financial liberalization in Europe would certainly eliminate an important asymmetry and would in principle contribute to more uniform exchange rate movements. The question here is whether liberalization of capital controls is a desirable move, or whether capital controls are in some sense necessarily associated with the present exchange rate system.

To address the issue of the desirability of European monetary policies which result in asymmetric exchange rate fluctuations, we first have to ask how monetary policy is run in a system such as the EMS. Central to the working of this system is the issue of symmetry versus asymmetry. With n interdependent countries, only $n-1$ policies can be set independently: the system therefore has a built in tendency to work asymmetrically. Symmetry can be achieved only with one of two arrangements: either countries give up control of exchange rates, which are allowed to float freely – a solution which was clearly refused by participants in the EMS; or exchange rate and monetary policies are decided cooperatively. But if countries are unwilling to give up control of the exchange

---

[13] Glassman (1984) contains a first empirical model of the bid-ask spread in the foreign exchange market.

rate, and policy is set non-cooperatively, the system works asymmetrically: one country can set its own monetary policy but has to relinquish control of the exchange rate, while the other countries independently manage their bilateral exchange rate vis-à-vis the 'nth' currency.[14]

Although the EMS was originally designed to work as a cooperative system, its experience has been characterized by widespread asymmetries. On the one hand, the practice of intervening when a single currency reaches its 'divergence indicator' is such that Germany almost never had to intervene to defend a given parity. Moreover, while decisions about exchange rate realignments are usually the result of negotiations, these negotiations fall short of including Germany's monetary policy.[15] The best characterization of the current working of the EMS seems therefore to be that of a system of managed exchange rates in which the mark effectively plays the role of the nth currency.

In a system of managed exchange rates, parity realignments can be of two types. They can either be an optimal cooperative response to local disturbances, or they can be the outcome of non-cooperative 'beggar-thy-neighbour' policies. When countries are subject to idiosyncratic local shocks and production cannot easily be relocated, we know from Mundell (1968) that exchange rate realignments (as long as they have some real effects) can be the optimal way to redistribute the costs of such shocks. But if monetary authorities do not cooperate, exchange rate realignments may take place even if countries are perfectly symmetric and are hit by common exogenous shocks. For example, after a common supply shock, such as the rise in oil prices, exchange rate appreciations enable countries to disinflate more easily by transmitting higher prices abroad through exchange rate appreciation (see Giovazzi and Giovannini, 1985b).

We do not know what are the payoffs to 'beggar-thy-neighbour' policies and hence what is their empirical importance. However, this analysis suggests a possible interpretation of the long term fluctuations of real exchange rates since the inception of the EMS. Table 4 shows that competitiveness among the EMS partners France, Germany and Italy has changed since 1979. The oversized appreciation of the dollar is accompanied by a significant improvement of Germany's competitiveness relative to Italy and France. Because the dollar appreciation can be seen as a supply shock common to all European countries, we can

---

[14] The issue of symmetry versus asymmetry lies at the heart of the Bretton Woods system and was at the centre of the debate over the reasons why it collapsed. For an illuminating discussion see v. N. Whitman (1974).

[15] See, among others, the discussion in Emerson (1982) who points to the leading role of West Germany in setting European interest rate policy. Micossi (1985) provides further evidence in support of this view.

Table 4. Long-term trends in competitiveness (Relative value-added deflators)

	United States	Belgium	Denmark	Germany	France	Italy	Netherlands	United Kingdom
1973Q2	114.9	104.6	104.8	96.9	93.9	90.3	107.9	69.4
1979Q1	100.0	110.3	111.9	106.2	94.0	90.4	106.5	73.1
1985Q2	142.9	80.9	95.8	89.1	86.0	100.2	86.8	91.9
% changes in competitiveness relative to Germany: 1979 to 1985								
	59.0	−10.5	1.8	—	7.6	27.0	−2.6	42.1

Source: IMF *International Financial Statistics*, relative value-added deflators computed using multilateral trade weights. An increase in the index is a real exchange rate appreciation.

interpret the data in Table 4 as documenting a non-cooperative response to such a shock by Italy and France.

The fact that the EMS works as a system of fixed but adjustable parities raises the issue of its viability in the absence of capital controls.

The anticipation of exchange rate realignments induces balance of payments crises, whenever monetary authorities try to minimize the volatility of short term interest rates. In order to avoid undesired fluctuations in domestic short term interest rates, strong currency countries can neutralize speculative attacks in various ways. In contrast, weak currency countries are not able to offset large reserve losses for prolonged periods of time, and therefore can only use capital controls to stabilize domestic interest rates (see Wyplosz, 1984). The evidence in Section 3.2 on the movements of offshore rates indeed confirms that expectations about EMS realignments could induce large changes in short-term interest rates in the absence of capital controls. The likelihood of large interest rate fluctuations is enhanced by the possibility that expectations of realignments be self-fulfilling, and that speculative attacks take place in the absence of changes in 'fundamentals'. In the present system weak currency countries have to choose between the welfare losses associated with capital controls and the losses arising from the volatility of short-term interest rates, and, as the evidence shows, overwhelmingly opt for the former. Thus capital controls appear to be an important feature of the EMS, which allows weak currency countries to take part in the exchange rate arrangement, without suffering from excessive domestic interest rate fluctuations.

In summary, the discussion in this section seems to suggest two policy lessons from the recent experience of European exchange rates.

First, the evidence that the EMS may not be working as a cooperative system implies that fluctuations of European exchange rates can be the result of beggar-thy-neighbour policies. New 'rules of the game' for the EMS are desirable. These new rules should enhance cooperation by establishing that monetary policy targets for all countries be updated whenever exchange rate parities are adjusted. Such rules would eliminate one source of asymmetric movements of European exchange rates.

Second, the observed exchange rate asymmetries are likely to be associated with the presence of capital controls. However, our discussion has shown that undiscriminating, across the board, liberalization of capital controls can have disruptive effects on the present exchange rate system. Hence the EMS, by itself, cannot be thought of as an intermediate stage which endogenously brings about monetary unification. The reason is that capital controls appear to be adopted by the weak currency members in order to keep some control over domestic interest rates and at the same time to be part of the parities agreement. Capital controls, however, prevent further integration. Once again, this seems to suggest that progress towards monetary unification can be achieved only if more integrated capital markets are accompanied by more integrated techniques of monetary management across Europe.

Discussion

David Begg
Worcester College, Oxford, and DEPR

Let me begin by restating the central argument of the paper. Dollar fluctuations are correlated with, and perhaps induce, changes in bilateral European exchange rates. Indeed, a sharp dollar depreciation has been almost a necessary condition for EMS realignments. Existing portfolio models of exchange rate determination at best only partly explain the pre-EMS period and fare poorly since 1979. To explain recent exchange rate behaviour it is necessary to recognise the vital role of controls on capital flows. Not only do such controls help explain the asymmetric behaviour of exchange rates but also, in the absence of complete European policy coordination, they allow member states to limit fluctuations in domestic interest rates and are thus intrinsic to the existing working of the EMS. Hence the EMS is not a stepping stone along a smooth path to exchange rate unification in Europe, but a cul-de-sac. It will be difficult, and may be undesirable, to scale the brick wall which Giavazzi and Giovannini identify as foreign exchange controls.

Dealing as they do with short run exchange rate determination, a subject of some controversy, the authors are skating on rather thin ice. Serious skaters get scored for technical merit and artistic impression and I shall try to award marks for both. I begin with their presentation of the compulsory figures.

Tables 1 report the data correlations between the effective dollar exchange rate and individual bilateral exchange rates. I gloss over technical considerations such as whether *differences* in correlations are statistically significant and whether movements were pure surprises or partially anticipated. The central message is that effective dollar depreciations tend, in the short run, to be correlated with mark appreciations against particular European currencies. To think this through, consider three shocks. A France-specific shock might lead to a franc depreciation against both the mark and the dollar. Since the latter implies an appreciation of the effective dollar rate, there would be a *positive* correlation between the effective dollar and the mark/franc rates. A Germany-specific shock might raise the mark/franc rate and the mark/dollar rate, thus inducing an effective dollar depreciation and a *negative* correlation between the effective dollar and mark/franc rates. A US-specific shock which changed both the dollar/mark and dollar/franc rates but left the mark/franc rate unaltered would imply a *zero* correlation between the effective dollar and mark/franc rates. Overall correlations must therefore depend on the source of the shocks (and of course the weights used in computing the effective dollar rate). The findings of Table 1 are necessary but not sufficient for establishing that the EMS is buffeted by external dollar-related shocks.

Next, I turn to the authors' attempt to investigate whether actual correlations can be explained using modern notions of international portfolio diversification. They are disappointed that portfolio models do not fit the data very closely. Personally, I should be rather disturbed if they did, at least in the form in which the authors (and everyone else) typically apply them. Sophisticated portfolio models are used to predict the equilibrium real exchange rate but then, to convert this to a model of nominal exchange rates, trivial money demand equations are postulated and then inverted to obtain the nominal exchange rate from relative prices and the underlying model of the real exchange rate. Since we have massive evidence that no nation's money demand equation resembles the naive form in which these equations here are specified, it would really be quite disturbing if the authors managed to fit actual exchange rate behaviour in this way. In fact it would be incontrovertible evidence *against* the underlying model of real exchange rates. Fortunately this is not the case.

Thus I reject the premise that it is necessary to introduce capital controls to 'explain away' the failure of the portfolio models. To be sure, I concur that such controls are important, and I welcome the approach advocated by the authors. They emphasise the fixed cost of transactions when controls are present, and show that this approach can be used to determine endogenously the number of traders, the

thinness of the market, and the degree of asset substitutability. I find
this appealing and promising as a line of research. And it could provide
a reason for asymmetric responses to exogenous shocks. Whilst the
authors agree that it would be desirable to augment a (realistic) portfolio
specification to incorporate capital controls, at present it is simply too
difficult to put together the data which would be required to do empirical
justice to this approach.

Instead, the authors – erroneously in my view – try to stand the
argument on its head. Perhaps exchange controls, and the imperfect
asset substitutability thus induced, explain why earlier portfolio models
failed to fit the facts. Sterilized intervention (central bank swaps of
domestic bonds for foreign exchange reserves) is known to be ineffective
when assets in different currencies are perfect substitutes but can provide the government with an independent lever over the exchange rate
when substitution is imperfect. Hence the authors wish to argue that
the proliferation of exchange controls under the EMS effectively gave
governments an additional weapon with which to bend exchange rates
from the underlying fundamentals which economic models would suggest. In my view this gives the game away. If sterilized intervention is
so powerful, governments can offset undesirable exchange rate changes
and any tendency to asymmetric exchange rate responses loses most of
its significance as a policy problem. Indeed, it may then be the outcome
of appropriate actions by national policymakers.

The authors offer two broad conclusions on policy. First, the implicit
rules of the EMS game accord to Germany the effective power to
determine monetary growth within the EMS but leave other countries
free, at least in part, to affect their own bilateral exchange rates against
the mark. Faced with a common price increase from outside, perhaps
because of a dollar appreciation, non-German EMS countries will have
an incentive to appreciate their currencies against the mark, thus exporting some of the inflation to Germany. If the authors are correct, this
suggests that the negative correlation between the effective dollar rate
and say the mark/franc rate, far from being a fact of life to which
European policy makers must devise an optimal response, is actually
the consequence of optimizing policy choices within the existing rules
of the game.

Second, and in consequence, this leads Giavazzi and Giovannini to
evaluate the rules of the game themselves. They have no answers, but
for those who wish to make the case for monetary unification, with all
the problems of monetary convergence and effective fiscal redistribution
that this entails, they draw attention to two features of the existing EMS
system which in themselves are undesirable: first, the beggar-thy-neighbour aspect of attempts to export inflation to partner countries (a

straightforward example of an externality), and, second, the extent to which foreign exchange controls, with distortionary implications for capital market efficiency, have been required to sustain the EMS so far.

In conclusion, I award our pairs skaters a silver for artistic impression. They have tried hard to get behind the casual impression that when the dollar is strong the mark is weak, and to identify the factors which might make this an important policy issue. They have also encouraged us to think afresh about the way that exchange controls actually work. On technical merit, they themselves have recognized the difficulties in translating their theoretical ideas into a convincing empirical performance. Many of the questions they raise remain to be answered.

Louka Katseli
Centre of Economic Research and Planning, Athens

Where is the EMS going? This question is at the centre of the policy debate in Europe. The most prominent issues are: whether capital flows in Europe should be liberalized; whether the pound should become a full member of the EMS; and whether the present EMS arrangements should provide the basis for an evolution to full monetary union in Europe. The paper should be seen against this background and, in presenting statistical evidence and an analysis thereof, it helps us answer some of the questions on which a final judgement of the above issues must rest.

The paper discovers an empirical regularity between an appreciating (depreciating) dollar and depreciations (appreciations) of the mark against other European currencies. But it demonstrates that this relation is less robust than is popularly supposed. It holds only in the very short run (daily but not monthly let alone quarterly data) and, since 1979, holds only during infrequent and short-lived periods of strain within the EMS. Some discussion is offered on the latter point but the authors never really confront the question of why, especially before 1979, there should be such a difference between results for daily data and results for quarterly data.

Since David Begg has already discussed the specific models of portfolio theory and capital controls which the authors use to try to gain insight on exchange rate behaviour, I will concentrate my remarks on the wider policy implications. First, I agree with the characterization of the EMS as a zone in which Germany effectively sets monetary policy. Exchange rate realignments occur as the outcome of negotiations in which all member countries participate, and tend to confirm the direction but not always the magnitude of the exchange rate changes desired by particular countries. However, unlike the fully optimal cooperative solution, it is quite clear that other countries exert only the smallest influence on German monetary policy. Under the existing system, asymmetry is a fact of life, and other countries have an incentive to attempt beggar-thy-neighbour policies to export inflation.

The paper concludes by highlighting the basic dilemma which lies ahead for those who seek greater monetary union. It argues that capital controls sustain the present EMS and are likely to prevent monetary union. To my mind, this claim is too sweeping. *Credibly* fixed exchange rate in perpetuity, the essence of monetary union, certainly deprive countries of their monetary sovereignty (though perhaps giving them a larger stake than at present in overall European monetary policy) and certainly eliminate the possibility of beggar-thy-neighbour policies. But it is conceivable that they would also *remove* most of the justification for capital controls. As the authors' own diagram suggests, the differential between onshore and offshore interest rates (the simplest indicator of how tightly capital controls are biting) is large when a realignment is imminent (or thought to be imminent) but is often close to zero when current parities seem defensible. To the extent that capital controls are required primarily to avert high exorbitant domestic interest rates when a devaluation is anticipated, monetary union is precisely the policy which will eliminate the most important reason for capital controls.

The more one believes that controls are distortionary in their effect on market allocation, the more one might wish to eliminate them by taking this route. On the other hand, I should like to stress that monetary union could have a very large cost. It would eliminate the possibility of using realignments to offset regional shocks within Europe. An efficient, Europe-wide, system of taxation, income redistribution, and indeed regional policy could compensate for the loss of the exchange rate tool, but it must be recognised by proponents of monetary union that existing European fiscal cooperation is nowhere near this point.

In the meantime, the issue for the UK is whether or not it should join the existing EMS system. Past experience shows that the sterling exchange rate tends to follow a path between that of the dollar and the mark, a pattern matched among EMS currencies only by the lira. Should the UK join the exchange rate mechanism of the EMS, one of two approaches should be followed. Either the pound should be allowed, as is the lira, to fluctuate within a wider band than other currencies, or the UK monetary authority should explicitly match German interest rates, thereby neutralizing the tendency for otherwise large capital flows between the relatively free markets in the UK and Germany. Indeed, in the absence of a wholesale readoption of foreign exchange controls in the UK, something akin to the latter outcome is likely to prevail.

General Discussion

Paul Krugman also emphasised the problems involved in constructing effective exchange rates. As an example he supposed that the US and Germany each produced 49.9% of world output while Grand Fenwick produced the remaining 0.2%. If the dollar appreciated by 10% against both the mark and the Grand Fenwick franc then Giavazzi and Giovannini's index would show 10% depreciation of the effective mark rate and a 5% depreciation of the Grand Fenwick franc while the bilateral mark/Grand Fenwick franc rate was unaltered. Such considerations had been important in assessing movements in the yen and the mark in the past. However the authors of the paper felt their empirical findings were robust to different methods of measurement.

Jacques Melitz disagreed with the authors' characterisation of the EMS and the discussion of 'beggar-thy-neighbour' policies. The EMS was not a fixed exchange system like Bretton Woods with the mark playing the role of 'nth' currency. There was much greater symmetry in the system. Nor was it the case that France could unilaterally control the mark/franc exchange rate. Consequently France was not able to pursue beggar-thy-neighbour policies in the face of external shocks by a parity realignment. Realignments were discussed jointly and were generally justified with reference to differing underlying inflation rates so as to maintain purchasing power parity. In response Giavazzi argued that although the system was nominally symmetric, the evidence suggested that 85% of central bank intervention occurred while currencies were still well within the prescribed bands and that it was not just the magnitude but the timing of realignments that mattered. The latter was open to influence even if the former was not.

Torsten Persson applauded the approach to modelling capital controls as a transaction cost which he thought very promising. It could explain the bias towards domestic assets in agents' portfolios for instance, something that was hard to explain in conventional portfolio models. However he felt the authors' discussion overstated the virtues of the dynamic portfolio model since the final equation (B2) looked very much like that which might be derived from much simpler models such as those with continuous market-clearing and a simple quantity theory of the demand for money.

Patrick Minford also questioned the relevance of the experiments with the complex dynamic portfolio model which was unrealistic in many ways such as its assumption that currencies are the only assets. Simple portfolio models could still be used to explain the correlations even if risk premia did vary over time, since they should do so only rather slowly. Movements in exchange rates could then be explained by movements in interest rates and expected money supplies. This could be implemented empirically.

Paul Krugman asked why the authors were using the models to explain correlations between exchange rates rather than movements in the exchange rates themselves. He suspected that this was because the models were not very successful at the latter task. In reply Giovannini said that they were merely trying to see which models of behaviour could shed light on the asymmetries in exchange rate movements. This might be worthwhile, even if the models did not provide a complete description of exchange rate movements.

Appendix A. The data

The nominal effective exchange rate of the dollar, used in the regressions of Tables 1 and 2 is constructed using as weights the ratio of the dollar value of GNP of each country to the dollar value of GNP of all nine countries for which we run bilateral exchange rate regressions. GNP and exchange rates are averages over the period 1973 to 1984. They are obtained from *International Financial Statistics*. The weights are: Belgium 0.027, Canada 0.075, France 0.150, Germany 0.192, Italy 0.091, Japan 0.282, The Netherlands 0.039, Switzerland 0.027 and UK 0.118.
Exchange rates are noon-time New York bid rates for the dollar from Data Resources Inc., FACS Databank.
Money stocks (M1) from IMF, *International Financial Statistics*. Industrial production is used as a proxy for monthly GDP.
Real exchange rates are constructed using relative wholesale prices from IMF, *International Financial Statistics*.

Appendix B. Numerical simulations with the intertemporal CAPM

The assumptions of the international and intertemporal capital asset pricing model of Lucas (1982) are as follows. There are N countries $i = 1, 2, \ldots, N$ inhabited by risk averse, infinitely lived families. Tastes are identical across the world. In each period each family receives an exogenous stochastic endowment of its own country GDP and a lump-sum transfer of its country's money. Money growth and output follow a joint first order Markov process. Each family maximizes the following time-separable utility function:

$$V = \sum_{t=0}^{\infty} \delta^t U(c_{1t}, c_{2t}, \ldots, c_{Nt}) \tag{B1}$$

where δ is the utility discount rate, and c_i is consumption of the output of country i. Wealth in each country is the sum of holdings of the monies of the N different countries. Money is the only outside financial asset. In this model it is held because the currency of each country has to be used to purchase that country's GDP. This transactions constraint implies a constant-velocity demand for each country's money. As Svensson (1985) and Stockman and Svensson (1985) show, however, it is possible to extend the model to allow for interest elastic money demand functions. In every period, equilibrium in the goods and assets markets implies:

$$E_t^{jk} = \frac{M_t^k}{M_t^j} \frac{y_t^j}{y_t^k} \frac{U_j(y_t^1/N, \ldots, y_t^N/N)}{U_k(y_t^1/N, \ldots, y_t^N/N)} \tag{B2}$$

Where E^{jk} is the nominal exchange rate, expressed as units of currency k per unit of currency j, M^i is the stock of country i's money, y^i is country i's GDP, and U_i is the partial derivative of U with respect to good i. The marginal rate of substitution enters formula (B2) because in equilibrium it is equal to the real exchange rate.

Equation (B2) is a model of the nominal exchange rate that resembles the traditional monetarist equation of Frenkel (1976). The similarity is mainly due to the equilibrium assumption; the unit velocity money demand prevents future money stocks in the two countries from affecting the current exchange rate. The difference between Equation (B2) and the monetarist model of the exchange rate is that output fluctuations affect marginal rates of substitution between output in different countries, and therefore change real exchange rates. In the monetarist model, instead, the real exchange rate is constant. Furthermore, all countries' output levels in general enter (B2), whereas the monetarist equation admits only output of the two countries to which the exchange rate refers.

In order to construct the theoretical correlations, we need assumptions about the utility function. We assume the following two-level CES function:

$$U^\rho = [(c_1^\alpha + \cdots + c_7^\alpha)^{1/\alpha}]^\rho + [(c_8^\beta + c_9^\beta)^{1/\beta}]^\rho \tag{B3}$$

which implies a constant elasticity of substitution α among European goods, c_1 to c_7, a constant elasticity of substitution β between American (US and Canadian) and Japanese goods, c_8 and c_9, and a constant elasticity of substitution ρ between the two groups. Using data on money supplies and output, and equations (B2) and (B3) we construct theoretical exchange rates. Their correlations are obtained exactly as in Table 1.

Appendix C. A model of international capital controls

Assume $N+2$ assets: N risky assets, a riskless bond and a 'market' asset, with which all rates of return on risky assets are correlated. Every asset j's payoff is made up of three components:

$$x_j = \bar{x}_j + b_j z + \xi_j \tag{C1}$$

where z is the market rate of return, with $\text{Cov}(\bar{x}_j, \xi_j) = E(\xi_j) = \text{Cov}(z, \xi_j) = 0$. $E(\cdot)$ is the expectations operator, and b_j measures the 'systematic risk' of asset j. Let there be L investors who maximize the utility of final wealth, which is a function of its expected value and its variance. Investors' demands for the N risky assets are set equal to their (fixed) supplies F_j to determine the standard equilibrium asset pricing equations:

$$q_j(1+r) = E(x_j) - b_j \pi_z - (A/L)F_j \text{ Var}(\xi_j) \tag{C2}$$

where q_j is the price of asset j, r is the riskless rate of interest, A is the coefficient of risk aversion, and where the market risk premium π_z is equal, in equilibrium, to:

$$\pi_z = (A/L)\left(\sum_{j=1}^{N} b_j F_j\right) \text{Var}(z) \tag{C3}$$

What is the effect of transactions costs? We assume for simplicity that investors demand positive quantities of each asset (Mayshar, 1983 shows that the analysis can be extended to the case where asset holdings can be negative). Investors have to decide whether the cost of trading in assets with transactions costs are worth the expected return on these assets, given their market price. The cost associated with trades in assets which have transactions costs is made up of two components: a lump sum component and a component that is proportional to the value of the trade. Lump sum costs differ across investors: for example, commercial banks have significantly easier access to Eurocurrency markets than nonbank institutions, or private individuals. We order investors by increasing cost of trading. In equilibrium, for every asset k for which there are transactions costs the following condition has to hold:

$$E(x_k) - b_k \pi_z - q_k(1+t+t_k) = \phi_k(l_k) \tag{C4}$$

where $\phi_k(l_k)$ is the lump-sum transaction cost associated with asset k, incurred by the l_kth investor. We assume a continuum of investors for analytical tractability. $\phi'_k > 0$, l_k is the number of active traders, and t_k is the proportional cost. As shown in Mayshar (1983), Equation (C4) together with:

$$q_k(1+r+t_k) = E(x_k) - b_k \pi_z - (A/l_k)E_k \text{ Var}(\xi_k) \tag{C5}$$

determine the number of traders in the market for the kth asset, together with its equilibrium price. All other assets which have no transactions costs are priced according to (C2).

Equations (C4) and (C5) can be used to show that when transactions costs are significant, the number of active traders l_k decreases. More importantly, in the presence of transactions costs assets become less substitutable: i.e. a change in their outstanding supply has a larger effect on their price. By differentiating (C4) and (C5), the effect of changes in the supply of asset k on its price is:

$$\frac{dq_k}{dF_k} = -(1+r+t_k)^{-1} \frac{(A/l_k)\,\text{Var}\,(\xi_k)}{\left[1+\dfrac{A}{l_k^2}\text{Var}\,(\xi_k)F_k\psi_k'\right]} + b_k\frac{\partial \pi_z}{\partial F_k} \tag{C6}$$

where ψ_k is the first derivative of the inverse of the function ϕ_k, and measures the potential number of entrants in the market when q_k decreases.

Notice that, in the absence of costs,

$$\frac{dq_k}{dF_k} = -(1+r)^{-1}\left[(A/L)\,\text{Var}\,(\xi_k) + b_k\frac{\partial \pi_z}{\partial F_k}\right] \tag{C7}$$

Comparison of Equations (C6) and (C7) shows that transactions costs affect the response of prices to a change in asset supplies in two ways. Lump-sum costs, by decreasing the number of market participants, tend to make prices more sensitive to changes in asset supplies. If lump sum costs are such that l_k is small relative to L, and if the potential number of entrants in the market is small (ψ_k' small), then changes in F_k have a larger effect on q_k compared with a situation where asset k can be traded costlessly. The presence of proportional transactions costs dampens this effect, but is unlikely to reverse it, if the number of active traders is very small.

Equation (C6) is interesting because it sheds light on an important effect of capital controls. Foreign exchange market operations which affect the supply of assets are likely to be more effective in the presence of capital controls. As we already stressed in the text, this result does not in any way depend on the presence or lack of political risk.

Finally, consider two assets which have identical systematic risk, but have different proportional transactions costs. Equations (C4) and (C5) show that an identical increase in their expected rate of return, or a change in the market risk premium, have a larger effect on the asset which is more freely tradeable, i.e. the asset with smaller proportional transactions costs.

References

Adler, M. and B. Dumas (1983). 'International Portfolio Choice and Corporate Finance: A Synthesis', *Journal of Finance.*

Aliber, R. Z. (1973). 'The Interest Rate Parity Theorem: A Reinterpretation', *Journal of Political Economy.*

Baer, G. U. (1982). 'Some Reflections on a Coordinated Dollar Policy; the Pivotal Role of Germany in the EMS', *Aussenwirtschaft.*

Baffi, P. (1978). 'I Cambi: Ieri, Oggi, Domani', *Bancaria.*

Black, F. (1974). 'International Capital Market Equilibrium with Investment Barriers', *Journal of Financial Economics.*

Claassen, E. M. and C. Wyplosz (1982). 'Capital Controls: Some Principles and the French Experience', *Annales de l'INSEE.*

Cumby, R. E. and M. Obstfeld (1985). 'International Interest Rate and Price Level Linkages Under Flexible Exchange Rates: A Review of Recent Literature', in J. F. O. Bilson and R. C. Marston (eds.) *Exchange Rate Theory and Practice*, Chicago University Press, Chicago.

Dennis, G. and J. Nellis (1984). 'The EMS and UK Membership: Five Years On', *Lloyds Bank Review.*

Dornbusch, R. (1982). 'Exchange Risk and the Macroeconomics of Exchange Rate Determination', in R. Hawkins, R. Levich and C. Wihlborg (eds.) *The Internationalization of Financial Markets and National Economic Policy*, JAI Press, Greenwich, Connecticut.

Emerson, M. (1982). 'Experience under the EMS and Prospects for Further Progress towards EMU', in M. T. Sumner and G. Zis (eds.) *European Monetary Union*, St. Martin's Press, New York.

Frankel, J. (1980). 'Tests of Rational Expectations in the Forward Exchange Market', *Southern Economic Journal.*

Frankel, J. and C. Engel (1984). 'Do Asset-Demand Functions Optimize Over the Mean and the Variance of Real Returns?', *Journal of International Economics.*

Frankel, J. (1985a). 'Comments on Williamson and Giavazzi and Giovannini', in A. Giovannini and R. Dornbusch (eds.) *Europe and the Dollar*, Torino.

Frankel, J. (1985b). 'The Implications of Mean-Variance Optimization for Four Questions in International Finance', University of California, Berkeley.

Giavazzi, F. and A. Giovannini (1985a). 'Asymmetries in Europe, the Dollar and the European Monetary System', in A. Giovannini and R. Dornbusch (eds.) *Europe and the Dollar*, Torino.

Giavazzi, F. and A. Giovannini (1985b). 'Monetary Policy Interactions Under Managed Exchange Rates', unpublished.

Giavazzi, F. and M. Pagano (1985). 'Capital Controls and the European Monetary System', in *Capital Controls and Foreign Exchange Legislation*, Occasional Paper, Euromobiliare, Milano.

Giovannini, A. and P. Jorion (1985). 'Interest Rates and Risk Premia in the Foreign Exchange Market and the Stock Market,' Columbia University.

Glassman, D. (1984). 'Exchange Rate Risk and Volatility: Evidence from Bid-Ask Spreads,' Department of Economics, University of British Columbia.

Hansen, L. P. and R. J. Hodrick (1983). 'Risk Averse Speculation in the Forward Exchange Market: An Econometric Analysis of Linear Models', in J. A. Frenkel, (ed.) *Exchange Rates and International Macroeconomics*, Chicago University Press, Chicago.

Hodrick, R. J. and S. Srivastava (1984). 'An Investigation of Risk and Return in Forward Foreign Exchange', *Journal of International Money and Finance.*

Kaufman, H. M. (1985). 'The Deutsche Mark Between the Dollar and the European Monetary System,' *Kredit und Kapital.*

Kouri, P. J. K. (1977). 'International Investment and Interest Rate Linkages Under Flexible Exchange Rates', in R. Z. Aliber (ed.) *The Political Economy of Monetary Reform*, Macmillan, New York.

Lucas, R. E. jr. (1982). 'Interest Rates and Currency Prices in a Two-Country World', *Journal of Monetary Economics.*

Masera, R. S. (1981). 'The First Two Years of the EMS: The Exchange Rate Experience', *Banca Nazionale del Lavoro Quarterly Review.*

Mayshar, J. (1983). 'On Divergence of Opinion and Imperfections in Capital Markets', *American Economic Review.*

Micossi, S. (1985). 'The Intervention and Financing Mechanisms of the EMS and the Role of the ECU,' Bank of Italy.

Mundell, R. A. (1968). *International Economics*, Macmillan, New York.

Mussa, M. (1979). 'Empirical Regularities in the Behavior of Exchange Rates and Theories of the Foreign Exchange Market,' in *Policies for Employment, Prices and Exchange Rates*, Carnegie-Rochester Conference Series on Public Policy.

Obstfeld, M. (1982). 'Comment on Claassen and Wyplosz', *Annales de l'INSEE*.

Obstfeld, M. and A. C. Stockman (1985). 'Exchange-Rate Dynamics', in P. B. Kenen and R. W. Jones (eds.) *Handbook of International Economics*, vol. 2, North-Holland Publishing Company.

Padoa Schioppa, T. (1985). 'Policy Cooperation and the EMS Experience', in W. H. Buiter and R. C. Marston (eds.) *International Economic Policy Coordination*, Cambridge University Press, Cambridge.

Pagano, M. (1985). 'Market Size and Asset Liquidity in Stock Exchange Economies', unpublished Ph.D. dissertation, Massachusetts Institute of Technology.

Russo, M. (1984). 'Cooperazione Monetaria Europea: Cinque Anni di Esperienza dello SME', EEC Commission, Brussels.

Stockman, A. C. and L. E. O. Svensson (1985). 'Capital Flows, Investment and Exchange Rates', National Bureau of Economic Research, W. P. No. 1598.

Stultz, R. M. (1981). 'On the Effects of Barriers to International Investment', *Journal of Finance*.

Svensson, L. E. O. (1985). 'Currency Prices, Terms of Trade, and Interest Rates', *Journal of International Economics*.

Thygesen, N. (1981). 'Are Monetary Policies and Performances Converging?', *Banca Nazionale del Lavoro Quarterly Review*.

v. N. Whitman, M. (1974). 'The Current and Future Role of the Dollar: How Much Symmetry?' *Brookings Papers on Economic Activity*.

Wyplosz, C. (1984). 'Capital Controls and Balance of Payments Crises,' INSEAD, Fontainbleau.